TRAVELING
at the
Speed of
LOVE

Also by Sonia Choquette

The Answer Is Simple . . . Love Yourself, Live Your Spirit!

The Answer Is Simple Oracle Cards

Ask Your Guides: Connecting to Your Divine Support System

Ask Your Guides Oracle Cards

Diary of a Psychic: Shattering the Myths

The Intuitive Spark:
Bringing Intuition Home to Your Child, Your Family, and You

Soul Lessons and Soul Purpose:
A Channeled Guide to Why You Are Here

Soul Lessons and Soul Purpose Oracle Cards

The Time Has Come . . . to Accept Your Spiritual Gifts!

Trust Your Vibes at Work, and Let Them Work for You

Trust Your Vibes Oracle Cards

Trust Your Vibes: Secret Tools for Six-Sensory Living

Vitamins for the Soul:
Daily Doses of Wisdom for Personal Empowerment

CD Programs

Ask Your Guides: How to Connect with Your Spiritual Support System
(6-CD and 4-CD sets)

Attunement to Higher Vibrational Living,
with Mark Stanton Welch (4-CD set)

Meditations for Receiving Divine Guidance, Support, and Healing
(2-CD set)

Trust Your Vibes at Work, and Let Them Work for You (4-CD set)

Trust Your Vibes: Secret Tools for Six-Sensory Living (6-CD set)

All of the above are available at your local bookstore,
or may be ordered by visiting:

Hay House USA: **www.hayhouse.com**®
Hay House Australia: **www.hayhouse.com.au**
Hay House UK: **www.hayhouse.co.uk**
Hay House South Africa: **www.hayhouse.co.za**
Hay House India: **www.hayhouse.co.in**

—❤—

TRAVELING
at the
Speed of
LOVE

SONIA CHOQUETTE

HAY HOUSE, INC.
Carlsbad, California • New York City
London • Sydney • Johannesburg
Vancouver • Hong Kong • New Delhi

Published and distributed in the United States by: Hay House, Inc.: www.hay house.com • *Published and distributed in Australia by:* Hay House Australia Pty. Ltd.: www.hayhouse.com.au • *Published and distributed in the United Kingdom by:* Hay House UK, Ltd.: www.hayhouse.co.uk • *Published and distributed in the Republic of South Africa by:* Hay House SA (Pty), Ltd.: www.hayhouse.co.za • *Distributed in Canada by:* Raincoast: www.raincoast.com • *Published in India by:* Hay House Publishers India: www.hayhouse.co.in

Interior layout design: Bryn Starr Best

Library of Congress Cataloging-in-Publication Data

Choquette, Sonia.
  Traveling at the speed of love / Sonia Choquette. -- 1st ed.
    p. cm.
  ISBN 978-1-4019-2402-7 (hardcover : alk. paper) 1. Love. 2. Conduct of life. 3. Parapsychology. 4. Spiritual life--Miscellanea. I. Title.
  BF575.L8C555 2010
  170'.44--dc22
                                                    2009035443

ISBN: 978-1-4019-2402-7

13 12 11 10   4 3 2 1
1st edition, March 2010

Printed in the United States of America

This book is dedicated to Bruce Anthony and Paul Choquette, my angels in heaven, and to earth angel Shamrock Holtz, who picked me up when I had crashed and showed me how to fly once again.

Contents

Introduction

Last May I found myself boarding a flight, this time from London back home to Chicago, after having taught several small workshops in several different venues in the city over the weekend. I felt energized, fatigued, satisfied, relieved, excited to get on board, eager to be home, and thrilled at the wonders, both inside me and all around. As soon as I received my boarding pass, I got a call from my sister and soul friend, Cuky.

"Where are you?" she asked, not knowing, as she usually finds me in transit.

"I'm in London," I answered.

"Well, you must have been very busy, because your guides, your nonphysical spiritual helpers, have been trying to get ahold of you and have had no success, so they contacted me instead."

Grinning, I said, "I'm not surprised. I have been rather deeply involved in teaching. What do they say?"

"They told me to tell you the name of your next book. It's called *Traveling at the Speed of Love*."

Looking at my boarding pass as I was rushing to the gate at that very moment, I laughed out loud. "Well, that's what I'm doing right now," I answered. "Did they tell you what it's supposed to be about?" I asked.

"No. They just said, 'You'll know.' That's all."

Just then, as I boarded the flight, my phone disconnected. How dramatic of them. Settling into my seat, I began to ponder the message I had just received. It may seem odd to some to have guidance delivered that way, but it's actually very common. If intuition and guidance can't get through to you directly, they often gravitate toward other openings, such as into the awareness of others who are on the same frequency, who then can reflect them back to you. It happens to me all the time, and probably to you as well. We are telepathic beings. We share thoughts, ideas, and inspirations far more than we know, and often deliver messages from higher sources to one another without ever realizing it. Receiving messages like this is actually one way in which we (or at least our higher awareness) do travel at the speed of love.

Continuing to smile, and to ponder my new marching orders, I buckled up. Traveling at the speed of love. Wow! What an appealing notion. As a traveler who has crisscrossed this planet for more than 25 years—doing stints as a flight attendant years ago—and a true gypsy at heart, I couldn't think of a better way to go.

As we lifted off, floating through the gray London drizzle, rising above the thick blanket of clouds towering overhead, and finally emerging into a crystal blue sunshine-filled sky, I realized that we are all travelers, and we are all on a journey of one sort or another all the time.

Whether we're taking a simple stroll from the living room to the kitchen or a trek across Nepal, every single one of us inhabiting a physical body here on Earth is also a spirit traveler journeying through the earthly experience.

Life itself is a journey and has been noted as such by poets and philosophers throughout history. As a matter of fact, the moment my eldest daughter was born and took in her first breath, the doctor looked at her and said, "Hello, little traveler. Welcome to life."

Life is an adventure, and we are free to travel this earthly journey in any way we choose. Our daily life unfolds; we are always in motion. Whether it's with our feet, our mouths, or our minds, we are on the go, pushing forward to another, and another, and yet another experience. At least I know *I* am, and looking out my airplane window, observing figures, cars, people, trains, and other airplanes darting all around me, on the ground and in the sky, I knew I wasn't alone.

Traveling is what we earthlings do. Having an earthly journey is what our spirits commit to when we are born. The earliest human beings were nomads, hunter-gatherers. They traveled by foot from place to place in search of food and didn't settle down in one place until they invented agriculture. Starting with these ancient adventurers, we've journeyed by canoes across lakes, by horses across plains, by ships across oceans, by trains across continents, by cars across town, and now, even by rocket ships across galaxies.

We enter the journey at birth, and this portion of the trip ends at death's door, although I'm sure the journey continues in a new shape and form after that.

Although we are all traveling this Universe together, the speed, the tone, and the quality of our journey differs greatly from person to person. We choose our way just as when we travel on airplanes we choose our class: first class, business class, economy, or even standby.

In the journey of life, the destination is always the same—our death. What makes each life unique is the means by which we arrive there. Do we plan an adventurous, exciting itinerary with stopovers in exotic locales; or do we join a package tour and stick with the crowd? Do we take the risk to venture into the unknown, explore the beauty, experience the variety, and connect with the wonderful diversity of people we meet along the way, making new friends who enrich our lives and bring us new awareness? Or do we stay on the beaten path, have a superficial drive-by experience, with the windows up and the AC on, keeping to ourselves, shunning what is different, and viewing the world around us through the isolating windows of our fears and negative beliefs? Do we have a rich experience filled with discovery and excitement; or a bleak, boring, and dreary trip that rarely takes us out of our comfort zone but fails to expose us to the wonders of the world?

Perhaps it's time to reevaluate the speed and level of awareness of heart at which you choose to travel through life. It's easy to do. If you love your life, and every day bears unimaginable gifts, exciting opportunities, blessings, and deep soul connections, and you wonder how much better it could possibly be, you are presently traveling at the speed of love. Whatever you are doing, keep doing it. It is working, and you know it.

If, on the other hand, every day is a drag and you feel victimized, ripped off, despairing, disappointed, shut down, cynical, frustrated, or depressed, then it's time to reassess your travel plans and consider an upgrade.

Traveling at the speed of love means being liberated from the fear that plagues this planet and robs us of a joyful journey. Shifting from a paradigm of fear to a paradigm of love is what this book is all about. Using the metaphor of air travel, it's a practical guide to upgrading your life from being mired in the drag of fear to cruising in the jet stream of love and flow.

In this book, I will share ways to elevate your life's journey immediately, from the planning stage clear through to reaching your destination and everything in between. I will address unpacking the baggage and negative souvenirs of the past, and help you more mindfully discern what baggage to carry into the future.

I discuss ways to get your body and mind in shape for a lighter-hearted journey so that you feel great as you go. I write about how to check in with life, manage insecurity, meet the pilot who assures your progress, and even make contact with the control tower of the Universe so that you safely navigate the chaos of life and stay on course to attain your highest dreams.

I also address how to manage unexpected turbulence, deal with occasional diversions, handle challenging travel companions, cope with unexpected mechanical problems, and even avert attempted hijackings of your peace of mind so that you travel the friendly skies of love throughout your life's journey.

At the end of each chapter, I present practical tips and tools to sharpen our ability to fly above the fray, catch the jet stream of joy, and have a delightful and wondrous adventure. We are intended to flow with the forces of goodness, beauty, creativity, and abundance that are our birthright as Divine Beings. Once we find our way out of the quagmire of negative, fear-based consciousness, we can soar to heaven. Loving life is what our journey is all about. If you're ready to travel through life in the best possible way, buckle up and let's take off.

How to Use This Book

Each chapter in this book addresses one aspect of life's journey and how to shift from the drag of fear-based traveling to traveling at the speed of love. At the end of each chapter, you'll find a series of questions called "In-Flight Check-In" for you to reflect upon in order to help you recognize the particular fear-based patterns that may be keeping you from having a less-than-joyful journey. Take your time in reflecting on these questions before answering them in a notebook, a process I'll describe in more detail in a moment. Travel at your own speed through this book; it proposes a way of life, inviting you to enter into it at your own pace and in your own time.

Following each In-Flight Check-In is a set of tools called "Flying Lessons," designed to reconnect you with Divine flow. There are two levels of these tools, Basic and Advanced, to help you continually upgrade your journey in every way.

The Basic Flying Lessons are easy first steps to help you rise above the fearful drag of negative energy before it sucks you in. The Basic Lessons open the way to experiencing what it means to be in the flow of love.

The Advanced Flying Lessons focus on building up an even stronger resistance, an energetic immunity against negative influences that can interrupt your loving flow, and helping you to avert problems before they arise.

Using these tools regularly creates a powerful shift from fear to love in how you respond to all conditions and situations in your life. They steer you around drama, sabotage, psychic ambushes, and energetic disruptions, and keep you in the flow. They also teach you how to begin the day with love over fear so that you lift off each morning into another beautiful adventure.

Start by working with the Basic Lessons for two or three days, and then use them anytime you find yourself losing altitude in life. Some of these Basic Lessons are so fundamental to traveling at the speed of love (especially the breathing lessons) that you will want to practice them regularly so they become a habit.

Graduate to the more Advanced Lessons once you feel comfortable with the Basics. Work with these tools to more quickly elevate your journey to an all-new level of peace and joy. They, too, are quite simple, yet powerful, so you will find using these tools a welcome support to your life. View them as trip insurance, helping guarantee that you get the most out of your life experience.

Use either a Basic or Advanced tool at least once a day, and even better, several times during the day as the need arises. In fact, use these tools anytime you feel you're spiraling downward into victimhood and negativity. They quickly reverse negativity and realign you with the flow of love.

Some of the Basic and Advanced Lessons require writing, so I suggest that you get a small journal as well as a small pocket notebook to carry with you in which to record your efforts as you work. Keep your journal by your bedside, along with this book and a pen so you can freely write down your lessons every evening; and carry your small pocket notebook in your purse or briefcase so you can record insights as you go. These notebooks will soon become your valued personal in-flight training manuals for keeping above the clouds and in the light.

The book is filled with a lot of information, so read it through once then keep it on hand so you can reread it often. New ideas and suggestions are assimilated best a little at a time, so revisiting the book frequently and rereading a few pages at a time is the best way to learn how to master traveling at the speed of love.

In fact, consider this a reference book, and refer to it as a compass to get back on track when you lose your way and remap your itinerary when you're lost. Traveling at the speed of love is a spirited art and takes practice to master. The fear-based world is a mighty foe, so you must pay attention, keep on your toes, and be fully prepared to dodge its many traps in order to remain above its ugly seductions. That is why it's best to refer to this book often, so you have constant support and guidance in ensuring your joyful journey.

The only thing between you and a first-class spirited journey through life is the awareness and intention to live your life to the fullest. If you want to travel at the speed of love, you can. I believe it's the only way to fly while on Earth. So insist on an upgrade today and get ready to bring a whole new level of joy to your life.

CHAPTER 1

Flying First Class

When on life's journey, you have a choice in the manner in which you choose to fly. You can travel on standby, waiting for others to give you permission to get onboard; economy class, which allows you to get where you want to go without any frills, comforts, or ease of flow; or first class, which makes the trip a real pleasure.

No matter what class you choose, the flight pattern is the same: you are born, you live your life, and then you die. How you travel, however, is up to you. Standby is a gamble. Economy is a struggle. First class is a joy. Although going first class provides a more beautiful and comfortable journey, it also asks more of us, the travelers, to have this experience. Economy class, on the other hand, is a far less consciously demanding way to travel. It gets us where we want to go, but often involves—even encourages—a lot of drama, discomfort, and indifference with respect to the joyful spirit of life. Standby, the least creative way to live, is life lived completely unconsciously. It is the default option for those who are unreflective, irresponsible, and ill prepared; and is the choice of those suffering from addictions or other self-destructive behaviors.

What is important to remember is that it's not the destination, but the journey itself, that our conscious awareness affects. As the saying goes, "You get what you give." While economy class might seem more accessible, the experience along the way will most likely be far more energetically costly to you, fraught with far more irritations, aggravations, disappointments, missed opportunities, and psychic insults to the spirit than a first-class trip would embody.

The good news is that when it comes to the journey of life, anyone can travel first class. Although it may feel as if you have no choice in how you journey, that standby or economy is all you can look forward to or all you can afford, that's not really true. It is really all you are affording *yourself.*

Let me be clear—I'm not suggesting you must physically travel on the Earth plane in first class, because that's not the point. What I am suggesting is that the quality of your spiritual journey, your experience of life, can be first class if you want it to be.

And that offer is not one you can buy. Traveling first class in life is a privilege you must earn, and you do this by choosing love over fear. It doesn't always come easily (although it gets easier and easier), but it does allow you the finest quality of experience on your journey. To travel first class in life is to travel at the speed of love. It requires that you travel much more consciously, making a far greater effort to be in charge of your experience, yet it is open and available to anyone willing to make the necessary effort to upgrade.

To travel at the speed of love is to decide that the upgrade is worth it. To travel at the speed of love is to confront your fears, including defensiveness, anger, judgment, abandonment, and insecurity; and consciously reject those patterns in preference of a better, more loving attitude.

How to Upgrade

Can you upgrade your journey? *Yes!* Anyone who is willing to ask for more from life and make the effort to get it, who wants to enjoy his or her life experience rather than suffer and be a victim of it, can travel at the speed of love. The only requirement is that you be open to loving life—your life—fully, and view everyone and everything as a learning opportunity for your soul. Yes, everyone and everything!

To love something doesn't mean you have to like it, approve of it, or even desire it. It simply means to accept that this is what is happening, and if it's not happening in a way that uplifts you, know that you have a choice in how to respond. You can be a victim of it or send it and yourself more love so that your response to it will transform into one that is proactive, creative, and ultimately right for you.

It is challenging to travel first class in life, as I'm sure you can think of many people and things you do not love. I'm not suggesting that you love being in pain, or love the awful and even evil things that can be a part of life, but rather that you love that you are alive, and that you respond to all your life experiences with love. Once you decide to love your life and accept it all with the choice to respond with love, you will never turn back and ride the coach class of fear again. Once you've experienced this more liberated and peaceful way of living you'll want it, crave it, and insist that it's the only way to fly.

Yes, I know loving it all seems like an impossible order, and it is certainly a challenging one. I can think of quite a few things in front of me right now, both on the personal and political horizon that, from an ego viewpoint, frustrate and even enrage my sense of righteousness, and I don't love them all. And yet, the energy of anger and resentment only throws my personal flight into a tailspin.

For example, you may hate your body. To project this energy onto your body, however, causes depression, anxiety, embarrassment, and low self-esteem, all of which we know will not create a peaceful, loving flow. Because of these negative frequencies traveling through your body, you may be attracted to negative choices, such as eating a pint of Häagen-Dazs ice cream while watching reality shows on weight loss, staying up and playing computer games into the wee hours of the morning instead of getting a good night's rest, or sneaking cigarettes while walking the dog—choices that only cause your body to feel worse than before, creating a vicious downward spiral.

To love your body, on the other hand, and accept *what is* with your body at the moment will start to free the blocked and stagnant energy that keeps your body from being the vehicle you prefer. When you treat your body in a loving way—nurturing it with healthful foods, giving it the exercise and sleep it needs—it will respond by becoming a body that you *do* love. The key is to shift the focus of your attention to ways to love your body by treating it in a way that serves its needs best.

Another way to love your body is to appreciate how hearty it is, even if it isn't exactly behaving or looking the way you'd like it to. For example, if you're chubby around the middle, acknowledge that you can still be mobile and get around. Then, in appreciation of this fact, go for a short walk every day. If your teeth are crooked and a little stained, be grateful that you have teeth at all, then take a little more time brushing and flossing in appreciation of that fact. If you have digestive problems that cause you to be bloated and gassy, be glad that your body lets you know what isn't good for it, therefore probably saving you from much more serious gastric conditions later. In appreciation of that fact, be a little more mindful of what foods cause your body to react so negatively. The point is, whatever your dislike or frustration, it could be worse, so turn your attitude around and love the full human experience, including the challenges and frustrations you may be experiencing.

Flying First Class Is Natural

Choosing to travel through your journey in fear and negativity, as most people do, goes against the flow of nature, against the flow of life, and against the flow of Divine grace. It causes you to remain below the clouds of doom and gloom and prevents you from reaching the higher altitude where the sun really is always shining.

So in the long run, the seemingly easier and more seductive way of living in fear is actually very expensive. It costs you positive connection, synchronistic support, ease, flow, grace, and personal joy. It will cost you present relationships and prevent positive future ones. It costs you health, vitality, good humor, creativity, and intuition. It costs you your life.

I just spoke with a client recently, Linda, who was married to a highly negative and fearful man, although he had many positive things going for him in life, including a beautiful 100-acre farm; a family of six devoted and healthy children who helped him on the farm in their spare time even though they had families and children of their own; and his loving wife, who stuck by his side in every way. They had no money problems, no addictions or dramas among their children, and they had a lot to be thankful for. And yet, in spite of his blessings, he was the bearer of an endless litany of doom and gloom, singing what Linda called the "lions and tigers and bears . . . oh *my*" blues. He was dreary, miserable, and ungrateful for everything in his life. He blasted the government, the economy, the neighbors, the weather, and anything else he could conjure up. All was fair game for his assaults and insults.

Linda lived with him as long as she could, but after she had a breast-cancer scare, she decided she'd had enough of his misery and moved into an apartment of her own just to get away from him. After she left, so did the kids, one at a time, because without her they found him even harder to bear. Eighteen months after she left, she received a call from the neighbors. Her husband had suffered a stroke and was on his way to the hospital. He was so debilitated that he was put in a nursing home. "Now he has created the misery he always feared," said Linda. "It's a shame it had to be this way."

Other Classy Travelers

One of the bonuses of choosing to travel first class is that you meet the best fellow travelers. Because like attracts like, people who choose to travel in first class meet kindred spirits, like-minded souls who share the same values and priorities. These are giving people who are generous of soul and full of heart and make your journey through life richer in every way. They make great traveling companions, and open doors to wondrous new opportunities.

Just last week I was given an example of the kind of open-hearted kinship that traveling at the speed of love can attract. The publicist for Hay House South Africa, Michelle, one of the most loving souls I know, took a trip to the United States for the annual Hay House business conference. Upon returning, she and three other Hay House employees decided to stop over in Singapore for a short three-day visit just for fun. After having a tremendously good time, they showed up at the airport to check in for their flight home when, to Michelle's horror, she discovered that her passport was missing. She was not permitted to get on the plane. None of her Hay House colleagues had time to assist her, as their flight was boarding, so she was left at the ticket counter without any apparent way to get home.

The ticket agent, clearly traveling at the speed of love, noticed Michelle's predicament and immediately stepped in to help her get an emergency passport and to change her flight for the following day. But his kindness didn't stop there. He insisted that once Michelle collected her new passport, she should spend the night with him and his family. Due to his gracious assistance, what could have been a disaster turned out to be the best part of her entire journey abroad. Her loving heart attracted another loving heart to her. That is how it works when traveling at the speed of love. You will always be helped, and often in surprisingly wonderful ways, even when things appear to go wrong.

Seats Are Available

It's easier than you think to reevaluate the level of awareness of heart in which you choose to travel day to day. There is plenty of room in the first-class cabin of life. It offers more friends, more room to be yourself, more ways to relax, and better nourishment. An upgrade is always available. To apply for such an upgrade, you must shift your perception from head to heart, from fear to love, from withholding to giving, from "no" to "yes," from negative to positive, and from "me" to "us." The benefits of your upgrade will be immediately felt.

This is your life, and the manner in which you travel through it is up to you. You can have a terrible experience or a phenomenal one, depending on how you choose to fly: open, accepting and loving; or closed, suspicious, and withholding. The external world will bring what it brings, both good and bad, to all. That is the terrain of the human experience. Just as there are valleys and mountains, deserts and oceans, so too are there peaks and valleys in the terrain of human life. That is just the way it is. How you navigate that topography determines the quality of your trip. Fly under the cloud of fear and drama and you will most likely slip into a negative tailspin, causing the journey to be a first-class drag. Fly above life's struggles with an open and loving heart—and a commitment to love life, come what may—and the entire journey becomes an enlightening adventure for the soul, a heavenly trip.

Instant Upgrade

I just read an article in the *Chicago Tribune* this morning about a doctor whose attitude dramatically changed once he nearly faced the end of his journey in a terrible and unexpected way. A self-acknowledged cynic who was known as the hospital curmudgeon where he worked, he was dropped off at the elevated train station to catch a train to O'Hare airport last winter at six in the morning. Crossing four lanes of traffic in a dark underpass leading to the train-station entrance, rolling his suitcase behind him, he was suddenly hit by a speeding SUV, which sped away and left him for dead.

Thanks to the expert response of the paramedics who arrived at the scene, within minutes he was properly transported by ambulance on his back, with his neck and head protected, to the hospital—which, coincidentally, was the same one where he worked, Illinois Masonic.

Once he arrived, he was met in the emergency room by a team of his own colleagues, who painstakingly devoted themselves to saving his life. Miraculously, only six short weeks later he was walking again, and six months later was fully recovered. Not only was his life spared, but it was also transformed.

Knowing that he came very close to losing his life on that dark and dreary morning, he now celebrates every moment on Earth as the best one ever. His peers at work cannot believe he's the same man who was once so negative that people went out of their way to avoid him. Today, he is so bright and loving that he is the star of the hospital. Grateful for his life, he encourages those he encounters day after day in the hospital to be the same. He nearly died in his own misery, but was given a second chance to journey in a different way. Filled with love for himself and all of life, he's now dedicated to awakening that love in everyone he touches.

In-Flight Check-In

Take a few moments and quiet your mind. Breathe in deeply, and relax. Get out your notebook, and write down your answers to the following questions:

- Looking over your life so far, would you say you generally travel first class, at the speed of love, or would you say it's time for an upgrade?

Maybe you travel first class in some areas of your life but could use an upgrade in others. To discover the answer, consider the following questions:

- Do you love and respect your body?
- Are you traveling in a solid vessel that gets you through each day's journey effortlessly, or could you use an upgrade in your body and health?
- Do you love your personal life?
- Are you surrounded by joyful friends and family members whom you love; or are you surrounded by people traveling standby through life—waiting to take your seat, your energy, your resources, and your time to use for their own benefit?

- Do you love your job?

- Are you engaged in your work and treated respectfully by your peers; or are you suffering at the back of the plane, near the lavatories and the galley, feeling cramped, unloved, and overwhelmed?

- Do you love yourself? Do you feel competent, confident, and in control; or are you wishing you were someone else living some other life than your own?

Basic Flying Lessons

Applying for an Upgrade

Looking over the answers to the questions above, can you identify any area(s) in which you are traveling at less than first class? You can change this and apply for an upgrade by answering, out loud, the following: "I love and I am grateful for . . ."

For example:

- I love and am grateful for my children's toes . . .

- I love and am grateful for spice markets . . .

- I love and am grateful for the smell in the air after a spring rain . . .

Do this ten times every day. Each time you fill in the blank, name something new. It will uplift your spirit and redirect your compass so that you start to notice all that is worth being grateful for now. If you remember what you love and go there first, not last, day in and day out, you will automatically be uplifted.

Improve Your Attitude

Where in life can you use an upgrade in attitude? Are you a complainer? Do you feel sorry for yourself? Are you chronically irritable and self-indulgent? A drag? Today, you are going to change your attitude and behavior. If an apology to someone is in order, make that apology today. If you've been treating someone rudely, ask for his or her forgiveness right away. If you've been complaining, stop immediately and count your blessings. Give yourself and those who must listen to you a break from your negativity, starting now.

Advanced Flying Lessons

Take Life as It Comes

Spend the day accepting whatever comes your way by saying out loud, "I accept this. I am learning from this. I am open to the purpose it serves. I love it. [Yes, I know. This part is highly challenging. But trust me and just give it a try. You'll be surprised by how things shift toward the better once you do.] Thank you for this gift."

This includes both the good and the difficult stuff that arises throughout the day. For example, if you end up stuck in the worst traffic jam of your life, say, "I accept this. I am learning from this. I am open to the purpose it serves. I love it. Thank you for this gift."

The same goes if you win the lottery, get a new job or a promotion, or have someone leave you. Always remember, when traveling at the speed of love, that everything is a gift, an opportunity, and something to grow your soul. If you accept and love it all, you will fly high indeed.

At the end of the day, review what occurred, what class you traveled in that day, and what you learned. If you're unclear about what you learned, be patient and sleep on it. Review it all again in the morning. Eventually you will see that traveling at the speed of love is a choice worth making.

A First-Class Day

All day today, view everything as a first-class experience. Start with a first-class shower, for example, remembering that there are those who don't even have water to shower in. Have a first-class breakfast, a first-class ride to work, a first-class workout. Make a special note of all the exciting, mystical, wonderful, surprising first-class blessings and gifts that come your way today as well.

From the smallest surprise, like finding a parking space right in front of your office just as you turn into the lot; to something greater, like being treated to a complimentary dessert after dinner by the owner of your favorite restaurant, notice all the perks of the first-class journey you're on. Notice the first-class beauty around you, whether in nature, in people, or even the "first-class" challenges confronting you. If asked, "How are you?" say, "I'm having a first-class day." You will.

CHAPTER 2

Travel Lightly

Before we can begin to travel forward in our lives at the speed of love, it is first necessary to stop and take an honest look at what is dragging us down today, and then let go of that which no longer serves us. In 2008, while I was attempting to travel full speed ahead toward my Divine reality, I was unexpectedly derailed by back pain, a kidney infection, extreme exhaustion, hospitalization, and two sudden deaths in my family. This train wreck of events caught me totally off guard. And yet it didn't.

I knew I was working too hard and was overextended. And I knew I was overly ambitious and said yes to way more than I should have. I was pushing myself too hard in my yoga practice because I like to be the best at everything I do. I also knew that I wanted to see my family more but kept working and postponing it instead. So when my energy gave up and my body became seriously ill, I was blindsided but not surprised. I was stopped dead in my tracks . . . and suddenly everything that had seemed so urgent and pressing became meaningless. I found myself without ambition, desire, motivation, or energy, as if someone had pulled the plug on the perpetual-motion machine of my mind. Everything stopped. And in retrospect, all I can say is, thank God it did.

Because along with my illness came the realization that so much of my life was flying by me at the speed of fear. It didn't feel like fear at the time. It felt like intensity, ambition, and urgency—even passion. But underneath it all, it was really more often than not well-disguised fear. One of the reasons I knew it was fear is that fear's main symptom is victimhood, and that's where I was more often than I care to admit.

I had fear that I had to say yes to all requests because otherwise I might turn someone away who needed my help, which would mean that I wasn't a truly spiritual person. I had fear of missing professional opportunities and felt that I needed to accept all that was offered to me. I had fear around the astronomical cost of sending two daughters to college. I had fear that I might disappoint a client. I had fear of getting older and didn't want to miss a thing in my life. I had fear about maintaining my standing among my peers at Hay House (my publisher), hoping I was acceptable to them and considered worthwhile. I had fear of being judged harshly or being misunderstood by people who read my books. I also had fear that I would not be as available to my daughters as I should be.

The deeper I dove, the more fear I uncovered. For years, it had driven me and kept me racing around at hyperspeed, pushing me forward, at other times pulling me so far backward that I dwelled on the past. That is, until I suddenly was confronted with two deaths and my fear was no longer disguised. Instead, I was face-to-face with the worst that could happen, and in one instant I became acutely aware of just how much fear tries to outrun death. Let me tell you something: it can't.

What Drags Us Down?

What I realized, to my great surprise, was that in spite of all my personal-growth work and deep spiritual awareness, I was still frequenting a neighborhood I had no business being in. I called it "victimhood." It is a place that seduces all of us, and promises to be a sweet place to travel to; but in fact, it is a dark, empty, sad neighborhood that looks appealing but delivers nothing. It doesn't lift you up. It only drags you down. Victimhood, or more specifically, victim consciousness, is the belief that life *happens* to you and that you are under constant threat. It is fear-based thinking that casts a shadow over every experience you have.

More than a set of beliefs, victim or fear-based consciousness is a soulless energetic frequency that pushes and pulls us in all directions, threatening, menacing, taunting, and robbing us of our free will and creative thinking. Fear-based victim consciousness is like a perpetual noxious gas that seeps into our brains and steals our vitality, our joy, our compassion, our tolerance, our generosity, and all the pleasure we get out of life. It drags us down, freezing us out of the flow of life, and throws us into cynicism, suspicion, and defense.

It keeps us from living joyfully in the moment and pulls us, instead, backward toward the past where it reminds us of our weaknesses, failures, and vulnerabilities. Even those events of the past that were positive and uplifting can be overshadowed by fearful thinking, while whispering in our ears that the best was nothing more than "luck" and should not be expected again.

How We Become Victims

Fear is like a virus that infects us through many channels. We are most intensely exposed to it through media bombardment such as television, newspapers, the Internet, and radio; and the constant stream of negative stories about global warming, school shootings, nuclear menaces, economic meltdowns, and terrorist threats.

We are fed fear through violence in movies, talk-show radio rants, video games, and music. We are trained to feel unsafe in our schools, hospitals, jobs, and neighborhoods; with respect to our food sources, and even in our churches.

This social and cultural fearmongering trickles down to affect us on an individual level as well. Because we feel so threatened externally, we look for ways to seek protection from these potential menaces in the safety of those closest to us.

Sadly, since others feel fear, too, relief is scarce. From this fear-based perspective, life seems as if it is something happening to us from the outside and from which we cannot be protected—that is, we feel like victims. This causes us to be on perpetual guard against injury, trying to win the love and approval of others while remaining in fear of getting it "wrong"—whether by what we say or do, or how we look or think, or whether we agree with those whom we feel possess the love we need. No matter how we strategize to run from fear, from a victim point of view, there is no escape.

In fact, fear-based consciousness is often subtly disguised as essential intelligence, common sense, street smarts, or when directed at our children, helicopter or "involved" parenting; so we view it as a positive, necessary approach to dealing with the dangers of the outside world. We meet the enemy, as Pogo would say, "and it is us."

Why Are We So Vulnerable?

People may wonder why we are so vulnerable to falling into the victim role that fear inspires in us. The answer is quite simple. The greatest reason we find ourselves ambushed by fear is that we do not want to be fully accountable for our choices and actions in life. Instead, we prefer to pretend we have no choice, that life happens to us, while lamenting its brutal and unfair affects. If we have someone or something else to blame for our unsatisfactory lives, we can step away from our responsibility and say it's not our "fault."

As long as we continue to accept the role of victim, we do not have to be accountable for our lives. Being held accountable is scary for most people. Yet while it is often difficult at first to take responsibility (meaning the ability to respond) for the affairs and conditions of our lives, once we do—and *only* once we do—we can turn life into something other than victimhood, into something positive that we love.

The good news is that we do not have to fight, outrun, or even outsmart fear to break free of its insidious effects. All we have to do is recognize how it has been running our lives and choose another way, a way rooted in self-love and love for life. Let us decide to be fully responsible for our lives, and protect and value them with our whole hearts and minds. We do this by making positive and loving choices toward ourselves and others in every situation. We can break free of old habits and establish new, better ones.

We can change the channel of our mind-set from a broadcast of fear to one of upliftment. When we do, we start traveling through life at a higher, lighter, more liberating frequency . . . a vibration that makes us utterly immune to every fear-based infection.

We can live lives that are peaceful and filled with joy; and be happy with who we are, happy with who we've been, and eager to discover who we are becoming. We can live lives where everything is perfect just as it is—and we can do it now. All we must do is shift from living in fear to living in love.

Let's Start

To begin traveling at the speed of love, we must embrace the challenge of recognizing and confronting our fears with the intention not to let them run or ruin our lives any longer. If we ever hope to rise above and break free of fear, we must recognize just how much it controls everything we do. Fear is something we've come to live with and accept as normal. We've been taught to hide our fear, deny it, or pretend it isn't there—all the while allowing it to influence every decision we make and every thought we have, often with disastrous results.

A client of mine named Kevin, a 47-year-old divorced man who worked as a computer programmer, was fearful of being too close to other human beings in case they might criticize him, hurt his overly sensitive ego, or take away his freedom. Consequently, every time someone did get too close for comfort or attempted to get a commitment out of him, he disappeared. He wouldn't answer e-mails or return phone calls, sometimes for days, even weeks. This infuriated and estranged those who could have been supportive of him. No wonder at age 47, after a lifetime of fear-based choices, he found himself alone, isolated, unsupported; and with many angry, disappointed people unwilling to do a thing for him.

His fear of closeness and commitment alienated everyone in his midst. When he became unemployed and sick with anxiety, there was no one to help him out. Fear robbed him of friends and family, and he suffered alone.

Another client of mine, Mary, a talented graphic artist and the only girl in a family of boys, was fearful of her femininity. Her mother told her that women were the weaker gender, and people would disrespect her because she was a female. Infected by her mother's perception, Mary refused to look, dress, speak, or act feminine in any way. She dressed in severe clothing, rejected all softness of character, and was dismissive of women who were more outwardly sensitive and feminine. Men found her harsh and aggressive. Women did, too. She was the first to be hurtful before she could be hurt. At 45, she developed cancer in her most outwardly feminine feature—her breast. Furious, she would allow no one to help her, neither man nor woman. As she became increasingly afflicted and enraged, she grew increasingly isolated. Battling her disease, she too suffered alone. Fear cut her off from friendship and support from either sex.

Nancy, a 37-year-old manager at an Italian restaurant in Chicago, was afraid of being alone. She believed that being alone meant no one loved her, and worse, that she was unlovable. Her fear drove her to seduce as many men as she could, hoping they would then stay with her and fill up her emptiness. By the time she was 30, she'd had so many sexual partners that she lost count, and lost her self-esteem as well. She became more and more needy and would attempt false or premature intimacies before any more authentic connection could develop. Her anxiety mounted and was felt by the men she dated, which sent them running in the opposite direction. This made her all the more stressed and drove her to self-soothe with alcohol. It didn't work. It only made her a lonely alcoholic. She was stuck in a vicious cycle of casual sex, alcohol abuse, and chaos. Now she was sad, sick, disruptive, angry, and alone. Fear took another victim.

As you read these three people's stories, it may seem obvious what their shared problem was, and you may wonder how they could possibly have found themselves so overrun by fear, so out of control. But take a moment to think about where fear sneakily infiltrates your own life.

You'll find it in feelings of low self-esteem or in the way you criticize your body. It may show up in your impatience with yourself or the way you treat others. It may show up in an addiction, such as overeating, drinking, or taking drugs—even over-the-counter drugs—that alter your mood and awareness. It may show up in sleeplessness, anxiety, depression, rage, manipulation, sexual promiscuity, overspending, or other crazy-making behavior. Once fear takes hold, it takes you and everyone around you down, unless, of course, you know how to rise above it and break free.

Love Is the Cure

The natural way to immunize yourself against fear and travel to a higher frequency is through love. Love is the only vibration that completely clears the toxic symptoms of fear. Love elevates all things above the vibration of fear. When you travel at the speed of love, fear falls by the wayside and dissipates, and you are filled with peace.

When you travel at the speed of love, you feel the opposite of being a victim. Look at the list below to compare and contrast the difference between flying in fear on the right or traveling at the speed of love on the left.

Speed of Love	In Fear
Relaxed	Tense
Present	Distracted
Grateful	Entitled
Optimistic	Pessimistic
Appreciative	Ungrateful
Forgiving	Begrudging
Compassionate	Indifferent
Patient	Impatient

Speed of Love	In Fear
Tolerant	Intolerant
Generous	Stingy
Humorous	Droll
At ease	Uptight
Light-hearted	Heavy
Timeless	Dated
Confident	Insecure
Alive	Dead
Humble	Arrogant
Accepting	Rejecting
Receptive	Tuned out

The more you love, the more you become immune to all the toxins and troubles of the "normal" world. And if do catch the fear "bug," you bounce back quickly because it cannot get a deep hold on you anymore. Fear drags you down. Love lifts you up.

In-Flight Check-In

Take out your notebook and spend a few minutes thinking about each of the following questions. Be honest with yourself and probe deeply beneath your fear-based defenses for the answers. Rather than simple *yes/no* answers, elaborate, and include examples of when you might have experienced these reactions or behaviors. The more effort you put into the exercises, the more benefit you'll get from them.

- In what areas are you most fearful today?

- What about health? Relationships? Work? Money? Family?

- Are you aware of when you are fearful?

- Do you criticize others often?

- Are you defensive?
- How quick to anger are you?
- Are you a worrier?
- Are you easily intimidated?
- Where do you become frozen with fear?
- How do you deal with your fears?
- How do you deny them?
- Do you foist them onto someone else?
- How fearful are those around you?
- Does this affect you or not?

Basic Flying Lessons

Lighten the Load

In your notebook, list your top ten fears from the slightest to the greatest.

1. I am afraid of . . .
2. I am afraid of . . .

. . . and so on.

After each fear, write down all the reasons you can think of for being afraid. For example:

1. I am afraid of not being able to pay my bills because I spend more than I make.
2. I am afraid of not being able to pay my bills because my ex won't give me child support on time.
3. I am afraid of not being able to pay my bills because my job is not stable.

4. I am afraid of not being able to pay my bills because my children's college education is so expensive.

As you write, think about coming up with a rational approach to deal with each fear. For example:

1. I can put myself on a budget.

2. I can put away a little each paycheck so that I have a cushion to fall back on.

3. I can rent a room in my home.

4. My children can apply for scholarships and grants.

Include the worst-case scenario with respect to your fears. What do you fear the most? What in this worst-case scenario is realistic? What can you proactively do to avoid this worst-case scenario? What can you do in response? Who might help you? And finally, look at the worst-case scenario and see that even if it all unfolded in this way, you would still be okay—maybe not happy, but okay—and realize you have choices in *any* scenario.

Keep writing down all the reasons you are afraid until you cannot think of any more. Once you finish this process, check in. Does your fear feel as large as it did before this exercise? Does it feel as intense? Do you still feel as afraid? Are these feelings yours, or are they someone else's? Is there any part of you avoiding responsibility for your life around this fear? And if you're not taking responsibility for addressing your fear, who do you believe should be taking responsibility for relieving it?

Write until you feel emotionally emptied. Then relax and do nothing more. Imagine love pouring into this newly emptied space in your heart and mind, filling you with energy, insight, and light. Take a deep breath and relax. Work on one fear like this each day. Watch what happens as you lighten your load. Record any changes you feel in your journal.

Breaking Free

To leave fear and begin traveling at the speed of love, it's necessary to first set your intention to do so. Start by fully focusing on the kind of experience you want to have *now*. The now part is the key to getting onboard the frequency of love. Fear does not travel in the now. It starts in the past and builds momentum and intensity as it travels to the future. In the present, it can and does carry you to places you do not want to go and into experiences you do not want to have.

So to free yourself from fear, decide what experience you prefer to have right now. Do you want an adventurous experience? A peaceful one? A learning experience? A relational experience? An intimate, loving experience? You can have any life experience you want, but not until *you* decide to have it. Tune in to your heart and your deeper authentic being for all of your decisions. Doing this will keep you from being pulled off course.

Advanced Flying Lessons

Color Your Fear

Fear is an energetic thought form that descends upon you like a dark cloud. It actually looks and feels a certain way in your mind's eye. Focusing on your fear, notice what color, shape, size, or tone your fear conveys to you. Is it a dense, dark form of energy blocking your flow? A sharp, brittle form hanging over your head? A gray blob with undefined edges? Face the fear head-on in an artful and creative way.

To do so, buy a package of crayons, the more colors the better, and a large sketch pad. Place your attention directly on your fear and, using the crayons, color your fear in the sketch pad. Be aware of its shape, size, and form; and depict it as best as you can. Does it shift as you color? Does it change shape as you identify it on paper? What color is it today? What size? The more you express your fear on paper with the crayons, how do you feel inside? Is your fear shrinking? If not, keep coloring. What thoughts are running through your mind as you color? Are you becoming more aware that fear has imposed itself upon you and can be easily discharged, released, reduced, reshaped, and reevaluated as you color? Let this happen and record your results in your journal.

Choose to Fly High

What experience do you want now? Make the distinction between the *experiences* you want and the *things* you want. For example:

- *I want the experience of joyful writing* vs.
  I want a completed manuscript.

- *I want the experience of loving intimately* vs.
  I want a soul mate.

- *I want the experience of learning from an inspired teacher* vs.
  I want a degree/credential/diploma/certificate.

- *I want the experience of strength, beauty, life force, and vitality* vs.
  I want to be a size six.

We are journeying on Earth to experience life, not just to purchase or accumulate stuff. To travel at the speed of love, focus on the experience you choose to create now, and you will catch a wave of love that will carry you there.

When you focus on simply *having,* you step out of the flow and slow your vibration down. You also set up the duality of *have* versus *not have,* thereby opening the door to repeating disappointments. On the other hand, choosing experiences puts you directly into universal flow, where everything you want begins to flow lovingly toward you.

CHAPTER 3

———·❤·———

Breathe: Your Ticket to Fly

This morning I overslept. I spent the weekend teaching a workshop in San Francisco and then caught a flight home that landed at midnight. By the time I collected my luggage, got to my car, and drove home, it was 2 A.M. I didn't mind. I still felt exhilarated from the workshop and the happy, joyful response that emanated from the people who attended. Their love carried me home on such a vibrational high that I didn't feel tired at all. That is, until the alarm clock went off at 7 A.M. and a wave of exhaustion swept over me as I reached over and pushed the snooze button. I immediately fell back into a deep sleep for another ten minutes when the alarm went off again. Struggling to wake up, I forced myself to open my eyes, stood up, and found my way to the shower. The deep satisfaction I had felt the day before still lingered, but my body was having none of it. It was tired and not ready to dive into another day's work quite yet.

Ignoring my body's needs, my mind pushed forward, and thus began a head-versus-body struggle that lasted all day. I had made commitments that I wanted to keep, yet physically I was running on empty. I pushed through to 4 P.M., then found my way home, where I could no longer put out any more effort, good intentions or not. I fell deeply asleep until 9 P.M.

As I pulled out of the heavy fog of such deep sleep, I realized that if I want to travel at the speed of love, I have to give my body more of a vote in how I pace myself, or I will not succeed.

My mind loves to create, and loses all sense of time and space when I'm possessed by an idea. My heart loves to connect and

25

to engage with others. And my body wants to share in the vibration of love as well, by "suiting up and showing up." But unlike my mind and heart, my body has a different set of requirements to keep up the vibration that my heart and mind seem to effortlessly maintain. I often forget to take these requirements fully into account as I arrange my day. And when I ignore what my body needs, my loving vibration takes a nosedive. I become agitated. I feel cranky and irritable. I have more difficulty listening or being present for others, and I overreact to noise and other dissonant energies around me.

I can't tell you how many times my family members, who witness me in an overextended, exhausted, and crabby state, have said, "I wish your clients and students could see you now . . . the way you really are!"

Every time this happens, I cringe a little inside because they're right. Coming off the vibrational high of an intense work experience, even work I absolutely love, I'm often caught by surprise by a negative mood, and I have no love or patience for anything.

If we try to do too much or have too many obligations snapping at our heels, the best of our loving intentions can implode into stress, irritation, and even depression because we simply cannot catch our breath. This is a tricky challenge, especially for the more ambitious among us, myself included. I love life and don't want to miss any of it, not a single moment. Yet if I cram my days chock-full of activities without allowing for what I call the three-dimensional physical needs of my body, I may be publicly loving, but privately guilty of downloading my stress and negativity onto the people closest to me.

Traveling at the speed of love is for the long haul. We must slow down and pace ourselves so that we avoid the emergency mode of breathlessness and exhaustion. As I write this, I'm shaking my head and smiling because this is so clearly a lesson I must learn. I know that my Higher Self is writing this chapter *through* me, *to* me.

I've read that the Dalai Lama is very mindful of the importance of keeping a sensible pace so he can travel at the speed of love every day. One time a reporter asked him how he remains so calm, so grounded, and so loving when his life can be so stressful and demanding.

He paused, gave the question some serious thought, and then answered, "I leave early for appointments." How sane. How realistic. How intelligent. And how loving to himself and the people who look to him for leadership that he paces himself realistically.

It is only when we refuse to allow our ambitious and overly active minds to bury us alive with their endless "to do" lists that we can genuinely travel at the speed of love for more than a sprint or a mad dash.

I received a call last night from my dear friend Julia Cameron (the author of more than 61 musicals, plays, and books, including *The Artist's Way*), who was in a fretful and unhappy frame of mind. Her "to do" list had grown so long that it seemed to be chasing her around her apartment, not allowing her a moment's peace. I could relate. I've been there a hundred times myself.

In an effort to help her slow down and catch her breath, I asked her to start listing all the things she had to do, all the things that were stealing her breath.

Her list unfurled. There were books to write, musicals and operas to produce, workshops to teach, interviews to do, calls to make, exercise classes to take, and social engagements to fulfill, but the one that she was most fretful over was that she simply wanted time to tidy up her apartment. No matter where she looked, her life seemed to be crowded, urgent, ungrounded, and in disarray; and her sleepless response left her frazzled and weepy.

The first thing I suggested to Julia was that she list her pressing obligations, one at a time, and contain them so they weren't racing all over her mind like runaway mice she couldn't catch. I learned from my teachers that containing overwhelming thoughts and pressures by naming them out loud is an important step to taking their power way. Just creating a list of demands gave Julia some relief. Yes, it seemed like a lot, she realized, but naming her responsibilities made them far more manageable, far less daunting than having them roll around her brain on the loose. She relaxed and took a deep breath. Next, I asked her what on that list she could tackle and see results from immediately. She didn't even hesitate. She replied, "Tidy up."

"Then do that," I said. "The rest will follow." So she turned off the phone and the computer, and plugged in the vacuum cleaner.

Just hearing the deep whine of the vacuum cleaner, she later shared with me, helped her to catch a breath. Pushing it around her apartment forced her to slow down a little. She surrendered. Her breath returned, and with it the remembrance that she loved doing all the things she had on her "to do" list, just not all at once. Without a breath, her mind had created the deception that her "to do's" were oppressive duties instead of creative efforts of love.

As she dusted, words and melodies for her next musical filled her mind and heart. When washing dishes, new chapter ideas for her next book popped into her head. As she folded her laundry, thoughts for an article she had promised to write flowed into her mind. Breath and grounding created an expanded sense of time. The more she breathed, the more time she had. It's funny how that works.

The slower she took things, the deeper she breathed, and the more the logjam of stress and emotion she had experienced hours earlier gave way to an inspired, easy, peaceful flow. All the things on Julia's list got accomplished once she gave herself more breath, and got organized and grounded by containing her runaway thoughts with a list. The emergency was over, and she was back in the flow.

That is what traveling at the speed of love is all about, staying in a peaceful, relaxed flow.

Emergency Alarms

We all struggle with assaults on our spirits that the vibration and tempo of the modern world impose upon us, especially those of us who are urban animals. In fact, we are so inundated with emergency sirens, especially in our cities, that we barely even register them on our conscious radar anymore. Yet alarms going off inside and out put stress on our bodies, make our hearts race, and steal our breath away, all without us noticing that it's happening.

Recently, I was driving through downtown Chicago with my friend Isabel, who moved here from the middle of Kansas five months ago. Sitting at a red light, an ambulance lunged across the road, as if coming from nowhere, and whizzed on by. She turned and commented that there seemed to be sirens screeching by all the time in Chicago. I hadn't noticed this until she mentioned it. Now, ever since she brought this to my attention, it seems that sirens and other loud noises are indeed going off nonstop. I also noticed how each siren or noise creates a sense of urgency in my body, a need to speed up.

Mental sirens such as "I should," "I must," and "I have to" can be just as anxiety provoking as physical ones. They put us on edge, making us feel as if we're overwhelmed with obligations that we don't have enough time to fulfill. They steal our breath as much as any rushing ambulance or air-raid alarm.

Although there may be an "emergency," it does not have to become *your* emergency. When hearing sirens or loud noises, whether inside your head or outside in the world around you, take a long, slow, deep breath. Stay calm and detached, and breathe slowly. If you hear the wail of an actual siren, the screech of a subway train, or any other sudden, dissonant noise, plug your ears and protect your nerves and your eardrums. If you feel inspired to do so, say a prayer for anyone experiencing a genuine emergency in that moment when you hear the siren. Then release it, as it's not yours to deal with. Breathe. Relax. That is the loving thing to do for you, for others, for everyone.

Exhale, Inhale

When internal or external noises throw you into a state of emergency and steal your breath away, let your awareness steal it back. When thrown off by noise or energetic dissonance, rather

29

than lurch forward in an anxious reaction, step back and exhale fully. Then inhale slowly and observe the disturbance, but do not allow it to affect you. This, of course, will take practice, but with a little effort it will start to become second nature. Say out loud, "There may be an emergency, but it is not *my* emergency." Then exhale deeply again, and follow with an even deeper inhale. The reason you exhale first is that the deeper you exhale and empty your lungs of stagnant air, the greater your capacity to inhale a deep breath and relax.

If, in fact, you are facing a real emergency, then it is all the more important to breathe before you respond. With breath you can make sound decisions, remain grounded and rational, and intelligently think through any challenge you face rather than blindly reacting in fear. Remember, when decompression occurs on an airplane, the first thing you're instructed to do is put on your own oxygen mask first, breathe in, and then respond to the emergency. That's because breath is power, and without breath you are at the mercy of circumstances.

Last week I was driving across Chicago to get to an interview when I hit an infamous Chicago pothole, causing my tire to go instantly flat, and I coasted to a stop. I could feel my heart pounding from the jolt and realized I was in trouble. Even though I had left early for my interview, I was most likely going to be late if I made it at all.

If there was ever a good time to breathe, this was it. My first instinct was to curse or scream or cry, just to release the stress streaming through my bloodstream at that very moment. But that would only make me look ridiculous and would not get me where I was going any faster.

And so, considering all my options, breathe I did, for a full three minutes as traffic whizzed all around me, many cars honking as they drove by. I continued to breathe as calmly as I could and surveyed the situation, looking for a way out of the mess I was in. To my great relief, I noticed a service station only a short block away.

Restarting my car while continuing to breathe slowly, I hobbled over to the station, the metal rim of the tire wearing through the deflated rubber as I drove. Within a minute of arriving, a calm older service attendant appeared from out of the garage and quickly assessed my woeful circumstance. He was definitely traveling at the speed of love when he spoke.

"These things never come at convenient times, do they?" he said sympathetically as he kicked my flat tire. "Got a spare?"

"I sure do," I nodded, relieved that he was able to help me.

"Sit tight and relax, ma'am," he continued. "We can fix this in a matter of minutes." And he did, in seven minutes, to be exact. Fifteen minutes later, I was back on the road.

And because I had left early for my appointment I arrived in time for the interview, even after all of that. No matter what occurs, stop and breathe—you can expect positive support to show up with confidence. You do not need to feel rushed or crushed by life pushing you past your comfortable pace. There is no need to lapse into emergency mode when dealing with new or unexpected situations. When traveling in the flow, there is no hyperventilating, breathless crisis—just life doing what life does, which is to challenge us while we endeavor to sail through it with calm, slow, peaceful, breathable ease.

Slow Down

The first step toward slowing down is to become aware of what in life falsely speeds you up; steals your breath; and ultimately throws you backward into a vortex of confusion, disorder, fear, disruption, and victimhood. Is it too little rest, too much noise, too many racing thoughts, too little time, too many opinions, or too many commitments? The second and final step is to guard against it at all costs.

I was reminded of this lesson just last weekend. I had been traveling week after week from city to city while on a workshop tour centered on my last book, *The Answer Is Simple . . .* , for three months straight, with very little time to myself in between trips. When I got to Denver, I went straight to bed, but when I woke up in the morning and began to get ready to teach, I realized I had packed one shoe each from two different pairs of shoes, both for the right foot, and those were the only shoes I had to wear to the workshop. I ended up hobbling to my workshop wearing two mismatched right shoes and feeling ridiculous, not to mention ungrounded and uncomfortable. In the end, all I could do was laugh, and realize that had I slowed down and given myself just a few more seconds to get properly packed, this silly situation wouldn't have occurred. A few more breaths would have allowed me much happier feet and a much more secure frame of mind.

So no matter what attempts to steal your breath and hurry you up—be aware of it and don't let it control you. Step back and catch your breath before it gets away from you and leads you into chaos. Whenever you feel rushed, or are challenged, caught off guard, taken by surprise, or met with unforeseen difficulties, before responding take a deep breath so that you remain grounded. Do this several times. Take your time and don't allow your mind to bully you into emergency mode. A few moments of conscious breathing sets the pace to keep you flowing no matter what appears on the horizon, and allows you to respond to any circumstances with love.

Fear of the Unknown

Fear is often rooted in the unknown, so try to be prepared for and anticipate as many eventualities as possible. This will help keep you calm, centered, and focused when the unexpected does arise. If you're dreading a phone call from someone, say an ex-husband or wife, or a client who has left a less-than-satisfied message, rather than wait for the ambush, take the bull by the horns. Call that person first, at a time when you feel calm and grounded. The point is to be proactive in assuring the peace and flow of your life by being prepared for the unexpected.

When I was in training to become a flight attendant, for example, 80 percent of our instruction involved being prepared for the unexpected so that we could fly with confidence, knowing that if something did indeed arise, we'd be able to handle it. Preparation is the best way to offset any potential stealth attack. Just follow the Boy Scout motto: *Always be prepared.*

Notice the difference in vibration between love and fear. Love expands, eases, relaxes, and opens the area around the heart, while fear accelerates the heart rate, contracts the chest area, implodes the lungs, agitates the nervous system, and makes life seem to go dark and threatening. Interrupt the vibration of fear by breathing slowly. I once heard that it is biologically impossible to breathe deeply and be in fear at the same time. I'm not sure this is accurate, but I do know that breathing deeply and slowly reduces fear and anxiety in the body more quickly than any other method. So begin to practice deep breathing, and pay attention to your breath.

In-Flight Check-In

Once again, it is time to take out your notebook and spend a few minutes thinking about each of the following questions. This time focus on your physical experience as well as the mental and emotional feelings you carry throughout the day. Rather than simple *yes/no* answers, elaborate, and include examples of when you might have experienced certain reactions or behaviors. The more attentive you are to these questions and exercises, the more benefit you'll get from them.

- Do you pay attention to your breath?
- Have you ever noticed how deeply you breathe?
- Do you notice how often you hold your breath as you go through the day?
- What sorts of situations cause you to hold or lose your breath?
- Do you generally feel calm, or do you feel anxious throughout the day?

- Do you often feel stressed or rushed during the day?
- What situations cause you to feel fearful or steal your breath away?
- Do you have quiet time?
- Do you allow enough time to flow through your life peacefully?

Basic Flying Lessons

Basic 6-4-6 Breathing

Start your morning with this basic deep breathing exercise. First, exhale all the air in your lungs. Next, breathe in deeply through your nose to the count of six. Hold your breath gently to the count of four. Exhale slowly through your mouth to the count of six. And then breathe in again and hold to the count of four. Do this at least 10 to 15 times. Be careful not to rush your count or your breath. Allow yourself to mentally relax and surrender to your breath. Try to stop thinking, and just experience this process. This basic deep-breathing exercise oxygenates the blood, relaxes the nervous system, and resets the fight-or-flight syndrome. Do this breath exercise every day. Breath is the foundation of and fuel for your life's journey. Without adequate breath, you are struggling in survival mode. *With* breath, you are in Spirit and flow.

Ahhhh Breath

Every time you find yourself in a stressful or anxious frame of mind, take in a deep breath through the nose, and then slowly exhale through the mouth, letting out the sound "Ahhhh" as loudly as you can. Repeat this until you feel calm once again. This breathing exercise interrupts the anxious mind, and fuels the nervous system with life force and fuel to reconnect to flow.

Embrace the Quiet

Give yourself 10 to 15 minutes a day of quiet time—time to listen to nature, to your breath, to your heartbeat. If you carry an appointment book or have a calendar on your cell phone, mark in "take a breather" at least once a day and allow enough time between other obligations to do so. Get used to being quiet and *enjoying* this solitude. This means turning off the iPod, the TV, the radio, the car, the computer, and anything else that makes noise. Relax, breathe, and listen to life without getting dragged into it. Hear the world from a detached state of mind. Notice the sounds you cannot control with calm breath. Learn to hear noise without reacting to it. Do this exercise a few times a day until you train yourself to enjoy more and more inner peace no matter what is going on around you.

Advanced Flying Lessons

Breath of Fire

The breath of fire is a wonderful breathing exercise to do when you are feeling weak, insecure, overwhelmed by life, or a lack of energy or vitality; or if you feel down, depressed, negative, or fearful.

Breath of Fire is a Kundalini yoga breathing technique that is centered in the diaphragm and floods the nervous system with oxygen and life force. To do the Breath of Fire, sit or stand, legs a small distance apart, feet comfortably flat on the floor, and your palms on your belly, your power center. Next, inhale and exhale rapidly, pushing the breath from your abdomen, like a bellows, through the nose 20 times, trying to eventually build up to doing this 50 or even 100 times before stopping.

Then exhale completely; and take in the longest, slowest inhale you can hold. Next, lock the perineum or Kegel muscle, located between the anus and your sexual organs, pull in your abdomen, slightly push your chin downward toward your throat, and close your eyes while holding your breath for as long as you can. Then, when you feel as though you're ready to burst, slowly relax the locked muscles in your body and fully exhale all the air in your lungs out through the mouth, from the bottom of the belly upward. You may feel ever so slightly dizzy or even nauseated as you exhale, but don't be alarmed. Just breathe normally for a few more moments and the feeling will pass; your body will feel purged of all tension. It will feel refreshed and renewed.

Soothing Breath

Whenever you feel as though you've had enough, or your emotional system is being flooded with a lot of upset, stress, anxiety, worry, or sadness, try using the soothing-breath exercise to get out of the emotional whirlwind and back into the peaceful flow of love.

Start by inhaling very slowly through the nose, filling your lungs to capacity without overexerting yourself or trying too hard. Once your lungs are filled, close your eyes and push the air out of your body, starting from the belly up, releasing the sound "Ahhh"—not by opening your mouth, but rather by allowing it to flow through your nose. It sounds a bit like Darth Vader's breath in *Star Wars,* or like the flow of the ocean in case you aren't a *Star Wars* fan. As you exhale and release the sound, you can actually feel your heart muscles vibrate and relax. Do this for several moments, and then for your final exhale, release an open "Aaaaahhhh" sound through your mouth, as though making a deep sigh.

Take Time to Breathe

Today, no matter what commitments you have, allow five to ten minutes more between them so that you can remain grounded and calm; and flow at an easy, relaxed pace. If you have too many commitments in a day to do this comfortably, let one or two of those commitments go for just this day. As you move through the day from appointment to appointment, take your time, breathe, and notice the world around you.

Relax and enjoy the scenery. Take an extra moment or two to say hello to people you normally whiz past. Notice who, what, and where you are in the world by moving more slowly. At the end of the day, reflect on your experiences and make note of what occurred as a result of breathing deeply and moving slowly.

Chapter 4

Check Your Baggage

Several years ago I was invited to teach at the Mind, Body, Spirit Festival in London. I decided to bring Mark, a musician whom I had recently met, along with me. Mark hadn't traveled much and had never been to Europe, so I was enthusiastic about showing him a new part of the world. He arrived at the airport nervous, carting a suitcase the size of a large steamer trunk. A seasoned traveler myself, I couldn't help but raise an eyebrow at the size of his baggage, and wondered what on earth he could possibly have brought along, and why. But I kept my mouth shut.

We were directed to take a tram from the domestic terminal to the international terminal, which is where our troubles began. As he was dragging the equivalent of this wounded cow of a suitcase onboard the tram, one of the wheels broke, and suddenly the 85-pound bag fell like a dead weight to the ground. With the tram doors closing, I lurched over and helped him shove the mammoth thing onto the tram and breathed a sigh of relief as Mark (barely) escaped getting smashed.

None too happy about having to lift such an overfilled bag, I voiced an annoyed "Good grief, what on earth have you packed in there? After all, we're only going for a few days." Mark didn't answer. In fact, he was completely unaware of the excessive nature of his baggage. Instead, he was tremendously distraught over the broken wheel and utterly disbelieving that his brand-new Costco suitcase could be defective.

"Don't worry about it," I dismissed. "You can check it soon, and it'll be out of your hands until we get to London." But he wasn't interested in being consoled, and fussed and fretted over that damn bag and its broken wheel the entire way across the pond.

I tolerated his distress for a while and then attempted to go to sleep, figuring that once we arrived in wonderful London, he'd forget all about his weighty and broken baggage and become enthralled with the city instead. But no, from the moment the defective beast came shooting out into baggage claim, Mark's focused frustration began anew. Loading the wounded cow onto a cart, we pushed it through customs and into a taxi.

Even then, Mark wouldn't lighten up and let the bag go. As we drove into London on what was a rare sunny morning, I played tour guide and pointed out various curiosities and landmarks to Mark's only half-listening ears. Believing his lukewarm interest was due to jet lag, I took the high road and decided not to be disturbed by what I felt was a significant lack of enthusiasm for the *fantastic* opportunity I had afforded him. That is, until he asked, "Do you think I can find a repair shop to get my wheel fixed on my suitcase today?"

Stunned that Mark was still obsessing over his stupid bag rather than engaging in the adventure at hand, I drew a breath in. Exercising, in my opinion, a great deal of self-control, I answered evenly, "Probably. But we only have one day to see London before we have to work and then return home. Are you sure it can't wait until you get back?"

"No," he insisted. "I would feel much better if I got it fixed. Would you mind?"

My patience was now at its limit, but since I didn't know Mark very well, I refrained from saying, "Are you an idiot or what? We're in London, for Pete's sake." Instead, I bit my tongue and said, "Okay. We'll ask the concierge for help."

Mark seemed relieved enough to look out the window. "Looks like Disneyland," he commented as we pulled up to the hotel. We checked in and then set off to bring the suitcase to the repair shop. Even emptied, the unwieldy cow was a pain in the neck for both of us.

Finally arriving at the shop, the repairman took one look at the suitcase, quoted an outrageous amount to fix the thing, and announced that it would take a week before it would be ready.

"Cripes," Mark replied, both shocked and insulted. "What a rip-off! That's more than I paid for this thing."

Nonplussed, looking at the bag and then Mark, the repairman replied in his most restrained British accent, "Why then, my good sir, you might ask yourself why indeed you have such a large yet inferior bag in the first place. Might you be better off casting this defective bag aside, and investing in something more well made?"

Mark, now frustrated to the limit, turned and said, "That's not possible. I need to carry all my stuff back home."

"Pity," said the bag man, clearly uninterested in Mark's plight, and the two of us altogether for that matter, since we weren't going to buy anything from him.

"Let's go," Mark snapped, grabbing his broken suitcase and dragging it behind him.

"Crap, now what do I do?" Mark wondered, once outside. He was so attached to his bag that he couldn't see beyond it.

"Throw the damn beast of a bag away and throw all your unnecessary stuff away as well!" I screamed, finally losing it. "Or don't. Just stop dragging this ridiculous problem around with us everywhere while we're here. We're in London, for God's sake, and all you care about is your useless baggage! Let it go."

Shocked by my outburst, he seemed to snap out of his obsession. "You're right. I'll let it go." And he did, albeit very reluctantly. Sadly, the greater part of our only day to visit London was now behind us, so we went back to the hotel too agitated to do anything more. We parted ways and headed to our rooms, missing London altogether.

Now, ten years later and really good friends, we both laugh at that situation. Never having traveled such a distance before, Mark had felt an overbearing need to pack nearly everything he could find to take along on the trip, just to ensure his comfort and security. He took his own pillow, blanket, song books, reading material, extra shoes, way too many clothes, and enough distractions and diversions to keep a person occupied in a deprivation tank for a year.

I laughed at myself for not cluing him in on how to pack, and for being so worried about missing opportunities because of his baggage. Happily, our friendship survived the challenge and, in retrospect, I learned a lot from that experience.

Anytime we carry too much psychic baggage, we risk not being present to the moment. Our insistence on dragging all of our stuff with us everywhere we go causes us to miss the magnificent life right in front of us. Psychic baggage comes in all shapes and sizes and demands as much, if not more, energy and work from us as any "mammoth" suitcase ever could. It comes in the form of our ego's beliefs and sensitivities, past dramas, secret agendas, subtle manipulations, petty demands, perceived injuries, "special" needs, comparisons, competitions, and other controlling negative patterns. It comprises all the filters that keep the light of our Spirit buried and our ego behind the controls. We expend a lot of energy carting this dead-end baggage around. It's heavy for us and for everyone else.

We know we're carrying too much baggage and failing to travel lightly by the amount of sighs, cries, and lies in our lives. Psychic baggage comprises the unspoken attachments, judgments, attitudes, disappointments, fears, discomforts, protective barriers, sarcastic remarks, isolating maneuvers, and dishonest and even unconscious agendas we are tempted to carry with us as we journey through our days. Needless to say, packing up all this unnecessary crap and carrying it with us wherever we go burdens us, slows our daily journey, and robs us of being present in life. It pulls us out of our flow and does the same to everyone around us. Psychic baggage is a huge drag on our wings and prevents us from gaining the kind of vibrational altitude required to travel at the speed of love.

Lost Baggage

Once, when I was flying to Paris, I waited patiently for my bags to arrive at the baggage-claim area only to have the belt stop after spewing out a hundred or so others, with mine nowhere in sight. Frustrated, indignant, and confused, I walked over to the baggage-claim rep and asked him to help bring my bags down. A quick search revealed that my bags had been put on the wrong flight and would arrive the following afternoon. They gave me 50 bucks to buy essential toiletries and sent me on my way.

After my ego indulged in five minutes of outraged indignation, I had to accept that there was no way my baggage would arrive any sooner even if I did throw a tantrum, so I took a breath, grabbed a taxi, and headed to my hotel. Somewhere between the airport and the city, I relaxed. In fact, I suddenly felt very light indeed. Knowing full well that my baggage would eventually be returned to me, I decided to enjoy the ease with which I could get around without it.

A quick trip to the local Monoprix, the French version of a Target or Wal-Mart store, yielded a hairbrush, a toothbrush, toothpaste, a bar of soap, a steaming hot cup of delicious café au lait, and money for dinner, all courtesy of United Airlines. Fortified both inside and out—and baggage free—my mind was freed up as well.

I actually liked being baggage free. In fact, it made life simpler. With my ego unable to have the comforts it was accustomed to, it actually quieted down. Being baggage free also freed up my time. Without the distraction of my heavy luggage, I felt liberated to completely enjoy Paris.

I casually walked through the neighborhood where I was staying. My heart was light; my attention was fully present; and my mind was quiet, alert, and completely engaged in the sights and sounds of the world around me.

Being relieved of my baggage, albeit temporarily, made me somehow more aware of the moment. Although I'd been to the same hotel and walked around the same neighborhood many times before, this time I noticed shops and people I'd never noticed previously. That is the price of baggage. It takes attention away from the present, condemning us to live in the past or future, rather than the moment at hand.

Unpack the Past

Perhaps the largest piece of psychic baggage we soul travelers unnecessarily lug around is the past. I was on a tour through India visiting ancient temple sites near the ancient city of Jaipur several years ago and met a young woman who talked the entire time about a lousy evening she'd spent on a blind date weeks earlier. She casually glanced over the ruins, snapped a few photos, and droned on and on about the evening's disastrous unfoldment. Her baggage was heavy indeed. So heavy that it affected everyone on the tour. Finally, my daughter Sonia looked the woman in the eye, smiled, and said, "Where are you from?"

The question jolted her from her monologue. "Los Angeles," she replied.

"Isn't this place gorgeous?" Sonia asked, distracting the woman from turning backward and reaching for the baggage once again.

She answered, "Yeah," as if seeing it for the first time. "It is."

Sonia stopped talking and looked back out the window. So did the woman. The tour then became peaceful, and everyone on it was able to resume the joy of the moment. The tricky thing about psychic baggage is that it is invisible to us (although not to others), and we are so accustomed to carrying it wherever we go that we actually believe it's normal and even necessary to feel so burdened.

Let Go of Control to Live in the Flow

I have a friend who seems to need to have a plan in place for every moment of her life, another type of baggage. Traveling with her to New York several years ago was a nightmare for me because she left absolutely no room for any spontaneity. She needed to know in advance where we were going to stay, at which restaurants we would be eating dinner, which areas we were going to visit, and what time we were to return in the afternoon for a rest.

Spending the day with her, I was constantly reminded about "the schedule," and how we must maintain it. I complied for a while, but finally rebelled when we happened upon a great little Italian coffee shop in Greenwich Village that screamed at us to stop and enjoy an espresso. I suggested this to her, but she nixed the idea in a minute because it wasn't on the schedule. I gave her a choice: lose the baggage or lose me as a traveling companion for the day. She chose to lose me and continued on her schedule. I had an espresso and wandered through the Village alone for the next few hours. She saw me as her excess baggage, and by dumping me, she enjoyed herself all day as well. By lightening our attachment to each other, we both received gifts, as do all who travel lightly. She had her fill of art, and I had my fill of homemade cannoli. It worked for both of us.

It's easy to figure out if you're packing too much on your life's travels. When we journey through life weighed down by unnecessary psychic baggage, our minds feel heavy, burdened, agitated, and irritable, while our hearts feel empty and closed off. The lighter we travel, freed of our own psychic encumbrances, attachments, expectations, and ego control, the more magical life becomes.

Traveling lightly is liberating. It creates a positive, openhearted vibration that literally surrounds your body and pulls positive, helpful, happy, supportive, and magical experiences toward you. This is because you are in Divine flow.

Don't Carry Others' Baggage

When you're about to board an airplane these days, one of the first things you're asked is if anyone else asked you to carry something onboard or in your baggage for them. It's extremely important to answer no to this question because things carried for others could potentially cause great harm. If you do answer yes, you must either get rid of it or risk being denied boarding. The same holds true for psychic baggage as well.

For example, I realized, after several sessions of therapy many years ago, that I was carrying my mother's bags from her war experience. She never asked me to, but I "volunteered," feeling bad about her difficult years as a child prisoner of war in Germany in World War II. I decided quite young that it was my duty to protect her and keep her from ever feeling vulnerable again.

I was so invested in carrying this baggage that my psychic sensors went on full radar mode, zeroing in on her every mood, thought, feeling, emotion, and discomfort. When she felt vulnerable, I was there to step in and stop it. Needless to say, it exhausted me and annoyed her to no end. After all, I kept trying to control her feelings and keep her from drifting into any emotions that made me uncomfortable. It was a clear case of us struggling over who was going to carry her baggage, and struggle we did, off and on for a few years.

Thankfully, with the help of some talented healers and therapists and quite a bit of reflection, I came to realize that I was actually being disrespectful of my mother's journey by trying to make it my own. *She* was the one who'd had the experiences, not me, and only *she* could decide whether to assimilate them into her life or let them victimize her. I couldn't undo her experiences or influence how she handled them. All I could do was respect her enough to trust that she would handle her emotions in the best way for her. I stopped trying to control her life so that she would always feel secure, and I stopped believing she couldn't handle life as it came. It was a relief for me, and from her response, I believe it was for her as well.

At the same time, she also learned to let the past go and live more and more in the present. She refused to dwell on the past, talk about it, or let it seize her emotions. She turned to the present, and with the help of *A Course in Miracles,* she became totally focused on the healing power of now. With awareness, patience, and prayer, we both learned to throw the baggage of her past to the wind. Now liberated, we travel to great and loving heights together, and the past is simply a bad dream we both choose not to recollect.

In the same way that allowing someone to convince you to carry their baggage across the border could land you in prison, allowing yourself to take on someone else's mental baggage could land you in *psychic* prison. My first intuition teacher, Charlie, emphasized the importance of this and cautioned me time and time again, saying, "Sonia, to travel lightly, mind your own business, and keep your paws off others people's business."

It has taken me a while to learn this particular lesson, but the advice has proven valid. Every time I've volunteered to carry someone else's baggage on my journey through life, it has gotten me into trouble, and was a thankless job at that. As I mentioned earlier, I'm not a master at traveling at the speed of love. I'm still learning, just like you.

Is It Your Baggage?

Many years ago, as I stated in the Introduction, I was employed as a flight attendant. One part of our uniform was a company-issued suitcase, or "crew kit," as we used to call it, to carry with us as we worked. This basic black bag was very useful because it held quite a bit of stuff, even though at first glance it didn't look like it would hold much at all. We were required to use these bags when we worked, but were allowed to use them for our personal travels as well.

This, of course, at times led to confusion, as all these flight bags looked the same, and heaven forbid if you grabbed the wrong bag and walked away with someone else's, or vice versa. It was disastrous because not only did you lose your belongings when you needed them, but you were also saddled with someone else's baggage, adding insult to injury. If this wasn't bad enough, if you were ever guilty of making this ultimate faux pas, word traveled quickly among the fellow flight attendants, and you were indelibly branded an idiot. Others would never let you forget it.

Once I went with my husband and kids to visit Disneyland. We arrived in Los Angeles at midnight, and were all extremely tired after our long flight, especially our kids, who were three and four at the time and up way past their bedtime.

To get on our way as quickly as possible, my husband, Patrick, and I decided to split up so we could accomplish more at once. I took the girls and went to get the rental car, while Patrick stayed back and collected the baggage. We reunited moments later; I had the car, and he had our bags.

When we got to the hotel, we opened the girls' bags, got out their pj's and put them to bed. Then I went to open my own suitcase, when to my horror, I realized it wasn't mine. Being a crew kit, it looked like mine, only upon closer inspection, it clearly wasn't. I opened it and discovered the belongings of a man with rather kinky sexual preferences, which I don't care to go into here. As grossed out as I was, I still felt a wave of anxiety sweep over me as I wondered where my own beloved and familiar stuff was. I could only indulge in this wave of terror for a split second, however, as I then realized that Patrick had committed the ultimate crime in taking a fellow flight attendant's suitcase in error. Granted, he wasn't a flight attendant so it was an honest mistake, but if anyone found out I was married to him, I would be blamed by proxy. Panicked, I sent him back to the airport at 3 A.M., undercover, of course, to hopefully find my bag and leave the errant bag behind without getting busted.

He returned two hours later, exhausted but successful. He said he'd found my bag sitting near the carousel all by itself, with no one around. So he switched the two, leaving "Kinky's" bag in its place.

"I was amazed your bag was sitting there all by itself," Patrick marveled as we drifted off to sleep, "You'd think someone would have taken it."

"I'm not surprised," I replied. "Other people's baggage is gross. Who wants it? It's basically dirty laundry, used underwear, cosmetics, and toiletries. Rarely is it the bag of gold and treasure it promises to be. Most baggage is of no use to anyone other than the person who packed it, and reveals way more than anyone else wants to know or should know about a stranger."

Own Your Baggage

Just because you have excess baggage doesn't mean you have to feel bad about it. We all drag around more baggage than we care to admit or even know we have. Yet it surfaces at the most inconvenient of times and is always obvious. When it does, just realize that you're dragging your stuff around with you. No one has to fix it or take care of it or relive it, not even you. Just see it for what it is: unnecessary old news keeping you from being in the flow of the present moment. Surprisingly, that is enough to minimize it, at least for the moment. Believe it or not, simply recognizing psychic baggage for what it is usually shrinks it down to a manageable size, where it doesn't stifle your every breath and leave you and those around you dragged down and bummed out. Try it. It lightens things up every time.

It's when you foist your baggage on others, expecting them to carry it while denying it's yours, that you drop out of the flow. Not only that, but you interrupt others' flights as well. It's not fair. It's like taking up the armrests on both sides of your airplane seat. And you're kidding yourself if you don't think your baggage is completely apparent to others. You can recognize your baggage if you want to, and you know what isn't yours. So own your stuff. When you do, you travel burdened but purposefully, and soon the baggage seems to drop away by itself.

The greatest challenge is to recognize whether or not you're carrying excess emotional baggage. Sometimes we get so used to our baggage and its burdens that we don't realize we even have it with us. Fortunately, this is where our traveling companions, usually in the form of friends and family members, clue us in. They do so with their feedback. They might say things such as:

49

- What's the matter with you?

- Are you all right?

- What's your problem?

- What are you angry about now?

- Have I upset you?

- Stop acting that way.

- Now what?

We can all agree that traveling with the least amount of baggage is the absolute best way to go. The exciting discovery when letting go of your baggage is that for everything you lose, the Universe will replace it with something much lighter, easier, happier, more loving, and joyful.

Let Go of Your Baggage

The best way to tell if you're carrying old baggage is by your overall feeling day to day. Allowing for the normal wear and tear of daily journeying through life, do you generally go to bed feeling happy; or are you bogged down, moody, resentful, angry, and drained beyond belief?

A light heart means that you're traveling without excess baggage. Chronic heaviness of heart suggests you should look at your attachments and consider letting some go. The beauty in all of this is that *you* are the one who decides how you travel in life. The quickest way to unencumber yourself is to practice simply letting things go. Say out loud: "I'm letting it go," and then do.

Here are some examples of excess baggage to leave behind:

- Wanting life to be predictable and suffering loudly when it is not

- Interpreting events such as unexpected upsets, changes of plans, disappointments, heavy traffic, and other people's moods as personal assaults

- Insisting that everyone do what you want, and pouting till you get your way

- Acting out when tired, hungry, or stressed, thus scaring everyone into submission

- Griping, moaning, complaining, criticizing, gossiping, brooding, sulking, pouting, giving the silent treatment, and withholding

- Not expressing your desires, leaving others to figure them out telepathically

- Bitterly suffering from the past and expecting every present moment and person to deliver the same all over again

- Being excessively accommodating and secretly resentful

- Refusing to accommodate or adapt at all

- Acting like only *you* matter

- Acting like you don't matter at all

- Being defensive

Now, of course, we all pack a few of these behaviors from time to time. We have our moments, even our days, when we're feeling a little insecure or needy for whatever reason, and resort to old baggage out of habit. It's when we do this every day or most days that excess baggage becomes toxic.

In-Flight Check-In

It's time now to take out your notebook and spend a few minutes thinking about each of the following questions. Be honest with yourself and look deep within for the answers. Rather than simple *yes/no* answers, elaborate and include examples of what creates such thoughts and reactions from you. Visit this check-in more than one time. Answer these questions over the course of a day or two, or even several times during the week, to get even more accurate insight into your baggage. As always, the more effort you put into the exercises, the more benefit you'll get from them.

What unnecessary psychic baggage weighs you down? To find out, simply fill in the following:

- I am upset about . . .

- I am worried about . . .

- I am angry about . . .

- I feel resentful about . . .

- I feel responsible for . . .

- I am annoyed about . . .

- I think it's unfair that . . .

- I think it's rude that . . .

- I can't believe that . . .

- I feel guilty for . . .

- I put up with . . .

- I feel unworthy about . . .

- I feel scared of . . .

Either use your small notebook to record your answers, or if that feels like too much effort, write your answers directly in this book. If you're afraid to write in the book, then write that down as well.

What you write reveals what you pack into your mind as you journey through life on a daily basis. Are your thoughts and mind heavy and burdened, or light and loving?

The key to traveling light is to check in with yourself often to see if you're carrying anything unnecessary. If you do discover that you're dragging old baggage, simply remind yourself to set it down by letting it go.

I just did. Aahhhh! It feels good. Try it now and see for yourself.

Basic Flying Lesson

Drop It

If you are drained, dragging, and worried, you're carrying unnecessary psychic baggage that needs to be dumped. Recognizing it is more than half the battle.

All you have to do to eliminate psychic baggage is to mentally drop it, just as if you were dropping a heavy suitcase full of dead weight. That's it. In fact, you might want to carry a small, heavy rock in your pocket, and whenever you feel the need to lighten the load, reach into your pocket and pull it out. Then simply drop the rock as a reminder to drop the problem, complaint, worry, burden, stress, need to control, angst, indignation, or whatever is dragging you down. You choose what you carry in life. You don't have to lug around any burden you don't want to carry. It is *not* nobler or spiritually superior to drag a heavy load with you in life. It just brings you and everyone around you down.

Tag It

In order to travel at the speed of love, we must dump our "stuff." Just as we must remove liquids and volatile substances from our baggage before we check them at the airport, so too must we remove toxic and volatile attitudes from our behaviors before we can lift off into a higher vibration. Our immature self-centered ego stuff is contraband and dangerous to elevated flight. It comprises our negative beliefs, patterns, and expectations and the habits that keep us grounded in fear, such as:

- Feeling entitled
- Believing that we're special
- Judging others as stupid, crazy, or worthless
- Being impatient
- Feeling superior, better than, and controlling of others

- Feeling inferior and being controlled by others
- Seeing the darkness, not the light, in life

Whenever you find that you're not in the flow, ask yourself what unnecessary psychic "stuff" you're carrying. Remove these things from your psychic baggage with awareness and a desire to live a more peaceful and loving life. Once you make the decision to dump the toxic behaviors, you and those around you can take a deep breath.

Distract Yourself

A quick way to release unwanted psychic baggage is to distract the ego from holding on to it by involving it in something far more interesting. You can do this by picking up a good novel, watching a funny movie, listening to an educational radio program, going to the gym, engaging in an interesting conversation about something other than the problems you're dwelling on, learning something new, or visiting a new place—just involve your mind in something other than drama. Just like distracting an infant who's clinging to his "blankie" and screaming his head off by diverting his attention to something more exciting (like a new toy) works well, so too does distracting the ego from its unhappy baggage with something more exciting.

Advanced Flying Lessons

Clear It

Getting rid of excess baggage is one aspect of soul work we all must do, without exception. We can do it in several ways. We can go to therapy, sort methodically through the bags with a skilled therapist, and pick and choose together what to travel with and what to leave behind. I've done this several times in my life and highly recommend it.

You can dump a lot of negative psychic baggage by attending a cathartic healing workshop, like the Hoffman Process (**www .hoffmaninstitute.org**). I've done this as well. It helped shed tons of emotional baggage for me.

You can attend 12-step programs such as Alcoholics Anonymous (AA), Al-Anon, and Co-Dependents Anonymous (CoDA), which are free, anonymous, and also work wonders. I've gone to Al-Anon over the years and found that it, too, relieved me of baggage I didn't even know I was carrying.

You can even attend the six-day healing event that I offer in Kauai every year called Translucent You: Becoming Energetically Iridescent and Divinely Alive. My team of 11 highly gifted healers and I devote the entire six days to cleansing and clearing all the negative debris of your past and restoring you to the light and bright beloved being that you naturally are.

Purge It

In Kauai, I visited a Hindu monastery where the monks set out pieces of paper and pens for people to write down their burdens and unwanted baggage, and then burn the paper. The Hindu monks believe that this practice relieves the subconscious mind of these patterns and problems; and in doing this daily, unwanted baggage is discarded and released over and over again. Over the years, I've had other spiritual teachers suggest this same method of relieving baggage, and I have done so with great success, finding that things that once bothered or burdened me almost seem magically lifted away after a few cathartic burnings.

Blow It Off

If your life force, your essential Divine Spirit, lies in your breath, then this is a wonderful way to use your breath to release old baggage. Go to the novelty section of the local grocery store and buy some kids' bubbles. Go outside and take a moment to feel all of the energy your psychic baggage consumes. Not wanting to travel a step further unnecessarily burdened, open your bubble container, take out the wand, and visualize the baggage you want to let go. Next, blow through the wand and see the luminous, bubbly orbs carry your concerns away. Put the rest of the jar in a handy place so that you can do this often.

Pray for It

Prayer can also relieve you of excess baggage. When you pray, you stop wrestling with old and burdensome baggage and turn it over to God instead. Prayer alleviates psychic baggage because it invites Divine power to come in and neutralize it or transform it into something new, fresh, and useful. My favorite prayer is "Let go, let God" when it comes to relieving myself of emotionally draining baggage. To use this prayer when faced with the stress of psychic baggage, simply say out loud: "I let go of this and let God take over." And then open your hands and fingers wide as though letting go. Shake your fingers, as though shaking your attachments off, which is all that baggage is. This works fast if your prayers are earnest.

Chapter 5

In Security

Several months ago I traveled from Chicago to Kansas City. After I checked in at the airport, I entered the security line especially designated for frequent travelers. Usually this line moves faster than the line for regular travelers, but that night it was so long that it wove around several posts like a line at Disneyland, packed with "special" travelers who were extremely irate and indignant that they were made to wait so long. Travel is stressful, no matter what, but standing in line with the "premier" people who weren't getting their expected first-class service was intense, and after several moments, got worse.

It began with the gentleman directly behind me. At first he moaned about how he couldn't believe how slowly the line was moving, darting his eyes around the line looking for others to agree with him. It wasn't hard. Two or three other "elites" heartily joined in the moment he opened up.

"Yeah, this is disgusting," agreed one well-dressed businessman in a beige overcoat, tapping on his BlackBerry in annoyance.

"It happens every time I come to O'Hare," sharply agreed a woman with a large black briefcase and pointy stilettos.

"You're right," chimed in a petite woman with a roll-aboard suitcase. She shook her head as though insulted to the core.

The crowd shuffled forward, getting more and more riled up by the conversation as everyone inched ahead. The five or six people engaged in this discussion used their agitation as fuel. They got louder and started looking at others, directly egging them on to join the protest (although airport security has absolutely nothing to do with the airline; they are a totally separate entity, as any frequent traveler would know).

I held my tongue as the collective dissent grew in strength, although I was certainly tempted to join in. The litany of complaints mounted, and so did the indignation in the line. Just then I caught the eye of the guard checking IDs. His head was down, his shoulders slumped. There was no question he was hearing the crowd's growing complaints as he concentrated as hard as he could on his task, with negativity and contempt raining down upon him. I simply couldn't be a part of it. He was clearly just trying to do his job, amid the psychic grenades being tossed his way, and I couldn't add to his misery.

I finally stepped up to the podium where the security guard sat. Smiling, I handed him my ID and boarding pass and said, "Tough night tonight?"

"Yeah," he sort of grunted, keeping his head down. "One of the x-ray machines is malfunctioning, so it's unusable. Backed things up quite a bit."

Feeling sympathetic toward him, I had to fight every impulse not to turn to the crowd and scream, "Shut up, you whiners! Can't you see these people are trying?" Turning with a whoosh of spiritual superiority, I marched like Joan of Arc through the x-ray machine, with a nod and a kind word toward each security guard on the job as a vote of solidarity with them.

They were indifferent. All they wanted was to keep the line moving, and my support only seemed to slow it down. I didn't even merit so much as a glance. I collected my things on the other side of the x-ray machine with a mishmash of feelings: frustration for being slowed down, agitation from the crowd, and irritation from the obvious lack of appreciation from the security guards for my heroic attempt to side with them. On top of that, I was late.

I glanced at my watch, expecting now to have to bolt to my gate like an ambulance racing to a crash scene, when I noticed to my utter amazement that in spite of the security line's bottleneck pace, I still had a full 25 minutes left to get to my gate before I had to board. What's more, it had only taken 15 minutes total from when I entered the security line to when I exited, which is only 5 minutes more than normal.

"All that for five minutes?" I marveled, still coming down from the stress. I couldn't believe it. Looking around, all the passengers who had only moments ago infuriated me with their bad behavior had now scattered like mice in different directions, never to be seen again. All that was left was the negative, stressful vibration pouring through my body.

In reality, there were no "bad" or "good" guys here; just a bunch of really insecure and frustrated travelers fearful that they would miss their flights. That's all it ever is. Although we were traveling by air, we were hardly getting off the ground because we were playing the game of victimhood, falling prey to our fears and insecurities.

Once I boarded, I felt my anxiety ease up, replaced by the relief of being back on schedule and away from that whirling dervish of anger and frustration. It had exhausted me. I was so relieved to be free of that psychic storm, safely in my seat, and back in the flow of going where I wanted to go.

See the Humor

The truth is, no matter where our life's journey takes us, when we do get sucked into the vibration of insecurity, frustration, negativity, and blame, the only thing we can do to find our way out and get back in the flow of love once again is laugh. Humor is a sure way to higher ground. So whenever you find yourself feeling unexpectedly insecure or upset, try to see something funny in the situation. It will be easier if you start by trying to see the humor in all situations all the time. If you're already in the habit of appreciating the lighter side of life, laughter will come quickly when you need it most.

When she was little, my sister laughed at her insecurity about her thick eyeglasses by jokingly saying she wore them to see through walls. My brother, Neil, laughed at his insecurity about losing his hair in his 30s by joking that he no longer needed mousse to coif it. My best friend in high school, Sue, made fun of her weight, her complexion, her thin hair, and her lack of interested suitors by writing hilarious stories spoofing herself for teen magazines and submitting them month after month. She never got a story published, but we laughed till we cried reading them. I give her a lot of credit for instilling in me my love of writing and humor to this day. I was insecure in high school for being at least six inches taller than most of the other students until I learned to laugh at my own height and make jokes about being able to see what was coming before everyone else—not because I was intuitive, but because I stood a mile high. Lame joke, yes. But it was high school, and it worked.

The point is, we all have insecurities, we all face insecurities, and we all feel insecure at times because we're human and that's what happens when life feels threatening or out of our control, which is often. Until we cut our insecurities down to size by laughing at them, they control us and keep us in a state of fear. If you've lost your sense of humor or cannot seem to find it, cultivate it again by watching funny YouTube videos and visiting other humorous Websites. Read funny novels, or watch silly movies and TV comedies. A sense of humor is cultivated, like a garden. Remember to laugh daily so that when you feel insecure or frustrated, your laughter reflex is well oiled. Humor shuttles you back to security quickly, so you will hardly notice the bumps along the way.

See the Light of God in Everyone

When we begin to overcome some of our insecurities, our attention is freed to see the hand of God at work in our own lives as well as in those around us. Look beyond the outer surfaces and appearances of things, especially other people. Look beyond their behavior, appearance, attitudes, ethnic background, apparent financial status, and age; and see the Divine light of God inside. This light gives us all life. We all share it, and we all have the same amount of it. Life force is life force. Even death doesn't extinguish the light in us; it merely frees it to assume another form.

If we practice staying aloft, day in and day out, by remembering to see the light in ourselves and in everything around us, it keeps us from feeling insecure. Better yet, if we choose to see the light of God in all things, when we encounter darkness in others, our own reflection of Divine light will actually restore theirs to full brightness.

I was just reminded of that recently. I was flying home from Portland and sat next to an extremely obese, negative, cranky, defensive, unfriendly, and clearly insecure woman, whom I would have ignored the whole way home, except that she was so miserable that she kept complaining to me. Every time she spoke, I chose to see the light in her and say so. She needed a seat-belt extension, something she asked for in a very irritated way. I could tell she was defensive about it—she didn't want to be judged or laughed at, and I completely understood. Once I traveled with a friend who also needed a seat-belt extension, and he shared with me just how painful it was for him to ask for one, so I imagined it might be the same for her.

I chose to be friendly and aggressively complimented her in response to everything she said, a technique I learned from my mother. She complained about her seat, and I complimented her on having the intelligence to ask for an aisle seat. She complained about the lack of leg room. I complimented her on wearing travel support hose for good circulation. She complained about the food; I complimented her on having the wisdom not to eat it.

I told her she was a pleasure to talk to. She seemed surprised and relaxed, and so did I. Two hours into the four-hour flight, she began to tell me about her work with mentally challenged adults. She helped them find housing and jobs. Her light suddenly became brilliant, and all insecurity vanished. I was humbled in her presence; what a saint she was to devote herself to such loving, compassionate work. It was a gift to be able to be with her.

I thanked my mom, in my heart, for having taught me to see the light in all beings as we parted ways. It was one of the best flights I'd had in a long time. In choosing to see the light in the woman next to me, I was actually able to experience a brilliant and uplifting person who inspired me as I traveled across the country.

As Always . . . Pray

Prayer is another powerful strategy to stave off insecurity when it descends upon you. We can become easily infected by insecurity over the slightest provocations, mentions of self-doubt, or sudden shifts in expectation, and it can really drag on our engines. A friend of mine who is overcoming many addictions gets insecure very quickly when someone makes a comment about his appearance or his work or his nonexistent love life, and he can easily spiral into self-doubt and anxiety—that is, until he was taught to pray by his sponsor at AA. Now, whenever he receives or perceives a negative comment (because he is prone to misinterpret things at times), he simply prays: "Lord, take this away from me right now. It's not me. It's not mine. Don't let it stick." Then he shakes his praying hands off, and he is free. I've followed his example, and I must tell you, it really works.

It is amazing how willing we are to believe that all negative comments are true. Just mention to people, for example, that they look fat or have bad hair or have something in their teeth, and they spiral downward at lightning speed. I remember running into an old school friend one early morning who asked me if I had been overworking lately because I looked "really, really tired." I must have looked at myself in the mirror five times after hearing that comment that day because her comment made me feel so insecure. It took me until the evening to realize that her comment wasn't about me at all, but rather a projection from her *onto* me. I was feeling great. She was the one who was tired and worn out. Besides, it didn't matter how I looked. Tired or otherwise, I was still lovable. We all are, all the time.

Prayer creates a protective energetic field that surrounds us and protects against unwanted infiltration of frightened and negative frequencies, those energies that cause us to doubt ourselves and feel insecure. Prayer assures us that no matter what occurs or what others think, we are, and will continue to be, okay. We may run into difficulties or trouble and not know what to do, but our hearts will guide us, and God will protect us. That is what prayer does. It reminds us that we are safe, we can relax, and we can trust what unfolds, in confidence that we are loved and will be taken care of. Always.

My favorite prayer is the serenity prayer used by those in 12-step programs. It goes like this: "Dear God, give me the serenity to accept the things I cannot change, the courage to change the things I can, and the wisdom to know the difference." It's short, sweet, and to the point, and it works. It is useful to anyone, anywhere, anytime, to rise above all insecurities and stay in the flow of love.

Another prayer that works is: "I am surrounded by light, protected by light. I see only the light in all things. I live only in the light, now and always." This is the most healing, empowering, confidence-building prayer I know. It is also the one that takes the most discipline and commitment to call upon, so it takes daily practice. Daily prayer, hourly prayer, ensures that when you are accosted by negativity and fear, when you are exposed to the demons of insecurity and they threaten to get ahold of you and cause you to doubt yourself or your trust in life, you can call upon the light of God automatically and chase these demons of darkness away.

In-Flight Check-In

Get out your notebook now and spend a few minutes thinking about each of the following questions. Take a few minutes to do some deep-breathing exercises before you begin, and then breathe deeply again between questions as you go. These questions are there for your own benefit, and the answers will not be reviewed by anyone other than you, so be fully honest as you explore your answers. Rather than be satisfied with simple *yes/no* answers, elaborate and include examples of what evokes certain feelings and behaviors in you. Take your time, and do not feel as though you must answer all the questions at one time. You can also answer them over a period of days if you prefer. The more effort you put into the exercises, as always, the more benefit you will get from them.

- What causes you to feel most insecure?
- What threatens you most?
- Where do you feel invisible?
- Whose approval do you seek?
- Whose approval do you fail to receive?
- What is your major source of stress?
- Where do you feel disrespected or not heard?
- How does your stress and insecurity affect other people?
- How do you generally handle your stress and insecurity?
- Do you lash out?
- Do you feel sorry for yourself and try to get others to do the same?
- Do you complain to anyone who will listen?
- Do you become aloof and distant?
- Do you become critical?
- Do you get defensive?
- Do you check out?

Basic Flying Lessons

Respect Yourself

Every day, after a few minutes of deep-breathing exercises, or at any time you feel insecure, state out loud all the things you love and respect about yourself. For example:

- I love and respect my work ethic.

- I love and respect that I am such a good friend.

- I love and respect that I am honest.

- I love and respect that I am a responsible caretaker of the earth.

- I love and respect that I am kind.

Keep on listing these things until you start to reconnect with your Divine Spirit and remember your worth.

Breathe and Sing

A lovely way to break out of insecurity is to sing. Yes, that is correct: sing. Singing reconnects you with your heart, strengthens your inner light, and restores your joy. It doesn't matter what you sing. As long as you sing with your heart, any song will do. And you don't have to sing out loud. You can sing silently, as long as a song is in your heart.

A few years ago while teaching a workshop in New York, I was surrounded by so much negativity, insecurity, and fear in the class that I asked my musician, Mark (he of the big bag), to write a song for everyone's inner victim. The lyrics went like this:

I'm a victim
People walk all over me
I'm a victim

65

People do just what they please
I'm a victim
I have no boundaries
So please, please . . . please hear my story
I'm a victim

We sang and danced that song facing one another with great gusto for more than 20 minutes. It was embarrassing to see just how much passion the class felt in belting out this song when only moments earlier they couldn't even register their voices above an audible whisper. We went from an anorexic whimper to a zeal that would have given the Mormon Tabernacle Choir a run for its money, such was the commitment they had to their suffering. Yet soon they laughed about their own silly song and forgot all about being victims. They were restored to the light, and we all moved back into the flow.

So back to my point: sing. If entrenched in ego misery, sing the blues, like the victim song I just shared, until you're tired of it. Then sing "Zip-a-Dee-Doo-Dah" or some other lighthearted and joyful song. It will escort you back into the ease and flow of love.

The Sound of Music

If you can't think of any song to sing, there is one that is guaranteed to lift you up immediately. The best news is, it's a song you most likely know very well. It is "Do-Re-Mi" from *The Sound of Music*.

There's a reason this song is such a potent detour around all the insecurities that threaten to block your journey. The notes in this song correspond exactly with, and instantly balance, your seven chakras or energy fields. Balanced chakras build an immunity to the negative undertow of life and release your insecurities. When you sing this song with gusto, you immediately take off at the speed of love.

In case you've forgotten the song, let me refresh your memory. The chakras correspond with the lines in this way:

- First chakra: *doe*
- Second chakra: *ray*
- Third chakra: *me*
- Fourth chakra: *fa*
- Fifth chakra: *sew*
- Sixth chakra: *la*
- Seventh chakra: *tea*

If you aren't familiar with this song, Google it on the Internet and you'll find it. Once you listen to it, you'll either remember it, or if you don't know it, you'll learn it in two minutes. It's catchy, witty, and it brings you into the vibration and flow of love quickly.

Advanced Flying Lessons

Take Control

Make a list of three things you do not like or respect about yourself. Be realistic and honest. List only those things that genuinely fail to meet your approval and that you're interested in changing. For example:

- I do not like or respect that I am a pushover.
- I do not like or respect that I do not speak my truth.
- I do not like or respect that I am in unmanageable debt and don't or can't pay my bills.

Next, pick one of these three things and make a commitment to change it. You may require support to succeed; and if so, get it. For example:

- If you are a pushover, you might want to take a martial-arts course and learn to set healthy personal boundaries.

- If you do not speak your truth, you may engage the help of a therapist to guide you in how to express yourself authentically.

- If you are in debt, you can attend Debtors Anonymous meetings and get a sponsor to help you get your debt under control.

Work on only one issue at a time until you feel as though you are breaking through and gaining self-respect in this area. Love yourself enough to stop complaining, and take action toward improvement. When you decide you want to respect yourself, you will follow through and do what it takes to succeed. As we all know, if you don't respect yourself, no one else will either.

Write Your Own Song

Music changes and elevates the vibration of a person so quickly that it can be used as a powerful means for traveling at the speed of love. Write a song or ditty of your own that sings the praises of life, the joys of being alive, and the fun of being human. Write a song about the blessings you experience, the fun of learning soul lessons, and the beauty in those you love. Write a song about your kids, your dog, your best friend, your most delightful surprises, or your adventures. Keep the melody simple and singable, and sing it often. Here's a favorite song of mine, written by my friend Mark Welch, called "Every Step I Take." It goes like this:

Every step I take is the best one (for me)
Every move I make is the best one (for now)
Life it keeps on flowing
If I only keep on knowing
That I'm always on the bright side
The sunny light side
(repeat)

Sunshine
I'm always in
sunshine
I make my own
sunshine
Ahhhh ahhhh . . .

If you think it's a corny song, that's okay. It is. That's why I like it. I like corny things. Always have. They make me laugh. That's the beauty of writing your own song. It speaks to you, using your language, your melody, and your imagery and metaphors. Besides, it's fun to write your own song, and having fun is essential to living in the light.

Sing Your Inner Child into Life

This beautiful Native American ritual is another powerful way to launch a life of love. When a woman is pregnant, she chooses a special song for her baby and sings to her unborn child during labor, delivery, and after the baby is born. This song becomes part of the child's identity and holds great power throughout his or her life.

You can do this for your inner child as well, especially if you feel you weren't welcomed in a loving way or did not receive the love and nurturing you needed as a child. Pick a song you love and sing it to your inner child whenever you feel insecure, agitated, worried, anxious, uncomfortable, and unloved. Let it be your signal to go back to your breath and leave all negative thoughts behind. Sing it silently or out loud, as the situation allows. Hum your song at work. Sing it out loud in the shower. Sing it to yourself as you exercise. Sing it all the time. It too will become a powerful mantra for you the more you sing it over time.

See the Light

For an entire day, practice seeing the light in all people, no matter how they behave. This includes family members, neighbors, the barista at your local coffee shop, the mail carrier, your hair stylist, and even the guy who cuts you off in traffic or takes your seat on the subway. Separate what they *do* from the Divine light of who they *are*. This lesson includes *you*.

Be Self-Respecting

Stop criticizing yourself or diminishing yourself in front of others. Never say a disparaging thing about yourself as mindless conversation. Think, believe, and speak lovingly *of* yourself *to* yourself and others. No need to brag or be grandiose, which are just cover-ups for feeling insecure. Simply be self-respecting.

Chapter 6

Meet the Pilot

Recently, as I was boarding a flight from Los Angeles to Chicago, I noticed a young mother with her three-year-old son just ahead of me. As we got on the plane, the captain greeted the young boy and asked if he'd like to see the cockpit. He squealed with delight and raced right in. I found my seat and was just about to settle back when all of a sudden, I heard the same three-year-old screaming and crying with rage. Wondering what could have possibly upset this child so much in the space of about three minutes, I looked up and listened.

"I want to fly the plane!" he screamed. "I want to fly the plane!" It was ridiculous, really, watching as both his mother and the captain tried to calm him down. Finally, the captain reached inside the cockpit and grabbed his hat. Placing it on the child's head, he said, "I'll tell you what, you can't really fly the plane, but you can pretend you're the captain and wear my hat during the flight as long as you give it back when we land." This seemed to be an interesting enough alternative that the boy stopped screaming. "Okay, I promise," he said.

The captain plopped his hat on the boy's head, and it promptly fell over his eyes, preventing him from seeing anything at all.

The entire scene was hilarious, and everybody who witnessed it laughed out loud.

Settling in after takeoff, a thought flashed across my mind: *Thank God there's a captain in charge of this flight, because God knows if I flew it, or anyone else onboard for that matter, we'd crash in a matter of moments.* A ridiculous thought, I know, because of course the captain is in charge. If he weren't, we would never board the flight. Similarly, on our life's journey, something greater than us is behind the controls. We need to trust the one who can get us safely above the clouds and on to our destination, and let that person do the job.

On another flight, this time on Southwest Airlines (where the flight attendants are funny and joke with passengers all the time), just as we were about to close the door and get going, the flight attendant got on the public-address system. "Everyone sit down, buckle in, and do what you love least in life," she said. "Surrender control, because right now you have none. Trust us. We'll get you where you're going, so relax while you can."

The entire cabin laughed out loud, mostly because it was absolutely true. We got onboard, but we weren't in charge of flying the plane. We had no choice but to let go of control and trust the captain in charge.

Traveling at the speed of love requires the same surrender and trust from you. The only way to travel at this speed is to journey with an intention to have a safe and pleasant experience. In this case, you must surrender to the captain of love, which is your heart. To get into the flow and ride the wave of ease and grace through life, the ego mind has to recognize its limitations and completely surrender to a source higher than the intellect.

To our crazy, controlling human ego, that sounds extremely threatening, doesn't it? And yet, would you get on an airplane and insist on flying it, especially if you clearly didn't know how? Of course you wouldn't. You'd gladly surrender control over to the one with the skill. That's why it's so important to surrender, and to put your journey in the hands of the source that gets you to the highest altitude safely—and that is *not* your fearful, overactive, controlling, reactive, limited mind.

Surrender to Freedom

Most of us identify surrender with submission, even imprison-ment. That's why we fight it so much. We fear it will rob us of our freedom to be in charge of our lives. Does it? Well, yes and no.

If you look up the word *surrender,* it means to yield or give power over to another. While this could disguise a scary "surren-der Dorothy" moment, such as in the classic movie *The Wizard of Oz* when the wicked witch tries to frighten Dorothy, it can also connote a spiritual surrendering. When traveling at the speed of love, you are not being asked to surrender to an outside oppres-sive force that will take your freedom away, but rather, you're asked to turn your trust over to your own source of intuitive wisdom, your heart.

Turning the controls of your life over to your quiet, loving heart instead of your overthinking, overcontrolling mind—that is, surrendering your ego to love and flow—is no less necessary than the three-year-old surrendering to the captain of our Los Angeles flight. And yes, if necessary, your ego can wear the captain's hat and pretend to be in charge, but only if it buckles in, quiets down, and tunes in to the loving guidance of your heart's wisdom. It's the only way you'll get off the ground.

Easier Said Than Done Sometimes

Surrendering control of the mind over to the heart can seem easy in some ways, and virtually impossible in others. It's almost comical to me at times how my need for control can take prece-dence over love.

We are in the midst of renovating our 100-year-old home in Chicago. It's been a long, disruptive process that has dragged on for more than a year. It has been carried out in two phases. In phase one, which lasted six months, we gutted the first floor, in-cluding the kitchen and the basement, which meant figuring out how to eat, cook, store food, and even get drinking water without a kitchen.

Option A was to move out, but we decided that was too expensive, so we chose option B, which meant eating out of a Crock-Pot, barbecuing, and ordering out frequently. We had to surrender to the situation to make it work, which for some members of my family was terrifically unpleasant, but for me wasn't challenging at all.

After six months of that craziness, the renovation moved to the second floor, where we gutted the bedrooms and bathrooms, requiring us all to move into the basement and live dorm-room style, sharing a single bathroom for another six months. Again, I was easily able to surrender and go with the flow—I grew up in a small house with a large family and limited privacy, so it was familiar and at times even fun, at least for me.

After it was all over, I was feeling rather proud of my ability to travel in cruise control over the previous 12 months. Yet all of a sudden, I was pulled into a vortex of panic and the need to take over control when Patrick placed three very ugly (in my opinion) bathroom mats that he'd purchased at Costco on "my" newly renovated bathroom floor. *How dare he even think of putting something so ugly* (they were orange-gold-puke color) *in my beautiful space?* I thought. I went ballistic and into a tailspin of indignation faster than I could scream "Help!"

I snatched them up, marched them directly over to his office, and said, "No way, José! These are gross!"

Those were, of course, fighting words, and he instantly rose to the challenge. "Oh, really?" he retorted. "Well, I like them. They stay!"

"No, they don't," I snarled back, my voice rising in pitch. "They go and so do you . . . if you try to keep these disgusting insults to our gorgeous bathroom in the house. Take them back."

Then the most devastating blow came as Patrick hurled the words, "I'm so sick of your controlling ways!"

"And I'm sick of yours!" I threw right back as I stormed out to lick my wounds, as soon as I was out of sight, of course.

I fumed all day. *How dare Patrick pick mats without my approval?* I thought. *Who does he think he is?* Now of course, I'm not proud of any of this. It's actually very embarrassing and highly unbecoming of my spiritual-teacher persona, don't you think? But I have to share it because it's true, and as I said, I'm on this journey with you. If I hid it, I'd only be protecting the very ego that keeps me—keeps all of us—from soaring to the heights of love.

The problem was that I really didn't want to have those ugly mats around, control or no control, so what was I to do? How is a person supposed to travel at the speed of love and still get what she wants? Especially when it is clearly not what someone else wants? Isn't that the million-dollar question? I pondered this with my own "captain's hat" covering my eyes. Then I remembered to turn the situation over to my heart and let it captain me back into love and flow. It worked. My heart told me loud and clear that I just had to let it go. I could sit with my own misery-making thoughts over something so silly, or give them up and soar back into a loving higher elevation.

My heart said I had a choice. Allow the mats to stay and travel in the ease and flow by surrendering control, or get rid of them and enter the downward tailspin of being alienated from my husband and, more important, from ease and flow. It was that simple. That's when I laughed. *Wow! The ego frequency really is willing to fight to the death to get its own way!* I thought. So I surrendered to the captain of my journey—my heart—and asked it what to do.

Nothing, was its answer. *Just breathe, relax, and enjoy your day.*

The answer was surprising, but resonated deeply throughout my entire being. *Nothing* was the best thing to do. Nothing I could do would allow the adrenaline surging through my bloodstream to mellow out or alleviate the pressure to "win" the battle. I had to "do" nothing. Once I accepted this, I forgot about the mats and went with a friend to see a funny movie. By the time I got back home, I didn't care about the mats anymore. I was no longer invested in the need to be right. I just wanted to take a warm, relaxing bath in the tub I was so grateful to once again be able to enjoy, and go to sleep.

When I walked into the bathroom, the puke-orange mats were gone. I hesitated at first to believe it, but then said to Patrick, "Sorry

I so overreacted about the mats. I don't like them, but if they give you pleasure, you can put them back down on the floor."

He laughed and said, "No. They were ugly. I already returned them."

I share this ridiculous and unflattering story because all ego battles are ridiculous and throw us into downward spirals of negativity, and we are well served to remember that. There is ultimately nothing rewarding about controlling life with our fearful thoughts and beliefs. It's just the three-year-old control freak in us trying to fly the plane.

Pilot Checklist

There are three ways to verify whether you are successfully connecting to your heart's wisdom. The first is that the guidance you receive relaxes your body. The heart's vibration is one of love, and love calms the nervous system and eases tension.

Second, the heart is brief and to the point, not verbose, while the intellect is full of words. The heart communicates with few if any words, communicating with loving energy instead. For example, it might say:

- Relax.
- Breathe.
- All is well.
- Let go.
- Do nothing.
- Allow.
- Wait.
- Begin.

These are the signature instructions of the heart. It may not sound like much, but it is perhaps all you need to get back to ease and flow.

Third, you may occasionally get what my friend Julia Cameron, whom I mentioned earlier, calls "marching orders." These are very distinct internal instructions guiding you to take a specific action when there is no logical reason for you to do so. Marching orders show up in our awareness like direct assignments. Julia was given the marching order to help me write my first book, and that was before I ever even knew (or would admit, anyway) that I had a book in me. She followed those orders by asking me over and over again where my book was. And then she finally convinced me to write the book to her. I did, and now *The Psychic Pathway* is winging its way around the world. Her Higher Self asked for my book. Mine answered with one. It surprised us both. That's how the Higher Self works. It bypasses the logical brain and communicates directly from Divine Source. When it does, it compels you to listen and follow, even if it doesn't make logical sense to do so. Once you feel the flow, go with the flow.

A friend of mine named Shamrock came to Chicago for a visit last fall with plans to stay only a week or two en route to Palenque, Mexico, where he planned to visit the sacred sites. This was something he'd wanted to experience for years and had made arrangements to do in depth. But as he was traveling to the airport to catch his flight to Palenque, his Higher Self said, *Don't leave.*

He listened to his inner voice and turned back to Chicago. Six months later, he had developed a flourishing healing practice, created a grounded home for the first time, and found a deep sense of purpose in his work. These are three things he had been hoping to achieve by going to Mexico. It surprised him that he actually achieved them by turning away from his original plans and surrendering control. Shamrock says again and again, "I could never have planned all the wonderful things now unfolding in my life. Only by fully surrendering control and going with my intuition, by ignoring my logical brain with all its questions and agendas, is my life unfolding as it is."

I realize this is an extreme example of surrendering control, but I've done it myself, when years ago my own Higher Self spontaneously guided me to move to France without reason, so I did.

I originally left with the intention of staying six months and ended up spending several years there, going to school, creating a second home, and developing lifelong friendships that are still very important and valuable to me to this day. So I understand.

This is a perfect example of the opportunity one gets: to make a choice to go with the intellect's plans and journey at the speed of the ego, or surrender ego control and go with the guidance of the Higher Self instead.

Follow the Flow

When life collapses under the pressure of the bullying logical brain, the only way up and out is to turn your life over to your heart, even if it may feel threatening or seem crazy to do so. When you are crushed by the weight of the world, become quiet. Pray, meditate, and humbly open to your heart and intuition for direction. Intuition is the true compass of your journey, but you must first be willing to consult it and follow its direction.

Surrendering control over to your heart and intuition can be challenging if you're not accustomed to doing so, but it can feel especially scary when under extreme distress. That's when your fight-or-flight reptilian brain pushes you most urgently toward controlling actions instead. For example, it may be hard for a mother to trust that her teenager is safe when he or she is not home on time, causing her to panic, imagine the worst, and call the police. It can be challenging when rumors of layoffs are whirling around the office, causing you to believe you'll soon be out of work, which makes you act angrily toward your employer and peers, further putting your job in jeopardy.

The best way around such a situation is to connect with your heart every day, even on the smallest matters, so that you establish such a strong and automatic connection with your heart that it becomes only natural to rely upon it in stormy circumstances.

Surrendering control to your heart is not a passive submission, even though the ego mind will tell you it is. Surrendering to your heart gives you access to your intuition, which is the radar your pilot relies on for guidance each day. Following your intuition is a tremendous act of conscious intelligence and takes dedication and practice, and is a topic I discuss further in Chapter 15. When you surrender your fears and turn to the heart instead, like a child passenger trusting the pilot, you take your seat in life, allowing a higher intelligence to carry you to your destinations throughout each day.

Allowing your heart to pilot your life raises you to a higher altitude and back into the jet stream of life. How the heart pilots your life journey is highly subtle. At first, you may not feel, sense, or hear a thing from your heart. But you *will* notice a difference in your daily life. You may, for example, spontaneously find yourself driving or walking in a new direction, speaking to someone by accident, or ending up at the right place at the right time. With no thought as to why you're doing what you're doing, life will simply fall into place better than ever before. With your heart piloting your life, you suddenly have less and less of an urge to think and obsess about things, or to try to figure them out. Answers seem to come before the questions even fully form. That's what being in the flow of love feels like. You have little or no anxiety or forethought as you move throughout your day. You just show up, and life moves you in the best direction for your soul.

Having no forethought doesn't mean that you're without goals or intentions. Having no forethought simply means that you're open to allowing the Universe to support your goals and intentions, moment to moment, in ways far superior to the plans your intellect can devise.

Another strong indication that your heart is piloting your journey is finding yourself suddenly attracting unexpected gifts. For example, in the most recent economic downturn, a client of mine named Marjorie lost her job at a hotel where she had worked for years. She was absolutely overcome with fear about the future. Exhausted from worry, she decided to turn off her fretful brain and listen to her heart for one full week without resistance, upon my encouragement, if for nothing more than to give her frazzled emotions a rest. Two days into her experiment, she received a call from a good friend asking her to visit Tucson where she lived.

Even better, the friend offered to use her free miles to buy Marjorie a ticket. Being unemployed, Marjorie was free to go and gladly accepted.

Once she arrived, a friend of her friend met Marjorie and invited her to lunch one afternoon at a beautiful local restaurant, her treat. Again accepting with pleasure, Marjorie met the owner of the restaurant quite spontaneously, and they struck up a conversation about her being laid off and out of a job. He immediately said he knew an elderly couple from New York who owned a house in Tucson and had just lost their house sitter for the winter. "I don't know if it would interest you, but if you have any plans to stay in Tucson, I believe you could house-sit for the winter in exchange for free rent."

Having nothing to race home to, Marjorie went for it. Not only did they engage her, the couple offered her their brand-new car to use in exchange for watching the house. Marjorie lived there rent free for six months, with a new car at her disposal. By the time they returned, she had met an entire new community of friends. She even found other houses she could take care of for the winter, only this time for a fee. Her heart encouraged her to take the risk even though she was apprehensive about all the changes. However, once she surrendered, her heart piloted her to a far better life than she could have ever dreamed of. That's how the heart works. It knows where to go to reach the highest level of life possible when the mind can't see it at all.

In-Flight Check-In

Take out your notebook now and spend a few minutes thinking about each of the following questions. Stretch and breathe for a few moments before you set about answering them. Be honest with yourself and probe deeply beneath your fear-based defenses for the answers. You may want to answer the question out loud before you write the answer down. Speaking out loud often opens the heart and frees information that the fearful ego mind blocks. Rather than simple *yes/no* answers, elaborate, and include examples in response to all these questions. Take your time and be willing to put effort into the questions and exercises, as they will greatly benefit you.

- In what ways are you controlling?

- Do others accuse you of being controlling?

- Are you open-minded?

- In what areas might you be overly presumptuous or hold strong and close-minded views?
  — In your religious views?
  — Your political views?
  — Your financial views?
  — Your social-status views?

- Are you in the habit of listening to your heart?

- How much does your heart influence your decisions?

- Can you differentiate between your heart and your intellect?

- Do you solicit others' opinions over the inner wisdom of your heart?

- What overrides your inner voice?

- Do you second-guess your heart's calling?

- Are you able to feel your heart wisdom?

- Do you check in with your heart when it comes to guidance and decisions?

- Are you aware of how it feels to allow your heart to guide you?

- Do you find yourself overthinking or obsessing with worry? In a particular area or in all areas?

- Do you forego thinking too far into the future and listen for inner guidance instead?

- Do you check in with your heart when you are peaceful, or only when you're feeling emotional?

Basic Flying Lessons

Name Your Pilot (Your Co-pilot, Too)

Take time to listen to your heart each day, to have a rendez-vous with your most precious and beloved inner guide. Listen to your heart with the same intensity you would listen for noises if you were all alone in a big house at night. Listen with more than your ears. Listen with your Spirit.

Many years ago, my spiritual teacher Charlie Goodman suggested that I name my heart and talk to it like an old and trusted friend. It was a great suggestion, which I followed, and to this day my heart, whom I named "Bright Light," and I are great friends. Whenever I need to check in with my heart, I ask Bright Light what she thinks. By naming my heart, I can more easily differentiate between my heart (pilot) and my head or intellect (co-pilot), whom I call "Poindexter." When I need my logical brain to register an opinion, I ask Poindexter for advice. If I'm looking for the best way to stay in the flow, I ask Bright Light. This simple system seems to work well. I am on a first-name basis with my heart, and we check in several times a day on every matter possible.

Breathe as You Listen

Breathe as you listen to your heart. You will know that you're tuning in to your heart's guidance by how you feel. When the heart speaks, you feel it vibrate in the center of your heart, where-as if you are in your head, your eyes roll up and all energy leaves your heart, leaving it feeling cold and empty. Try this right now and you will feel the difference yourself. If you're not accustomed to following your heart, this may all seem a little confusing and leave you feeling somewhat insecure. That is understandable. Don't worry.

Get to know the captain of your plane by experimenting with following the heart's guidance. For example, place your hand on your heart and ask it any question, such as, "What is the best way to handle my mother right now?" Then, with your hand still on your heart, answer out loud. Feel your heart as you speak. If you feel peaceful and calm, you know it is your heart speaking. Try this with several questions, always keeping your hand on your heart and answering out loud.

You need not go to your heart for everything. For those areas in life in which you feel peaceful and content, you're already in your heart and in the flow, even if you aren't aware of it. It's only necessary to check with your heart and let it captain your journey when you're in turmoil or are struggling. Turn to your heart whenever you're not feeling like your authentic self and aren't happy with your experience. These are the times when your captain can take you to higher ground and get you back into the flow.

Reach Out

The hands are often referred to as a direct extension of the heart, so reaching out with the hands opens the heart to life and keeps you in touch with it. Reach out at least once or twice a day and give someone you love a heartfelt hug. By this I mean a hug that allows you to genuinely connect heart to heart, and not the "burping" pat on the back that some substitute for a genuine hug. Don't overdo your hug, however, by clinging to the person you're hugging too hard or too long, as this doesn't feel genuine, but rather contrived and controlling, even intrusive and uncomfortable.

Be authentic and mindful; and give a hug that is real, warm, and comfortable for your "huggee." During the day, extend your hand when greeting another, and when shaking hands, offer a warm and solid handshake (not a limp fish [women] or death grip [men] handshake), but one shared with an authentic desire to connect with that person on a heart-based level. Breathe as you hug or shake hands, and relax. Don't force the hug or a handshake, as not all people will be appropriate to hug or shake hands with. Just be mindful of what feels heartfelt and authentic. Be genuinely friendly and let the heart lead you throughout the day.

Advanced Flying Lessons

Paging the Pilot

Whenever you need direction, call to mind the decision, concern, or topic you're wondering about and ask your heart to guide you on the best course of action. Next, voice out loud each option you're considering. If the decision, thought, or course of action you expressed is aligned with your heart and your greatest good, your body will feel a warm, energetic confirmation flowing from your heart and throughout your body. If the course or direction you're considering is not in alignment with your heart, you will feel a very subtle dissonance or agitated energy in your heart and throughout your body. Either way, resonant or dissonant, the response from your Higher Self will be subtle, at least as you are first becoming connected. With attention, and with consistent awareness of, and connection with, your heart, its guidance will become stronger and stronger. Finally, it will become the primary—and eventually, only—energy that moves you throughout each day. When this occurs, you will be traveling fully at the speed of love.

Give Up the Controls

Practically speaking, if your ego is throwing a fit and trying to take over your journey, it is emotionally worked up. In this case, you may have to expel some of the excess adrenaline it is pumping through your body before you can disengage from the ego's struggle. Here are a few ways in which you can do that:

- Scream in the shower (a personal favorite).
- Punch a pillow (feels really good).
- Go to the gym (does more good than just burning off negative energy).
- Go for a walk or a run.

- Watch a movie.

- Refuse to talk about the upset.

- Sleep.

- And, of course, breathe. Breathe. Breathe. Breathe. Breathe slowly and deeply until you calm down some more. This always works.

After you scream, punch, walk, sleep, and breathe, ask your heart to take over the journey and then relax.

CHAPTER 7

Connect with the Control Tower

I have a friend named William who is a commercial airline pilot. I once asked him if he ever worried that he might get confused when flying and not get to where he was going, given that there was so much he had to be aware of during the flight. He laughed and said, "Heck no, because I'm not the one guiding the plane. I *fly* the plane, but the control tower directs my course, from the minute I turn on the engine to the minute I park at the gate. In fact, it directs the flow of everything in the sky, not just me. From the driver's seat I can only see so much, even in an airplane. The control tower, however, sees it all. So I just listen, trust, and follow orders. With them guiding the way, it's easy to get where I'm going because I'm not the one figuring it all out."

Lately it has become apparent to me that just as we need a control tower at the airport to guide our external aircraft safely to their destinations, we also need to check in with a Divine control tower, something that sees beyond all of our limited ego perspectives to keep us safely traveling at the speed of love. Fortunately, we can all connect to the Divine control tower . . . it's called our Higher Self.

Your Higher Self Is Present

Every morning before I open my eyes, I lie in bed and make contact with my Higher Self through a silent inner conversation, centered in my heart. I've been conversing with my Higher Self through my heart my entire life and have felt her gentle voice ever since I was very young. But only lately, in the past few years, am I beginning to fully understand that just because she's my Higher Self doesn't mean she's far away, in some distant heaven that I can only aspire to reach when I die. I'm becoming increasingly aware that my beloved Higher Self, my essential Divine Spirit, is present at all times; and she is as close as my thoughts, my breath, and my beating heart. She is here, she is present, and she oversees my entire life's journey.

I now realize that the only way to travel at the speed of love is to maintain constant contact with the Universal Divine control tower and stay connected to my Higher Self throughout my journey in life. Only my heart, the pilot of my journey, can make contact with the Higher Self, and only this control tower can guide me seamlessly through the fog and pollution of *my* thoughts as well as others'. Only my Higher Self can steer me through the congestion of my emotional ups and downs; and toward a more beautiful, elevated frequency of love.

Making contact with my Higher Self is very different from listening to the vibration of my lower ego mind bouncing around my head. Just as the pilot of an aircraft cannot fly willy-nilly through the sky, going wherever he or she wants to go, so, too, must we not allow the ego mind to pilot our journey anywhere it wants to go without guidance from a higher source either. A pilot flying out of touch with the control tower is not only a danger to himself, but a danger to the world around him as well. A pilot who loses contact with the control tower—or worse, attempts to fly without direction from the tower—is in serious trouble and can head into disaster at any moment. And a person out of touch with his or her Higher Self is also, in many ways, in serious trouble. He is not only thrown off by his own errant thoughts, but can also be manipulated by the crazy and errant thoughts of others, which can cause a crash of a different sort.

Travel Warnings

One way in which the fearful ego tries to lure you off course and disconnect you from the control tower is to harass you about time. It tells you to hurry up and get busy, reminding you that there's so much to do and not enough time to do it all; or it tells you that no matter what you're doing, you're wasting your time, that it *is* the wrong thing to do, and you're missing the "right" thing to do.

Another indication that you've disconnected from your Higher Self is that your body feels heavy, even achy, as though all the sleep in the world is never enough to feel energized. Like a huge energy leak, fear can be so debilitating that it zaps all your energy and leaves you feeling stuck and unable to get through the day.

Yet another sign that you are disconnected from your Higher Self is finding yourself unable to speak your truth or express your authentic self with others. Rather than listening to your heart and expressing it, you focus on how to impress others instead. You speak to please or manipulate people in such a way that you avoid confrontation or risk receiving disapproval.

It's important to realize that it's not the authentic you that feels this way. Rather, it is the vibration of fearful energy moving through you, like poison flooding your system. All you need to do to break free of this draining force is to focus fully on your heart and make a call to your Higher Self to guide you above, around, or if necessary, *through,* the crowded mental skies in order to rise to a higher vibration.

The Higher Self Is Calm

Your Higher Self connects with you through your heart. When the channels are open, you feel a warm, open, light, calming vibration. This feeling reverberates throughout your body and into every one of your cells, like a Divine GPS broadcast moving your consciousness, directing you above the clouds and to the light.

You immediately begin to feel Source energy clearing your system, calming your fears, or guiding you through them.

Fortunately, with awareness, attention, and intention, you can tune in to your Divine control tower for direction. It isn't difficult. It is just new and different for many people to ask their Higher Self to guide them through their day rather than their intellects. You can shift your attention away from this lower broadcast and begin to follow the heart for instructions on how to lift off into flight. Although the control tower of your Higher Self may feel faint or distant to you right now, that is only because your attention gets stuck, even mesmerized, by the blaring bursts of negativity coming from the lower band.

A similar phenomenon occurs when you walk into a room full of people who are depressed or angry. The negative energy can nearly sucker punch the life force right out of you, even if you're not aware of it. That certainly was my experience when going to a dermatologist's office to get treatment for a mild case of eczema in Chicago last year. Although the office was close by and convenient to get to, the vibration of the people working there was so toxic that it nearly ruined my day almost every time I entered. I preferred the eczema! Now I just don't go there. I found another dermatologist's office that is a few miles farther away, but absolutely delightful to enter. The vibe is just so much lighter, happier, and more loving that I don't mind making the extra effort to get there. My Higher Self directed me to make the detour, while my ego mind would have denied the negative onslaught, telling me it's nothing, or at least nothing real or important enough to go to the extra effort to avoid.

It's not always practical to hopscotch around negative energy as a means to protect your flow, however. It's better to learn to recognize negative energy when you're in it, listen to your heart, and follow your Higher Self to higher ground instead.

Negativity—Love It or Leave It

When you encounter negative energy or thoughts and internalize them as your own, they will pull you down every single time. It's smart, therefore, to recognize where negativity gathers and avoid being in those places when you can. It is also good to know that no matter when or where negative, fear-based energy gathers, you can simply observe it from the perspective of your Higher Self and know that it is not about you. Detach, then broadcast love into the energy field.

I knew the negativity in the doctor's office had nothing to do with me, and using detached awareness, I did keep it from overpowering me like a noxious gas by sending love to everyone who worked there as I entered and exited. Eventually, however, my Higher Self said, *Time to leave the building.* So I did. But when you can't, your Higher Self can serve as a gas mask, too.

Here's how: simply know that no matter where you encounter negative thoughts and energy, if you send love to the situation and the people involved from the frequency of your Higher Self, the negativity cannot touch you.

This, of course, takes practice. We have not been taught, encouraged, or shown how to navigate around or above negativity, so it's not familiar. In fact, the last great role model for this was Christ, who said, "Love your neighbor as yourself." Yet many of those who teach his way don't really live it. He also said, "Get up and walk," and I think he especially meant for us to do this when surrounded by negativity. It's worth the effort to know you have a choice when you encounter negative energy; love it or leave it. Either way works. In fact, making that choice is at the heart of traveling at the speed of love.

A Clear View

Imagine looking at the world through ego mind, as though looking through a dirty airplane window as it sits at the gate in dense, polluted smog. Imagine how gray, dreary, sad, and stuck everything looks, feels, and is from this perspective. Next, imagine looking at the world from the same airplane seat, only this time you tuned in to the control tower, loud and clear. You are being guided above the pollution, through the clouds, and into a crystal blue, shining sky; and it is beautiful everywhere. That's how different traveling at the speed of love is from remaining stuck in the muck of the mind.

The point is to stay connected to your Higher Self all day, on all matters, until it feels like the most natural thing in the world and the only way to fly. Only the Higher Self can show you how to travel at the speed of love. The mind cannot go there. The mind can only surrender, get onboard, and go for the best ride on Earth. It can sit in the pilot's seat, but as my pilot friend William reminds us, it cannot go any which way it wants to. It must follow the direction of the Higher Self to have a safe and successful journey.

Dialing in to the Control Tower

The best way I know to dial in to your Higher Self is to spend a few moments in meditation or contemplating your Higher Self every morning. I rouse myself and begin to make contact with my Higher Self while still in a semi-dream state. In this half-awake, half-asleep frame of mind, I can feel the vibration of my Higher Self pulsing in my heart. I feel her wisdom, wit, beauty, and creativity. Best of all, I feel her love for me. And in this quiet space, before my eyes engage with this earthly, mundane dimension, we talk in my heart.

I ask her to remind me why she loves me. This is my favorite conversation, and every day new answers come. Sometimes they are deep, sometimes they are comical, and sometimes they are surprising, but they are always filled with love. My Higher Self gives me answers I would not think of myself. She tells me I'm kind. She tells me I'm creative and daring. She tells me I'm authentic and open to learning. She tells me I'm funny and lovable. She tells me I'm a creation of God. These are things my heart loves to hear and my mind easily forgets.

I also ask my Higher Self questions about my life, ask her to guide me through sketchy areas, and ask for protection from negative mental energy, especially my own, throughout the day. She tells me not to fear the mental realm. She advises me to be detached and not allow any negative thought or belief about myself or the world to be important, because in truth, it is not. Only love is important.

This morning meditation practice works well for me and is something I anticipate every day now. In the past, on days I didn't connect with my Higher Self, I always got ambushed by negative sniper energy and was completely derailed by it. So now I know. This early-morning connection is my way to ensure I have enough lift to live each day at a high altitude.

Mindful Meditation

Setting aside time for daily contemplation or meditation, such as the conversation I have with my Higher Self, is the foundation for connecting to your Higher Self. Without creating this connection intentionally through meditation, a connection with your Higher Self will remain vague. Having said that, meditation is not easy or appealing to everyone, at least in the conventional sense. Happily, we can also do something author and Buddhist monk Thich Nhat Hanh coined "mindful meditation," which merely means going about our daily tasks in a meditative state of mind.

I have a neighbor who connects to his Higher Self through selfless service. Every day he walks from house to house, watering and mowing lawns, sweeping sidewalks, picking up debris, and arranging flowers, all quietly and without the need for recognition.

He loves what he does and does it with love. He is, in fact, meditating in peaceful flow as he quietly serves, and his Higher Self is guiding his work. He is definitely traveling at the speed of love, and wherever he goes, whatever he does, whatever he touches, radiates with that love.

My assistant Ryan's mother, Ann, meditates by working in her garden. She spends hours and hours in the quiet beauty of nature; and the time there calms her mind and leaves her peaceful, grounded, and renewed.

My sister Noelle, an interior designer, meditates by taking long hikes in nature with her dog, Tux. She works as hard as anyone I know, and her mind is whirling a mile a minute on the design projects she undertakes, so a daily hike in the mountains where she lives is her mental escape. It takes her away from all the hustle, bustle, details, and drama that go along with her job; and leaves her calm, quiet, refreshed, and peaceful.

These are not complicated efforts. The key to success is to connect with the Higher Self regularly, consistently, and predictably. The daily contact, the consistent connection, strengthens you as you travel.

Journal Your Adventures

Another way to strengthen your ability to travel at the speed of love is to journal every day. Use your journal as another means to dialogue with your Higher Self.

I was taught how to do this by one of my great teachers, Charlie, when I was very young and apprenticing with him in the psychic arts. Back then we called it inspirational and automatic writing, and it seemed exotic indeed.

Write to your Higher Self as though you were writing to your best friend who loves you and knows you better then anyone in the entire world, and only wants the best for you in every situation. And then, without censoring, editing, or overthinking, allow your Higher Self to borrow your hand and write back. The logical mind tries to interfere with this by saying that you're making things up, but don't pay attention because it's not true. What comes through this effort, if done earnestly and (this is the key) consistently, is profound, truthful, life-changing, heart-opening, authentic wisdom.

Your Higher Self is present and will direct you if you allow it to do so. The decision to connect with your Higher Self and ask it to lead your life is a turning point, the moment when you lift off out of the swamp of negativity, out of the clouds, and into clear sailing at the speed of love.

The important thing is to make it a point to stay in constant communication with the Divine control tower during your life's journey. Connect with your Higher Self daily. Ask your Higher Self to open and expand your heart. Witness life through love rather than fight it with fear. It isn't complicated, just radically different from what you've learned and what the world does. Therefore, you must be on guard, work to strengthen your Higher-Self connection, and allow for the learning curve as you go. It will get easier and easier to make contact day by day. You'll see.

In-Flight Check-In

Take out your notebook and spend a few minutes thinking about each of the following questions. Before answering, take a few moments to do some deep-breathing exercises to help quiet all fears, activate your heart, and connect with your Higher Self. Be curious as you explore the answers. Do not settle for simple *yes/ no* answers. Use the questions as a springboard to have a personal conversation with your Higher Self. Feel free to allow extemporaneous writing to take over as you work through these questions. Enjoy the process, and be open to discovering information that will elevate your journey toward a great and loving altitude.

- Are you aware that you have a Higher Self?
- Do you make contact with your Higher Self now?

- Do you know how to meditate?

- Do you take the time to meditate regularly?

- What guidance have you received from your Higher Self so far?

- Can you tell the difference between your Higher Self and your mind?

- Do you have any sort of meditative practice in place in which you connect to your Higher Self through your heart now?

- If so, what is it? How often do you do your practice? Every day? When you can? When you feel stressed out?

Basic Flying Lessons

Heart to Control Tower . . . Come In

Make contact with your Higher Self first by doing a few minutes of breath work. Next, get a good meditation CD (see my CD suggestions at the end of this chapter) and a good set of headphones with which to listen to it. Next, in your journal, write to your Higher Self and allow your Higher Self to write back.

Set a regular time in your day during which you can connect with your Higher Self uninterrupted. For some, this is the first thing in the morning; for others, it's the last thing at night before sleep. I have found that when beginning to tune in to the control tower of Spirit, it works best to be consistent, at least until you establish a solid connection and have the habit of connecting all the time. Very early in the morning is usually best.

Like an astronaut in training, it's important to build up your capacity to journey at a high frequency by connecting every day, as much as you can, until it becomes a part of you. Using your notebooks, commit to at least one of the following practices for a minimum of seven consecutive days, or until you know you've made contact with the control tower of your Higher Self.

Daily Practice

Do one of the following for a week and notice the change it brings about:

— Using your journal, try automatic and inspirational writing. To do so, write your Higher Self a question, and then answer as though it is your Higher Self writing a response back.

— In your notebook or on a separate pad of paper, write down all of your fears, negative thoughts, feelings, and experiences that occurred that day or are hanging around in your mind, distracting you and keeping you from hearing your higher self. Once you have filled these pages, tear out what you have written, rip it up, and either burn it or throw it away.

— If you prefer a more techno-savvy approach, speak into a voice recorder and then, with your hand over your heart, allow your Higher Self to talk back. I've done this, and it works remarkably well.

— Dialogue with your Higher Self every day. All you need to do is set your alarm for half an hour earlier, and when you wake up, with eyes closed, feel the loving presence of your Higher Self. Sense his or her frequency and let the vibration of unconditional love sweep over you, around you, and through you, loving everything about you. Enjoy bathing in this love. Ask your Higher Self to remind you of all your Divine qualities so that you can use them throughout the day. Relish the peace and calm of your Higher Self. Be aware that it frees you of all tension, fear, and urgency. Breathe your Higher Self into your body and invite it to live in you this day.

— In your journal, write down all the beautiful things your Higher Self reminds you are part of you. Write down the appreciation your Higher Self holds for you. Write down all the compliments and inspirations your Higher Self offers as well. Read these at least once, preferably twice, throughout the day to remind you that the Divine control tower is watching over you.

— Set aside 20 to 30 minutes a day to meditate. Don't let your mind bully you out of this by telling you that you have no time. You do! Simply choose to use your time in this new way. Focus on your breath and watch it flow in and out of your body. A meditation CD helps keep the busy mind calm, but isn't necessary. It is lovely, however, to use music, as it acts as a beautiful bridge to the Higher Self. While meditating, thoughts will pop up. Watch them as though they are birds passing in the light. Some may stop on a branch or circle around, but eventually they will fly on. See the thoughts come and go, but don't focus on them. Focus only on your breath. You may want to engage a mantra to help quiet the mind. "I am [breathe in] at peace [breathe out]" is my favorite mantra. You can use this or another. It doesn't matter. What does matter is that you keep using it. Once you begin meditating, it will stabilize you, like a rudder on a boat, as you move through your sea of thoughts.

As I said, do at least one of these for a minimum of seven consecutive days in order to get a strong connection. To contact the Higher Self, you are opening new pathways from the Higher Self to the heart, and like creating new grooves on a road, you need to repeat the flow in this direction many times over before the mind can automatically connect. Seven days is enough to make an impression.

Advanced Flying Lessons

How to Enter a Meditative State

Here is an even deeper guide to successfully entering a meditative state to support your daily practice. Upon awakening, start the day with a few slow stretches and a couple of deep cleansing exhales and inhales. Take it easy with this. It is best to move slowly and quietly into your day so as not to cut yourself off too abruptly from the dream space, where you are in deep communion with your Higher Self.

Once you stretch and take a few awakening breaths, close your eyes and place your palms over your eyelids, cupping them gently, and then simply inhale and exhale for about two minutes. Next, keeping your eyes closed and your breath steady and even, place your palms face up on your lap. Then, call to mind your Higher Self as though you are calling to mind the one you love more than anything in the Universe, more than anything or anyone you can ever imagine loving more. Use every power at your disposal to conjure up this deep feeling of love for your Higher Self. Borrow from all of your senses to help you connect with and experience your Higher Self. For example, if you love your child, borrow this feeling and amplify it. If you love an animal, use the feeling of petting your animal to help you better connect with your Higher Self. If you love music or nature, use this feeling as your bridge. Use it all, as well as anything else that feels like deep love to you, as a means to feel the love you hold for your Higher Self.

Next, imagine with your continued focused breath that your Higher Self is responding to your love and approaching you with infinitely more love in return. Imagine, with each inhale, that your Higher Self is so delighted, so devoted, so dedicated to your heart that it is hard for it to fully contain this love. Without rushing or effort, using your breath to fuel your connection, continue to daydream about this Divine love affair between your conscious mind and your beloved Higher Self.

Trust that your Higher Self is becoming more intimately connected with you on a conscious level. As you breathe, feel loved by your Higher Self. Again, borrow from your imagination and from memories of other feelings of love to assist you in establishing this deep spiritual connection. Invite your Higher Self to override your conscious ego mind and take charge of your life. Give it your full permission to move you through each day toward your greatest, most expansive opportunities. Remain in this deep meditative state for as long as time allows. Do not rush. If you become distracted, simply return to your breath and relax.

When you are ready to come out of your meditative state, continue to breathe, and once again place the palms of your hands gently over your eyelids. Slowly, slowly, open your eyes behind the palms of your hands and open your fingers to allow the light in. Meeting the light of day with an inner connection to your Higher Self, take one last deeply cleansing breath and withdraw your palms altogether, greeting the new light of day with the eyes of your Higher Self.

Many of my clients and students have told me that they don't feel any inner voice, don't hear any deep and profound words, and worry that they will never attain this state. These thoughts are all ploys by the ego mind to discourage you. Ignore these random fears and keep your intention and focus on making this powerful connection. Remember, the Higher Self does not necessarily speak to us using language. The Higher Self connects through a warm and peaceful vibration that transcends words. This vibration resonates with a deep, loving, calming energy throughout the heart and body and will always occur if you are present to your breath and intention long enough and allow it to happen by not rushing.

Once you begin to invite your Higher Self to take over the controls of your life, you will notice your Higher Self in action through the many small, and then greater and greater, synchronicities occurring on a daily basis. This is your most definitive indication that your Higher Self is piloting your life and you are now in the flow.

Any amount of time spent in genuine, dedicated meditation will strengthen your connection to your Higher Self and get your life in the flow. The more time you commit, the deeper your connection will be. Again, the ego mind may try to manipulate you by rushing you through this process, telling you that you don't have the time today, or cause you to feel restless and impatient as you meditate. Recognize this for what it is, sabotage, and stay true to your intention. I recommend a 20-minute commitment to meditation a day in order to experience obvious shifts from head to heart, from ego to Higher Self, from stuck energy to traveling at the speed of love.

I have found that using specific meditative music can further deepen your connection with your Higher Self. There are so many beautiful selections to choose from. You may already have some music that works. If so, keep it in your meditative space and play it just before you begin. Headphones may help but are not really necessary.

Some of the music that helps to move me quickly into a deep meditative state are compositions by Deva Premal, Snatam Kaur, Steven Halpern, Jacotte Chollet, Tom Kenyon, and Karenush, to name just a few. I find their works extremely effective for creating a connection to the Higher Self quickly. Although this list is by no means complete, it is at least a start.

CHAPTER 8

Going Nonroutine

Last year I set off to the airport to board what was supposed to be a simple two-hour flight to Denver. When I arrived, I saw that the flight had been delayed. Planning to leave Chicago at 4 P.M., and arrive in Denver at 4:30 (with the time change), I was frustrated and a little annoyed. The plane finally arrived in Chicago at 5:20 P.M., and we didn't board until 6:15. Finally onboard, with the plane filled to the brim, the captain got on the sound system and informed us that a lavatory in the back was inoperable, and we were waiting for a mechanic to arrive to fix it. We sat for another 40 minutes before hearing from the captain again, this time announcing that the repair was not possible, and that all passengers would have to deplane and board a different plane to Denver. Now it was nearly 7:15 P.M. Needless to say, all my evening plans in Denver were quickly unraveling.

We boarded the new plane and took off fairly quickly, only to run into severe thunderstorms shortly into the flight. Rocking and rolling around the lighting bolts, we all sat with white knuckles and bated breath as the captain tried to outmaneuver the thunderheads. Soon we were told that the storm was bigger than we were. We were diverted to Lincoln, Nebraska, where we were unloaded and forced to spend the night.

My plans were trashed, my body was exhausted, and my mind was crazy with frustration—for about 15 minutes. Marching over to the Four Points Inn across from the airport, I happened to look up and see a brilliant display of stars dancing across the sky. The storm had passed, leaving the night air crisp, cool, and peaceful, inviting me to join in and be the same. I looked around and realized that I had a choice. I could remain stirred up and indignant or enjoy the stars and relax. Either way, I'd still be in Lincoln. So I took a breath and surrendered to the moment. I elevated my vibration by looking back to where this misadventure had begun, with a broken lavatory on the first airplane I boarded, and laughed out loud. "Yes, I know," I said to the stars. "Shit does happen, all the time and in many ways. That's life." And suddenly I was back in the flow, traveling toward my unexpected king-size bed at the Four Points Inn.

Traveling at the speed of love means, at times, being able to gracefully accept the unexpected. Because when it does happen, there isn't a single thing you can do to stop it or change it. It is what it is. But you do have a choice in how you respond. You can get up to your eyeballs in it by fighting it; add to your challenge by becoming enraged or indignant about it; get sucked into the undertow of angry, frustrated victimhood; or you can step back, accept what is happening as an unplanned adventure, and go along with it with an open and accepting heart.

You cannot stop the unexpected from arising. But you can expect and embrace the unexpected as part of life's circuitous path and let the journey unfold as it will.

Embrace the Unexpected

Another means of keeping in the flow of love is to embrace the unexpected as an important, even necessary, part of your soul's journey. Gratefully accept what is happening at any moment, rather than fighting or resisting it; and then apply a positive, loving acceptance and attitude toward the situation before you respond. This approach keeps you balanced and in loving flow with life no matter what is happening around you, but especially when things don't go your way, which if you think about it, happens pretty often.

When I was a flight attendant, we called the unplanned and unexpected "going nonroutine." While in training, we were advised to be ready for the unexpected every time we went to work. We were especially cautioned to be prepared for the worst when working what we called a "turnaround" trip—in other words, a working trip that leaves your city in the morning, and turns around and ends up back there at the end of the day.

One time I was assigned a short turnaround to St. Louis and back from Chicago, a working day that usually lasted only five hours from start to finish, so I took a chance and left without a suitcase. In fact, all I had with me was my purse. Almost as if on cue, after the first leg of the trip, another flight attendant called in sick and went home. I was now left to fill in for her and had to fulfill her schedule for the next four days without a change of clothes, makeup, a toothbrush, or anything to freshen up. It was the most challenging five days of my flight-attendant life, and a lesson well learned.

No matter what comes your way, always remember that the best way to quickly get back into the flow of love when life throws you a curveball, is—you guessed it—to breathe. The unexpected can steal away your breath and traumatize your nervous system, causing you to crash into anxiety and victimhood, so always remember to draw in a deep breath first whenever you get caught off guard. The "6-4-6" breath exercise I introduced in Basic Flying Lessons in Chapter 3 is a great one to draw upon when thrown off course.

Adjust your attitude and enjoy the unexpected, allowing for the possibility that with it will come exciting new challenges. Like expert skiers who joyfully navigate moguls on the mountain, learn to be flexible when you hit life's bumps. My a dear flight-attendant friend David met his wife, another flight attendant at the time, while both were stranded in the Pittsburgh airport for 21 hours together on a nonroutine flight during the worst snowstorm of the year many years ago. Although the situation itself was highly challenging, their meeting was the most delightful surprise either of them could have ever imagined occurring, and would never have happened if the storm hadn't thrown them together.

Find Gifts in the Unexpected

A change of plan or course of direction doesn't mean that what unfolds is necessarily "bad." It's just other than what your ego had in mind and could, in fact, bring about wonderful new surprises.

Just this year, my husband was given the Christmas gift of a three-week adventure to Mount Kailash in Tibet. He was so excited that he could hardly contain himself, and shared the news with everyone he knew. He even started to physically train for the trip, as part of the journey involved trekking across the Himalayas, and he wanted to be able to meet the demands of the trip.

He was to leave on May 30 and be gone through the greater part of June. Imagine his disappointment, therefore, when he was informed in April that the trip was called off for May, and perhaps for good, due to mass demonstrations against the Chinese government by the Tibetans in honor of the Dalai Lama's birthday. Patrick was devastated. He was so looking forward to the trip, and to have it called off for reasons way beyond his control really frustrated him. But he chose to go with the flow.

The trip organizers offered to return his money, but suggested that if he would just be open a little longer, and there was enough interest, perhaps they could arrange an alternative to the original plan. Almost everyone scheduled to go on the journey with Patrick canceled when the original dates had to be changed. This, at least in Patrick's mind, guaranteed that the organizers would cancel the trip altogether, because there weren't enough adventurers to justify arranging an alternative itinerary. Still he hesitated, waiting to see what the organizers would come up with, if anything, before he withdrew his interest. He was prepared to be disappointed, but he didn't jump the gun and cancel immediately, which is what most of the other travelers had done.

Today, he just received an e-mail from the trip organizers stating that even if he is the only one who comes, they're still committed to creating that journey for him. Wow! His willingness to go with the flow really paid off. He is now going on a private tour rather than going with a large group, which in his mind is far better than the original plan in every way. Had he cancelled his trip due to the change in dates, he would have missed out on this once-in-a-lifetime opportunity. By not overreacting, by being open to change, he is now going on his trip as a solo pampered guest. I assume he will have a great time. In fact, tuning in to my Universal wisdom, I *know* he will.

So even when something "bad" unexpectedly does happen, still trust that the Universe has a reason for this sudden change of course, and that it is happening to teach you something important on a soul level.

That doesn't mean that an unpleasant or sudden shift in your journey may not be a challenge to adjust to. So be kind to yourself and give yourself the room to adjust without the pressure to be happy. This can simply mean room to vent your frustrations or enjoy a few well-chosen curse words. If necessary, take a moment or two to dispel your ego's anger, but then move on. Get your upset out of your system in the quickest way possible and then breathe, accept, and get back in the flow. Any other reaction only drags you further down and will not change the situation. The journey takes you where it takes you. Sometimes it swerves off course and you find yourself going in a direction you didn't consciously choose. It's what is happening, and there isn't anything you can do to change it. So accept and flow with it. See what gifts may come.

The foundation of flow is being open to everything, learning from everything, and being willing to go along with life's surprises. Remember that soul growth is the point of this earthly journey and can come from anything, even disruptions.

Those who travel at the speed of love intuitively understand that behind all things there is a higher wisdom unfolding in our lives. Our world is not spinning randomly out of control; and the chaos, craziness, and disappointment we occasionally experience has a purpose, even when we cannot see it.

Vibe Check

A great way to stay connected with the flow when things get unpredictable is to do a vibe check on the situation. That means to intentionally take a close inventory of exactly what you are feeling, experiencing, and fearing in the moment before you react. Start by checking in with your body, mind, and spirit. Then assess what's going on around you; check in with the other people involved in the upset; and choose to respond in the best, most informed, grounded way.

For example, ten days ago my car got rear-ended on the way home from a wonderful evening with friends. The *crack* of a car ramming into mine literally shoved the breath out of my body, interrupted my evening afterglow, and sent my adrenaline surging. My immediate reaction was, "What the . . . ?" Followed by an angry, "Who did that to me?!"

Looking in the rearview mirror, I saw a car full of young kids, laughing and blaring music, apparently finding the situation funny. My initial response was to jump out of the car and angrily confront the punks who hit me. That's when I remembered that it was time for a vibe check. So I took a breath and did. It went like this:

Q: How are you feeling right now? Breathe. Check over yourself, and be specific.

A: Surprised. Irritated. Afraid of the damage to my car. Afraid of those young men who hit my car with theirs. Annoyed that my pleasant evening was so rudely interrupted. Victimized by these careless, irresponsible youths. Yet other than that, okay.

Q: What just happened? (That's when I got out and looked.)

A: I am physically unharmed. The night air is warm. The traffic is thankfully light. The car that hit me has six young men around the age of 17 in it. The back bumper of my car is slightly scratched and, looking at the kids that hit me, they looked scared and rather young. No one was hurt.

The next thing I did was call upon my heart for guidance. I asked it how I should respond to the situation. My heart could see that the fender was okay. It told me to look the driver in the eye and ask him to breathe, so I did. Then he did. Suddenly his eyes welled up with tears. His breath gave way to full-blown terror.

"Are you okay?" he asked, sincerely, his false bravado falling to the ground.

"Yes," I answered. "Are you?"

"Yes. Are you?" he asked again, which made me laugh. We were both okay.

So I made the choice to let it go.

"Just be more careful," I said. That came directly from my heart.

We then went our separate ways.

Telling the story later, almost everyone who heard it chastised me for not calling the police, taking down the young man's driver's license information, or reporting it to my insurance company. After all, that's what I should have done, right?

Except my heart said, *Let it go,* so I did. My choice left me feeling peaceful and in the flow. That's the choice we should always make.

In-Flight Check-In

Take a few moments to quiet your mind. Breathe in deeply and relax. Get out your notebook now, and in it write down your answers to the following questions:

- How do you generally handle the unexpected?
- How would your friends and family say you generally handle the unexpected?
- What unexpected occurrence has happened lately?
- What challenge are you facing now?
- How are you handling it?
- Can you tell the difference between your feelings inside and what is actually going on outside?

- When someone makes a mistake or upsets you, can you let it go?
- How do you handle disappointment?
- Do you look for the silver lining in the clouds?

Basic Flying Lessons

Rear-End Recovery

Think about all the slights, bumps, bruises, and injuries that have been inflicted upon you lately. They don't have to be as dramatic as my fender bender to impact you. More often than not, life gives you many more subtle, energetic taps than intense, overt collisions.

Energetic taps can show up as:

- Sarcastic comments from co-workers
- Rude interruptions by someone when you are speaking
- Unpleasant glares from unhappy service people
- Being blatantly ignored
- Condescending criticisms intended to make you uncomfortable
- Insults
- Vulgar language
- Negative remarks in general
- Sighs from others when you are speaking

These are all the psychic equivalent of getting energetically sideswiped or rear-ended by a fellow traveler's conscious or unconscious behavior. If you are not aware, any of these reckless travelers could take you out of commission, or knock you out of your balanced orbit, before you even know what hit you. So just as any good driver carries a first-aid kit in the car for just such unexpected collisions, I suggest you keep a vibe check in your psychic first-aid kit to help you stay in the flow. Here's how:

1. As always, first breathe. Next, acknowledge out loud exactly how you feel inside when encountering negative sideswipes.

2. Breathe again and acknowledge out loud what is actually going on outside of your life in your surroundings. Focus solely on the facts—what is real. Keep the "what if's" and "could be's" away. Only acknowledge what is actually so.

3. Breathe deeply and ask your heart: *What is the most self-loving way to respond to the challenging situation at hand?* Then listen for inner guidance.

Drama and fear get adrenaline flowing, so you may need to take several extra breaths just to neutralize those effects. Even a dire emergency is best handled with grounded breath behind it. Practice checking your vibes every day, several times a day, especially when you feel your engine seizing up or your altitude decreasing.

Enjoy the Unexpected

Make a list of all the things that didn't go as planned today and how you handled them. Were you going with the flow, even if the day was nonroutine? Or did you waste your emotions over the fact that things didn't go as planned? Write down not only the "bad," but also the unexpectedly good things that came along this day. You will soon see that good surprises are starting to come quicker and quicker, with less and less time in between.

Advanced Flying Lessons

Strengthen Your Core

When we get caught off guard and go nonroutine, it usually hits us in the gut first, scrambling our solar plexus and weakening our grounding and focus. Therefore, it should come as no surprise that strengthening the abdomen is a wonderful way to lessen or even prevent a psychic invasion of negative energy from flooding through your body when life does indeed go nonroutine. It certainly has proven to be a huge protective measure for me when life throws me a curveball. Engaging your core is a highly effective gut strengthener.

To do so:

- Stand up tall.

- Tilt your pelvis slightly forward and clench your buttocks muscles.

- Next, pull in your gut and hold it. Don't hold your breath while you do this. Just hold in your gut and breathe naturally.

Do this for a few minutes a day, every day, and whenever you get caught off guard or feel invaded, surprised, disappointed, or upset. A strong core serves as a protective shield and keeps you calm and centered when life goes crazy around you.

I know you may think this is odd, but believe me, it works wonders to keep your energy stable and grounded. It also gives you an impressive abdominal six-pack and a strong back as well.

Go with the Flow

Whenever you get caught off guard; go nonroutine; end up traveling at the speed of fear; and find yourself resentful about the way things are unfolding, get centered, follow your breath, and say out loud, over and over again: "I trust the flow. I go with the flow. I learn from the flow. I am protected in the flow. I am traveling at the speed of love." Let this be your mantra day in and day out. It will keep you in sync with whatever comes your way rather than struggling to fight against it.

Take the High Road

When things go wrong and mistakes are made, rather than seek to blame or play the victim, take the high road, give the benefit of the doubt, pick up the pieces, forgive and forget, and move on. Don't look back.

Chapter 9

The Guilt Trip

Several years ago I decided to take my husband, Patrick, and our two daughters on a trip to Morocco for spring break, starting in the city of Fez. I asked my brand-new and somewhat inexperienced assistant to book our hotel reservations. Boarding our flight, I assumed that everything was in place for our arrival. Imagine my surprise when we finally arrived at our hotel in Fez at three in the morning, after 22 long hours of travel, only to be told there was no reservation for us, and furthermore, no room at the inn—not there or anywhere in Fez because it was spring break and virtually all of Europe had just arrived.

Standing there with my exhausted family in this strange, exotic, and highly intimidating place in the middle of the night with no place to go, I begged the hotel clerk to please look again for our reservation.

He was reluctant to comply and seemed frustrated by my insistence as he typed away on his computer for several minutes when he finally found our reservation—only it was for the following year! We all burst into tears, except my husband, who whispered some choice curse words under his breath instead.

If ever there was a time not to fall into the undertow of victimhood, this was it. *What can I do to get back in the flow and in a hotel room, too?* I prayed, asking my Higher Self with all my heart. Walking away from my highly emotional family for a moment, I got very quiet. Suddenly the answer came: *Send the situation all the love you can summon, and go back and ask for help.*

It was a challenge to summon the energy of love when feeling so ashamed, and so responsible for the problem. I never double-checked the reservation. I never asked for an e-mail confirmation. I had never even looked over the itinerary. I handed it off to my new assistant and assumed all was set. Looking at my anxious daughters and exasperated husband, it was very challenging not to collapse into self-loathing and guilt for putting them into such a terrible predicament. Or worse, I could have gotten defensive and lashed out at the hotel clerk, my husband, or the kids as a way of deflecting the fact that I had, indeed, not been thorough and attentive; and because of that, put us all in this terrible pickle.

Again, my Higher Self clearly suggested that I summon all the love in my heart and call upon that love for help. So I did.

I took a deep breath and walked back to the hotel clerk. Opening the portal of love in my heart as I approached, I sent him, the hotel, myself, and yes, even my assistant at home, love and acceptance of the situation. Forcing myself to breathe and relax, I asked the wary clerk once more if he would help me.

"I really made a mistake on this reservation," I explained. "I put my family and myself in quite a predicament because of it, and I would very much love it if you could try to help me correct it and get us to a room, at least for the night."

He shook his head in doubt. "It is unlikely," he said, "as I explained before."

Refusing to succumb to the bleak outlook he was painting, I said, "I realize all this is true, yet I'd so love a solution, even if it is a miracle."

He laughed when I said that and replied, "Yes, a miracle is what it would take," as he tapped away at his computer, looking for openings at other hotels in the area. Continuing to send the clerk love, while ignoring the strong wave of irritation and annoyance coming toward me from him, my thoughts were suddenly interrupted by the phone.

"Excuse me," the clerk said picking up the phone.

He chatted for several minutes in Arabic, hung up the phone, and shaking his head in disbelief, said, "A reservation for a suite for the same number of days you want just cancelled. Your family can have this room."

"You're kidding!" I laughed out loud with relief. "Praise Allah. He called to give us a room. God is so good. He came through for us."

He laughed, too, still shaking his head, saying how unbelievable it was, and handed me the keys to the room with a smile. "Enjoy your stay, and welcome to Fez."

Turning around to my grim-faced crew I said, "You guys look so tired. Thank you for your patience."

"What are we going to do?" they cried.

"We are going to our room." I smiled. "Allah called and opened up a room for us." I laughed, flashing the key and reentering the flow.

Let's face it, we all make mistakes; we mess up, we drop the ball, we hand things off and fail to make certain they're done properly. We overlook responsibilities, miss deadlines, drop calls, lose keys, lose our minds, and open the door again and again for all kinds of miseries to descend upon both us and our fellow travelers. We do this because we're human, and we're in training to stay aloft. At times, although we have good intentions, whether through carelessness, lack of awareness, impatience, or just plain irresponsibility, we fail miserably. We leave the flow and end up in the badlands of our own foolish errors, with no escape in sight, just like when we landed in Fez.

The Trip to Hell

I had a client named Elise, a devoted mother of three rambunctious kids and a loving wife and business partner to her husband, Stan. She worked tirelessly to grease the wheels of their lives, and did an impressive job of it, if you ask me. She ran the house like a master; their home was spotless, the kids were doted upon, their schedules always orchestrated without a glitch. At the same time, she worked as the customer-service rep for her husband's furniture store. She was up at five in the morning, went to bed at midnight, and never stopped or paused during the day to take a moment to catch up.

I met her because in the whirlwind of her life, she backed out of her garage too quickly one day and didn't see her son behind her. She hit him, but fortunately not too hard. He ended up breaking his leg. She was devastated by her own error. Filled with guilt, shame, and remorse, she booked a one-way ticket to hell that very moment. She felt so worthless that she simply couldn't accept her error and forgive herself. Her son recovered, but she spiraled into a deep depression. This caused her to make even more errors in judgment. Distracted, she made mistakes at work, which caused her husband to lose orders and inconvenience customers. Another wave of guilt washed over her, and her shame deepened. This downward spiral took over her life. Now a *permanent* resident in hell, she tried to hide from everyone.

Her strategy was to push people away by being withholding, defensive, aloof, and preoccupied. Her energy was a drag to experience, but what she didn't know was that her behavior and her negative vibration were dragging her family to hell, also. Her shame rejected their love. Her guilt rejected their forgiveness. And her pride rejected a connection with them. One by one, she kidnapped her kids and husband and took them to hell with her. In trying to maintain contact, they went along with her vibration. The whole family was suffering unnecessarily. All she had to do to rescue them from hell and return to the flow was to accept her human error, forgive it, learn from it, review it from the most loving perspective, move past it, and ask the Universe to lift her back into the flow, now wiser for the experience.

This sounds easy enough, yet as we all know, the ego doesn't approve of this flight plan. It likes to keep us in unforgivable shame and guilt. It likes to fly us straight to hell and keep us circling there. It loves guilt, shame, and embarrassment more than life, more than love, and more than flow. In fact, the ego loves its own misery more than anything. Because misery loves company, it will try to imprison us along with it forever. And it will, if we aren't on full alert and remembering that the ego books our ticket to hell.

Let's face it. Bad things happen. It's just much harder when those bad things are our own fault. It is at these times, when our mistakes cause us and others pain, that we can get caught in the negative undertow of life—the vibration of embarrassment and guilt—and drift really far from the flow. In fact, shame and guilt over our own mistakes have delivered more people to hell than all other vibrations combined.

Hell is an overcrowded, dense, toxic drag of a destination that we are all at risk of traveling to if we aren't committed to love. Hell is the place in our minds and hearts where our human errors land us when we are unable or unwilling to forgive ourselves and others for errors. It's a place many of us unconsciously book a one-way ticket to because our egos, our pride, our false selves, or our erroneous past training cannot allow us to be anything less than perfect. It is the great no-man's-land to which we are banished when we cannot accept or forgive our humanness.

I've been diverted to hell enough times to know that it's a terrible place of fear, shame, remorse, regret, and embarrassment. There's nothing worthy about hell. It's the psychic outpost of the unworthy—those who mess up and won't forgive themselves for it. The hell of guilt, shame, and embarrassment takes us out of the flow and is the equivalent of sending ourselves to Guantánamo Bay. Only you can get yourself out. You do that by making the choice to love yourself, mistakes and all, no matter what. The interesting thing about trips to hell is that they are almost always fully booked. For most of us, even the slightest human error causes us to sign up for the next flight straight there.

Forgive and Forget

No matter what error occurs, ours or someone else's, we must always remember to send love and total forgiveness to ourselves and to others if we are to stay in the flow. And we must be alert for the dozens of shuttles to hell we could unconsciously take every day, and make certain we don't accidentally get on one of those guilt trips.

119

The guilt trip, or the trip to hell, is boarded anytime we fail to be perfect according to our ego's standards. We climb aboard when we punish ourselves for not living up to our, or another person's, expectations.

Only when we accept and forgive all that is or has been the good, the bad, and the ugly of our human lives can we get off the guilt trip and back into the flow. That means we must love our humanness and all of our failings; we must accept, learn from, and yes, even love our mistakes. We must accept our errors, our mess-ups, our foolish choices, our stupid actions, our negative patterns, and our failed efforts; and we must let them go.

One of my big shadow traits is being so overly busy and over-booked in my "save the world" agenda that I do not slow down and take the time necessary to pay attention to the small details of my own life that keep me and those who count on me grounded. I remember once, when in college and living in France, a friend came to visit me and the two of us took off to the south of France for a five-day holiday. My host family arranged for us to stay with their friends for the entire time, which, as poor as we were, was a tremendous gift. The only problem was that I left without the name or number of the friends awaiting us, and my host family was out of the country on that particular weekend and out of communication as well. This was before the days of cell phones and e-mail, so we got all the way to our destination and had no way of contacting them or knowing where to go. We never did make the connection and were forced to stay in a very crappy hostel instead. I felt like an idiot for my mistake and kept berating myself.

Finally, my friend said, "Enough already. I'm tired of listening to you. Let's just make the best of it." She was right. I took us on a guilt trip instead of our planned vacation, and I was ruining her fun. I tried to get over it, but my shame and embarrassment were pretty seductive. Needless to say, she couldn't wait to get away from me. Our friendship sadly ended, not because of my mistake, but because of my guilt trip. Who knows what might have happened if only I had been more tolerant of my own human mistake and lovingly forgiven myself for it and moved on instead?

Another friend, Grace, experienced a similar diversion to hell when she signed up for a trek in Machu Picchu with a spiritual group she had studied with for years. Halfway through the climb up the mountain, Grace simply could not continue. She was breathless, out of shape, and ready to pass out. A friend saw her struggle and offered to carry her backpack. Instead of enjoying the gift of being liberated from her burden, Grace immediately took a guilt trip to hell. She profusely apologized for her weakness and incessantly thanked her friend for the help for hours.

Finally, her friend turned to her and said, "Grace, stop. I'll carry your backpack, but I won't carry your guilt." That shut Grace up. She instantly saw how her ego was dragging them both down. She had to accept her limitations. She stopped talking and walked in silence. For Grace, this moment was the gift of the trek. She learned to allow the Universe to carry her back to the flow. It took a humbling of her ego to allow love and support in.

We All Make Mistakes

I have a dear friend who is a world-renowned healer and massage therapist. Flying high, he started to feel good, better, and then great about his ability to do such healing work. But along with that, he also began to develop an attachment to the accolades and flattery. More and more he found he was working for his clients' approval and attention, and less and less from a devotion to service. One woman was particularly flattering to his ego, and he found he spent more and more personal energy on her. One day his boundaries slipped a little, and he placed his hands on her breasts as he worked. At this point he was self-serving, not healing. Nothing occurred at that time, but six weeks later, she requested an appointment last-minute, which he couldn't accommodate. The next day she turned him in for the inappropriate touch. He was arrested and charged. He lost his license, his reputation, his income, and immediately boarded the bullet-train guilt trip to hell. His girlfriend left him and his friends were grossed out. He stayed in hell for quite a while, but then he brought love to his situation and asked God for help.

In the light of love, he saw his craving for approval, his loneliness in his previous relationship, and his secret low self-esteem. Once he viewed his mistake with more self-acceptance and self-love, he found far deeper self-understanding and wisdom than he ever knew. He saw how much fear and victimhood he had brought to his massage practice by constantly overgiving, becoming too interested and involved in his clients' lives, and not respecting professional boundaries. Now he is building homes; is in a new, more nurturing relationship; and is at greater, although humbled, peace with himself.

To travel at the speed of love and avoid the guilt trip to hell, we must make peace with our shadows, admit our errors and manipulations, and humble our egos to love. It feels uncomfortable, even unsafe, to admit those negative patterns within us that take us out of the flow. It's even more unpleasant to see our own negative patterns in action. But know that the light of love heals them. The light of love frees us. And when we view our shadows with compassion and self-love and ask our Higher Self for help, miracles do happen.

In-Flight Check-In

Let's go back to *you* now and spend a few minutes thinking about the following questions. Take out your notebook and prepare to answer each one. Be honest with yourself, and be aware of your body's reactions as you consider each question. Notice your breathing, and be sure to breathe deeply and mindfully as you address each inquiry. Probe far beneath your fear-based defenses for even deeper answers. Rather than simple *yes/no* answers, elaborate and include examples relevant to each question you're answering. And as always, the more effort you put into the exercises, the more benefit you'll get from them.

Recall your most recent or most frequent errors, mistakes, negative behaviors and patterns, and outbursts; and ask yourself how you handled them:

- Did you go into defensive mode?
- Did you hide in shame?
- Did you push them under the rug?
- Did you beat yourself up for being less than perfect?
- Did you blame others?
- Did you become mean and tell others to "get over it"?
- Did you shut down and act stoic, as though nothing was wrong, while internally feeling embarrassed and anxious?
- Did you replay and obsess the mistakes over and over again, amplifying them each time?
- Did you deny them altogether, hoping they'd go away?
- Did you drink, do drugs, go to sleep, overwork, or overeat to ease your guilt?
- Did you refuse to forgive yourself and hold on to your mistakes like a scarlet letter blazoned across your chest?
- Did you ask for help?
- Did you apologize?
- Did you let your mistakes go?

Basic Flying Lessons

Instant Replay

Now go back and shine the light of acceptance, forgiveness, humor, and love on these behaviors and take a deeper look. Ask yourself:

- What fear was underlying these behaviors?

- What negative patterns kicked in?

- What aspect of your shadow must you now love in order to be free?

- Were these onetime mistakes or a repeat pattern?

- What can you learn from your errors?

- What can you do to accept and let them go?

- Can you apologize to those you caused injury to?

- Can you offer to make amends?

- Will you forgive yourself?

Your Top Ten Worst Mistakes and Regrets

In your notebook or on a separate pad, make a list of your top ten worst mistakes and regrets ever. Include everything as far back as you can remember, even the names of all the people you've hurt with your mistakes. Next, write down what you learned from each mistake, as well as what you would do now knowing what you know. Write down the name of the person you hurt and ask the Universe for forgiveness. Then ask those involved for their forgiveness. Next, forgive yourself. Finally, tear up your list and throw it away. Refuse to look back or ever mention, or suffer for, these mistakes again.

Nitpick List

Get a small pocket notebook and use it to keep an ongoing list of all the small things you constantly hassle yourself over or pick on yourself for. This includes all the insignificant errors, mistakes, and irritating guilt- and defense-invoking behaviors that irk you and others, such as:

- Falling off your diet
- Being late for appointments
- Missing flights
- Forgetting your best friend's birthday
- Avoiding your commitments
- Overspending
- Telling white lies
- Putting a dent in your car or someone else's
- Forgetting to turn off the oven or water the plants
- Not keeping your New Year's resolutions
- Making excuses
- Missing deadlines
- Getting lost
- Forgetting to floss

Next to each item on the list, write down all the nitpicky, self-critical commentary running through your mind concerning these behaviors, such as *I'm so stupid for forgetting that, I'm really a bad person for making this mistake,* or *I'm so disappointed with myself I cannot stand it.* Then ask yourself, *If this were my last day alive, which, if any, of these "nitpickers" would matter?* Highlight the ones that *do* matter and strive to correct them. Cross out the ones that don't and give them no more attention. Doing this trains your mind to be more selective in what it focuses on, sorting between truly damaging behaviors that deserve your attention and self-criticism that only reflects the ego's vain and inane attempt at perfection. The poor behaviors that truly matter will soon start to bother you enough to stop doing them. The inane ones will soon stop affecting your peace of mind.

Advanced Flying Lessons

Make Mistakes

A teacher once told me that we learn best from our mistakes and so should intend to make at least one really good mistake a day to ensure we're learning as much as we can. With that in mind, stop thinking about your mistakes as something to be ashamed of or embarrassed about, and instead, perceive them as your greatest teachers. At the end of each day, review the events and write down, record, or share with someone you love what lesson you learned from a mistake you made and how.

Me and My Shadow

Focus your heart and ask yourself:

- Are you aware of any shadow behaviors? (They are shadows, so this can be tricky.) If so, what are they?

- If not clear about your shadow behaviors, where in life have you had persistent troubles?

- Where do you consistently make mistakes?

- What feedback do others give you about your shadow side?

- What criticisms do you receive? What complaints?

- Can you see the truth in any of these criticisms or complaints?

- What are you ashamed about?

- What do you feel guilty about?

- How do people treat you in spite of your mistakes and human errors?

- Is there a recurring theme in your life?

- Do you feel as though you're caught in any vicious cycles?

- What have others forgiven you for that you have yet to forgive yourself for?

- Are you angry that others have directed your attention to your mistakes?

- What overshadows you?

- How do you treat those whom you have affected with your mistakes?

- Are you apologetic?

- Did you treat these people as though nothing unpleasant occurred?

- Do you expect them to cover up your mistakes? Do you expect them to *fix* your mistakes?

Humble your ego when replying to these questions and ask your heart to respond: What is true? Remember, behaviors and negative patterns of the ego cannot control you once you recognize them and see the toll they've taken on you. Once you're willing to accept errors as part of your journey, the trip changes. You are no longer headed to hell. You gain altitude and are on your way back to enlightened flow. So breathe, and surround yourself and your mistakes with love.

When we make errors, we can learn from them, and we can stay in the flow in spite of them if we're honest and let the guilt around our errors evolve toward conscious responsibility. This means rectifying our course the minute we become conscious that we've gotten onboard a trip we don't want to take. Guilt and shame put us on the flight to hell. Love gets us off that freaky flight and puts us back in the flow of our truth. Love heals everything, and in spite of our mistakes, we can still be loved.

Visualization to Recover from Mistakes

Sit quietly and focus only on your breathing for several minutes with your eyes closed and your legs uncrossed. Review your most recent mistake. Be as detailed as possible. Continue to breathe as you reflect on your error, as though you're watching a very interesting movie. Imagine that seated next to you, viewing the movie with you, is your Higher Self. Together, review how things unfolded as neutrally as possible, and every time you arrive at the moment of the poorly fated decision, choice, behavior, or outcome, imagine turning to your Higher Self and asking, "What would you have done here?" Then listen for your Higher Self's response. It may come to you immediately and make perfect sense. Or it may come illogically and make no sense at all. Or you may just get a feeling, perhaps only a vibration instead of a specific answer. Just keep your heart open and listen and feel for an inner response. It will come.

Next, as though redirecting the movie, run the same scenario through your mind once again, only this time changing the sequence of events to correspond with what your Higher Self suggested. What new outcome presents itself? What element of surprise is connected with the new perspective? How do you feel internally, vibrationally, when considering your Higher Self's suggested course of action?

Next, take a deep breath and bring your awareness back to present time. Slowly open your eyes and look around the room. Continue to be aware of the presence of your Higher Self. Look at your world through its eyes. If time allows and you feel inspired, get out your journal and write down the thoughts, ideas, new perspectives, and energy that manifested through your visualization.

Make Amends

Perhaps the quickest way to gain altitude and recover from a diversion to hell is to promptly acknowledge your mistakes, seeing how they do affect others. Apologize fully and without hesitation whenever your mistakes have caused another harm, injury, deception, hurt feelings, upset, or confusion.

More than just that, however, also offer to make any appropriate amends to the person injured due to your error, and do so immediately if possible. For example, if you put a dent in someone's car, offer to get the damage fixed. If you put a dent in someone's heart, offer service and support to make up for it. Go to your heart and check in with your Higher Self for guidance on how to make the best and most healing amends to those you've harmed. Once this is done, once the lesson is learned, once amends are made, let it go and refuse to revisit this error again. It is done, so simply continue your journey in peace.

Laugh It Off

When you make a mistake, rather than hide it, put it under the bright light of humor and tell on yourself. Laugh about your mistakes with others. Notice how sharing your missteps defuses your embarrassment and shame and takes the sting out of your self-indictment. Laughing at your worst mistakes, especially with others, replaces self-criticism with lighthearted acceptance of your human foibles.

Chapter 10

———— ·~♥·· ————

Catching the Jet Stream of Grace

Grace is a Divine frequency and an incredible source of infinite love and blessing that is bestowed upon us by God to protect us, carry us, and lift us up through life's challenges. It helps us rise above the fray and the negativity all around us and catapults us to higher ground. Grace is a gift from God. It is a special Divine resource, the vibration of the all-loving, all-empowering, all-protective force that is available to all God's beloved children. It's like a nuclear battery pack, a special reserve; a concentrated, powerful fuel that sustains and supports without fail in every unexpected and uncomfortable situation. When Grace is with us, no matter how dire the circumstance, the outcome will be all right. Being filled with grace is like catching the spiritual jet stream of life. Our journey picks up speed and flows free from worry and fear over the worst of circumstances to the best of all possible outcomes.

For example, a dear friend's young son and his girlfriend accidentally (or carelessly?) conceived their first child this past fall. They had no careers, goals, money, nor a proper place to live. Ski bums, they lived in the mountains of Colorado and worked service jobs while paying very expensive month-to-month rent. They had no savings, no plan, and no focus when they discovered their unplanned baby was on the way.

My friend said to me, "My son has no plan, but he *is* full of confidence. His heart is open. He embraces the child as a gift, and he trusts that all will be okay. He is calm, while I'm an anxious, worried wreck. How can that be?"

I know. His heart is full of grace. Grace is the blessing of being in the moment, freed of the mind's fear. It is being connected to the breath, in flow with life, and secure in life's love and support for you. My friend's son had stepped aside and was now allowing grace to inform and protect him, step by step, through this part of his life's journey.

"Sometimes I get angry and think his calm demeanor is just plain irresponsible, naïve, and not at all realistic," my friend snapped. But she had to admit that his serene state of mind didn't seem rooted in denial. He was just confidently accepting the facts.

That is what grace does for you. It helps you accept and be at peace with what is, and trust that life will work with you rather than against you. So why do some people have grace while others don't? It's because you have to cultivate it, gather it up, and store it away so that you can draw from it when you need it. When all is going well, it hardly seems necessary—in fact, it seems almost silly to focus on a backup. But where would you be without the spare tire in the trunk? The extra battery in the case? The food stored in the pantry? They're reserves just in case you need them. More likely than not, you will need an emergency ration of grace at some point on your life's journey.

I have a client, a medical doctor I've known for years, named Brenda. She is a gentle, loving soul who, in her career as a physician, has devoted her time to the care of low-income men and women who have limited resources for their health care. She provides a dignified, loving environment for her patients to come for treatment and always has time and kindness for each and every one, regardless of their ability to pay. She works hard, long hours and barely makes ends meet with her office and staff payroll, but she is full of grace and, therefore, peace.

The last two years have been dreadful for Brenda. First, her beloved father was injured in a car accident in which he broke his neck, was left paralyzed, and ultimately died after a short but horrendous struggle. Then her brother took his own life. But even through burying her family members after such tragic and violent deaths, a deep and peaceful calm descended into her heart as she waded through these experiences.

"Sonia, I can't explain why, but after the initial shock and flood of tears, I've become strangely changed and peaceful," she told me.

I asked Brenda exactly how she had changed, partly curious to see if it reflected any of the changes I had experienced after my own losses.

"I feel free," she said. "I know that in spite of the horrors of these events, all is well. If anything, my brother's suicide left me with a gift. I don't worry about anything much anymore. Not money. Not work. Not my family. We will be all right. We are all right now. I just cannot get worked up about anything. I know we will all be fine, even in death and after."

Those words were a clear indication that grace had taken the controls and was giving Brenda a chance to rest. That's what grace is all about. It is our Divine relief pilot, our spiritual AAA. It is God in action, watching our backs. It is like traveling with a relief pilot who takes control when we're afraid of losing it, and a blessing to travel with. Feeling the presence of grace on our journey through life is one of the most reassuring and valuable gifts we can ever have bestowed upon us.

So it only makes sense that if we wish to travel through life at the speed of love and not spiral out of control when unexpected crises happen, we must think ahead and prepare stores of grace for ourselves. The good news is that cultivating grace is not difficult. All it takes is a little foresight and effort on your part. Don't be put off by the effort—if ever there was a backup pilot you would want to travel with to make your journey a blessing, grace is it. Grace is the spirit of love, and it can be intentionally invited into your life in very specific ways.

Be in Awe of the Beauty in Life

The first way to cultivate grace is to consciously and constantly appreciate the life your Creator gave you. Be in awe of God's beautiful world and aware of the blessing given to you to be part of it. View your world as awesome, because it is.

What is awe inspiring in your world today? I was in awe of the crisp winter air and the bright sun dancing across undisturbed blankets of snow sitting on the tree branches as I reached for the paper before I sat down to write this chapter.

I also found it quite awesome that my daughter's visiting boyfriend, Mike, brought me a beautifully prepared plate of food for lunch just at the moment I was about to pass out from a hypoglycemic meltdown.

I was in awe of the enthusiasm of the children playing in the snow as I walked to my office. And I was in awe of how oblivious they were to the freezing cold as they laughed and squealed with delight.

In other words, look around and bask in the goodness of life as it is happening now, even if everything isn't perfect.

My in-laws are a great inspiration to me when it comes to having awe-inspiring gratitude for life. Both up there in age, they've been through far more than their fair share of difficulties, including health challenges, deaths in the family, and serious accidents and illnesses over the past few years. They've been through some heartbreaking stuff, but they rally and find a way, through their tears, to be grateful to God and have a good laugh while crazy things are happening. It is awesome.

In the words of Albert Einstein, "He who can no longer pause to wonder and stand rapt in awe is as good as dead; his eyes are closed."

Follow the High Road of Kindness

Another way to invite grace to accompany you along your journey through life is by being kind to all God's creatures, human and otherwise. Being intentionally kind to others, even when it is challenging or they're not kind to you, amplifies the grace in your life.

My role model for undying kindness to all is my mother. I swear you could tell her you were an ax murderer, and she'd still treat you like royalty: with reverence, dignity, and well, yes . . . grace.

I've often marveled at how kind and patient she is with all people, even, and especially, those who have been quite snide to her. Being extremely hard of hearing, many times when people speak to her, she doesn't correctly hear what they say. Consequently, she might not answer quickly enough or may look at them quizzically and with a confused expression, especially in restaurants. This often solicits an aggravated remark, a roll of the eyes, or an impatient comment because they don't realize she's hearing challenged. Perhaps they think she's slow, not paying attention, or who knows what. Although their irritation with her is sometimes obvious, she never takes offense. She smiles and kindly asks them to repeat what they've said so that she can read their lips, without any sense of indignation or defense.

Once I asked her how she remains so kind to people, even when they are obviously less than kind to her. She laughed and said, "I have an advantage. I'm deaf, so I can't hear all the negative comments that come toward me that might make it difficult to be kind. And if they are rude or impatient or short of goodwill, then it's only all the more obvious they need some kindness to help restore their spirits."

What a wonderful outlook on life! Perhaps we should turn a deaf ear toward rude behavior, whether our ears are fully functioning or not, and just allow kindness to flow outward no matter what's flowing our way.

That is definitely a skill I've had to practice because I have a somewhat fiery temperament at times and have been known to flare up when provoked. But making the effort to be kind has calmed my excitable nature and awakened me on an even deeper level to just how sensitive all human beings are, even under their crusty shells. Kindness is a salve for the soul and heals many deep wounds. Being kind is a wonderful way to invite more grace into your life, and it works every time.

Give Others a Break

A third way to invite grace to journey with you through daily life is to be of service to others in everything you do.

"Wow! Now wait a minute! Slow down!" I can hear you screaming at the page. "How in the heck am I supposed to do that? Who's got the time? Who's got the freedom? And with all I have to do already, that sounds impossible. And besides, what if they don't appreciate it?" Admittedly, it can be difficult to be of service in all we do because doing so requires us to treat others with reverence even when our ego minds remind us that some don't *deserve* reverence. I had the "Whoa, too much" reaction myself when I saw this on the application form for grace. Yet if we would be open to seeing every situation as an opportunity to be of service, we could find a way to *be* of service, even if it's just to give a guy a break.

A client of mine, Colleen, was outraged with her husband, who seemed quite ungraceful the time he got drunk at a family wedding and insulted everyone there, from the bride's mother to the bride herself. The idea of holding him in reverence after he made such a rude spectacle of himself seemed like the last thing his bloated, alcoholic ego needed. But even so, there is a Divine Spirit in all beings, drunk or otherwise, and when the Divine seems least present is the time we most need to call it back home. Struggling between either lashing out at him for his vulgar manners, or being quiet and leaving him to stew in the aftereffects of his own rotten behavior, she chose to simply be calm and quiet and let him sober up to face his mistakes himself. He did end up sobering up and was so ashamed of his own behavior that he finally went to his first AA meeting. Colleen believes that because he was otherwise a basically good and helpful man who cared for others, it was the grace of God that got him there.

It absolutely takes effort—a lot—to achieve grace, and the root of that effort is to go the extra mile to help others. It takes self-control to let irritating things slide off your back rather than get worked up about them when others bother you with their mistakes.

I have a client, Janet, who's married to a very moody and mean-spirited man who often refuses to speak to her and the kids if he's had a bad day at work or something doesn't go his way. He yells at the children at the least provocation, slumps in his chair in front of the TV after work most nights, and takes little interest in anything going on in Janet's life. He is stingy with his money, never offers his wife a kind word, and is an overall grump in every sense of the word. Most people they know can't stand him and find him offensive and rude, yet she never takes offense at his behavior. She lets it all slide off her back and miraculously remains in good spirits regardless of how unpleasant he is.

When asked how she can possibly stand him and stay in such positive flow with life, she says, "I love him. He was sadly born with a lousy temperament and can't help it, so I just ignore it and try to be patient." She sets the standard for accumulating grace.

"At times I want to lash out and verbally let him have it. But that wouldn't help for a man who is already suffering, so I just let it go." She's right. Being tolerant and forgiving accumulates grace. Lashing out dissipates it.

Janet has been a huge teacher for me when it comes to accumulating grace. The foundation of grace is having the self-control not to "lose it" when the journey gets challenging, but rather to be patient and choose to let upsets move *past* you rather than *into* you. The less you react to what irritates, the quicker it flows by. Janet shared with me that even though her husband was such a troll by day, every night before he went to bed, he hugged and kissed her, apologized for his moodiness, and told her he loved her. "That's all I need," she said. "He's doing his best. What more can I ask?" She was right. In truth, no matter what we think of ourselves, we are all doing our best, even when that best doesn't look or feel very impressive to others.

So why take anybody else's struggles to heart? If other people are having difficulty gaining altitude on their life's journey and nearing a crash and burn of negativity, then compassion is what's called for. Janet knows this truth. She is aware that beneath the surface, her husband is in pain. She chooses to love him and step aside as he struggles to see what's happening. "He's just a 'slow learner' in the school of positive outlook," Janet says. Her wisdom and compassion have accumulated enough grace for lifetimes. She merrily cruises through her days without allowing her resident grump to rob her of her peace.

Spread the Light

Another very simple way to accumulate grace, and one that seems obvious but nevertheless is generally ignored, is to be genuinely respectful toward all people. Say "Please," "Thank you," and "Excuse me." Even throw in the occasional compliment, because we humans are sensitive and generally insecure beings, and appreciative words really elevate us all to higher altitudes and smoother waters in the journey in life. A heartfelt "My, don't you look beautiful today," not only accumulates grace, but spreads it as well, reminding others to feel positive and loving toward themselves by pointing out their beauty and worth.

Grace allows us to witness one another on a soul level as Divine players in the theater of life, and it pulls us out of the abyss of emotion, reaction, and fear when our journey gets so intense we risk getting sucked in and destroyed.

I have a friend from high school named Gloria whom I've known for over 30 years. She was devoted to her daughters, her husband, and her work as a spiritual therapist. She taught meditation classes, intuitive development, yoga, and breath work, so she was constantly reminding others to practice grace. She was lovely and loving in all that she did, and everyone who came into her presence felt her grace. Last year, her husband of 18 years lost his job and, in a moment of despair, overwhelming fear, and shame, killed himself. It was so shocking to Gloria and her children that she could hardly believe it. "He was so generous," Gloria said. "It was like Santa Claus committing suicide. How did this happen?"

Devastated, confused, and angry with God, she prayed for answers. Grace answered in the form of a dream. Her husband showed up, apologized, and explained that he did this to himself in a drunken, vain moment in which drama overrode common sense—a moment of "theater" gone too far. It was not something he had contemplated before. It was an act of self-serving passion. He asked for her forgiveness and encouraged her to set herself free from his error because she deserved to be happy.

She was "graced" by his visitation in a dream. She grieved for nearly a year, but was freed of any thought that she might have prevented this act or that she was to blame. Her grace saved her; thank goodness she had cultivated it to such an extent in advance.

Cultivate Grace

Our dignified behaviors; our choices to be kind, tolerant, and of service; and our approach to life with awe build up a large "stash" of grace to draw from at essential times. Grace is the equivalent of a psychic savings account: it is a resource we can intentionally cultivate, gather, strengthen, and develop. The more grace we create, the greater our ability will be to rise above the small indignities of life; stay in the flow of love; and not get sucked under and destroyed by fear, negativity, and disgrace.

When life does unfold gracefully, shout "Praise be to God!" count your blessings, and thank the heavens above for your good fortune. But when it doesn't—from the slightest provocation of someone snatching your parking spot to devastating events such as losing your job, your marriage, or a life—grace is the salve to heal all wounds and the Divine support to get you through it.

Grace coined the phrase: "This, too, shall pass."

Grace acts like the jet stream on your journey through life. It takes you higher, farther, faster, and more smoothly to the frequency of love and keeps you above the turbulence.

Grace is like accumulating frequent-flyer reward miles for the seasoned soul traveler. The more you practice accumulating grace, the more and more "free" upgrades you'll receive. These aren't actually free upgrades at all; they're the earned benefits of choosing, practicing, and cultivating an awe-inspired, tolerant, kind, service-oriented, polite, compassionate spirit toward all humanity.

A marvelous consequence of the continual cultivation of grace is that it elevates your vibration so much that your nervous system is liberated from almost everything that jangles your nerves and potentially disturbs your journey. Things that normally irritate simply don't anymore. Behaviors that push your buttons, test your patience, insult your sensibilities, or disturb your equilibrium cease to bother you, other than perhaps to make you smile. This is an exciting indication that you are in the jet stream of love and that your Higher Self is making direct contact.

Cultivating grace insulates you from the assaults of fear-based consciousness. That's why the prayer says, "Hail Mary, full of grace, blessed art thou." When you're full of grace, you're blessed with so much that it's hard to fully assess it all. You're blessed with humor, resilience, thick skin, short-term memory of upsets, and the capacity to easily forgive. When filled with grace, there is no room for the ego to hold you hostage with its litany of injuries, indignations, wounds, and demands, nor does it react to these behaviors in others. Grace allows you to witness the lower, fear-based, ego frequencies and thought forms of negativity, but insulates you from feeling—or worse, absorbing—those vibrations as your own.

In-Flight Check-In

Turn your attention now back to *you*. Take out your notebook and spend a few minutes thinking about each of the following questions. Be patient with yourself and the questions as you answer them. Don't rush through them. It may even be useful to discuss them with a trusted friend before you write the answers in your notebook. Experiment with this suggestion and see if it is useful. Contemplate each question with the help of a deep breath. Move past simple *yes/no* answers to elaborate, and include examples of when you might have experienced various reactions or behaviors. The more effort you put into the exercises, the more benefit you'll get from them.

Think about your own "grace account" honestly. Where does it stand? Don't judge. Just assess.

- Are you kind to all people? Sometimes? Rarely? Most of the time?

- Are you in awe of life, as a child might be? Sometimes? Rarely? Most of the time?

- Are you willing to be of service to all things and situations? Sometimes? Rarely? Most of the time?

- Are you good-humored about others' bad behavior, or do you let it bother you? Sometimes? Rarely? Most of the time?

- Do you easily overlook others' mistakes and give them a break when they goof things up? Sometimes? Rarely? Most of the time?

- Are you easygoing, and do you adapt quickly to new plans when things go awry? Sometimes? Rarely? Most of the time?

If your response to most of these questions is *rarely* or *sometimes,* the balance in your grace account is low. Practice cultivating grace this week. What's so uplifting is that grace is abundant. It's a guaranteed abundance you can most definitely go after with absolute confidence in your success. The more you intentionally cultivate grace, the more elevated your vibration becomes.

Basic Flying Lessons

Be Polite

This week, go out of your way to be extremely respectful of all people. Say "Please," "Thank you," "Excuse me," "Pardon?" "I appreciate that," "You are so kind," and "It's my pleasure." As you speak to others, remember that they are spiritual beings who deserve to be respected. Use any appropriate pleasantry, and smile, too. Don't interrupt when others are speaking, turn on or answer your cell phone at dinner, or text while having a conversation with someone. Address strangers as "Sir" and "Ma'am." Open doors and say "After you" when entering. These are all basic manners which, when used, show respect and consideration for others. They also build grace in your life.

Be of Service

This week, volunteer your services to someone. It can be as simple as offering a co-worker a ride home from work or inviting a single person home for dinner. Donate items to a food pantry, or your gently used clothing to a back-to-work program. You can send a college kid a care package or take an elderly person to dinner and a movie. Pick up garbage left on the ground, carpool instead of driving alone, offer someone gas money if they drive you, or stay late at work in order to finish a project on time. Volunteer your time at a local school, church, or neighborhood group. If there is a will, there are plenty of ways to be of service. Actually follow through on your intentions, and be modest about your service. Don't brag about your good deeds. Keep quiet and let the positive energy that flows from being of service be your true reward.

Give a Compliment

For an entire day, offer everyone you meet sincere, heartfelt appreciation and a compliment. Try to be original and relevant when offering your compliments. Do not be canned or insensitive, saying, for example, "Nice head of hair" to a man with a receding hairline. You can, however, say "Beautiful smile" without hesitation, knowing you made someone's day.

Be Kind

Today, open your heart and be extra kind to everyone you encounter. Breathe deeply and easily so that others can feel the ease flowing through your body. Open a door for someone and let them enter first. Help carry someone's groceries to the car. Empty the trash without being asked. Give someone a warm hug, or better yet, a back rub. Smile and ask interested questions when you speak to others. Ask about their family, their projects, their pets, or their vacation. Listen with patience, and laugh at their stories. Be genuine, be present, and give someone a few extra moments of your time to show you care.

Advanced Flying Lessons

Take a Vacation with Meaning

Consider taking a vacation with meaning this year. There are many options that invite participants to spend their vacation in service to poor people around the world. People do things like build houses or schools, teach kids to read and write, help out on farms, and teach young parents how to take care of their infants. A vacation like this can often be found in your own backyard, working with Habitat for Humanity, for example, teaching local underprivileged kids to read, or volunteering at a Boys & Girls Club. It's a vacation from your own concerns and opens your heart and mind to the benefits of serving others. If you are feeling more adventurous, check out the book *Mapping Your Volunteer Vacation* by Jane Stanfield. Based on her experiences, it is filled with ideas and guidance on how to take a volunteer vacation in many places around the world.

Visit a Nursing Home

For one month, spend an hour a week visiting your local nursing home. Bring newspapers, candies, fresh bottles of water, board games, magazines, and good conversation to those who may be neglected. Get to know a few patients and see them each time. It's a lot to ask, but the rewards are vast.

Donate Your Time

There are many poor and homeless people in this world who could use the interested support of someone like you. If possible, donate your time to a charitable children's organization or one that supports the underprivileged in your area. Foster a child, even if only by giving a small donation once a month. Better still, become a Big Brother or Big Sister to a local child for one weekend a month. If that's not possible, donate your time at a local school. Be a room parent, a crossing guard, or a sports coach. Look into assisting at the local YMCA or other children's afterschool programs. Volunteer to help this world in any way you can, and do it today.

CHAPTER 11

Travel Assistance

Years ago, when I first moved away from home to Chicago to become a flight attendant, I found myself filled with anxiety about my job and homesick beyond belief. I had never imagined it would be so difficult to make so many changes so fast, but it was. The stress of all the shifts manifested itself in my body as a severe case of sciatica, which left me in excruciating pain and barely able to walk. I was a new hire, and thus on call as a stand-by. I never knew from hour to hour whether or not I'd be called to work, and if so, whether I'd actually be able to get up and walk so I could work.

Young and overwhelmed, I had very few skills to cope with my physical stress and pain at the time, let alone the emotional challenges. Every day I questioned whether or not I had made a huge mistake in leaving home and taking the job at all. I was in deep confusion and despair, and all I could do at the time was pray and cry a lot. I was alone and in agony and couldn't see any way out.

One day as I once again found myself on standby, I lay down on the couch where I slept in the studio apartment I shared with two roommates and closed my eyes. I was, as usual, filled with fear and pain and didn't know where or how to get relief from my darkness.

As I lay there, eyes closed and praying, one of my roommates quietly walked into the room and, without speaking to me, covered me with a warm blanket. Her act of kindness had an amazing healing effect on me. It was so loving, so gentle and sweet, that it lifted the psychic pain and anxiety out of my chest. I didn't open my eyes; I just took in the love and let it fortify me.

This simple, kind gesture was all it took for my anxiety to quiet down and my confidence to return. Suddenly, I felt as though I could face the challenges at hand. Although I was on probation at work, I knew I'd be able to meet the job requirements and do just fine. As my fear subsided, my sciatica eased as well. It went from acute to dull, tolerable pain. I could stand on my own two feet and face whatever the unknown introduced without collapse. That blanket brought comfort, support, and reassurance—things I desperately needed but was too out of touch with myself to realize and far too insecure to ask for. My roommate's kindness pulled me out of the dark trenches of fear and anxiety and literally got me back into flight.

Although subtle, this was a life-changing experience. Up until this moment, I had been a solo flyer. I assumed myself to be self-reliant, self-sufficient, and self-sustaining and didn't ever consider the need, indeed the necessity, of receiving love and support from others. Only when I got it did I even realize it was missing from my life.

Tears rolled down my cheeks as I lay there quietly, pretending to nap. They were tears of gratitude, relief, and appreciation; and I opened myself to the love and support of others in that moment and have been aware of the importance of it ever since.

Many of us like to travel solo because we believe that it prevents us from ever being vulnerable, but the truth is, we are pack animals and are intended to travel in tribes. We need one another to reach our greatest heights. We cannot travel at the speed of love if we do not accept, embrace, and yes, love our vulnerabilities; and allow others in to share their gifts and strengths with us. We may travel only a little way, but not to great heights, if we insist on doing it all by ourselves. Even if we try, there are always those behind the scenes from whom we must draw support if we are to fully succeed in our journey.

It's important and natural to allow ourselves to drop back from the lead at times and follow the guidance, love, and support of others. This doesn't make us weak or dependent. It simply makes us human. Just look at geese in flight. They form a *V* and fly in unison, but the lead bird is in front for only a short while before it drops back and allows another to move up; all share the roles of follower and leader, equal in their grace and beauty.

As travelers in Divine flight, we must be vigilant in preventing our egos from blocking our need for support. We are not intended to be strong in every way. We are not designed to be totally independent, separate, and by ourselves. We are designed to be interdependent with all of life: people, nature, and God.

There are times in flight when we will be the head goose, leading the way; other times we might be in the middle; still others, trailing behind. All these experiences in our life's journey are beautiful. The difference between accepting our vulnerabilities by letting others assist us and stoically struggling is that being vulnerable and accepting helps lead us back to wholeness, while being stoic keeps us in fractured pain with no possibility of relief.

Don't Go It Alone

I can't tell you how many times I've seen people who have fallen out of flight and are stuck in absolute negativity because they insist on traveling solo rather than flying with a flock of Divine others, thereby allowing help to come their way.

Recently, my client Bernadette called me for a consultation. She had only one question on her mind: Where was the love of her life, her soul mate? It had been 12 years since she had been involved with anyone, and she wanted to know where "he" was and why "he" wasn't showing up in her life.

Using my intuitive scanner, I couldn't see any significant "him" on the horizon. Instead, I saw her living in such a self-contained bubble that she had the psychic equivalent of a "Go away" sign on her heart. She had fallen into such an all-encompassing, self-reliant mode that no one, male or female, could get close enough to her to make a connection with her heart. She was cloistered from life and looked to me like a hardy, prickly cactus in the desert, daring anyone to come near. She was surviving, but not in the flow of anything other than preserving her own defenses.

Sharing this with her was challenging. Every suggestion I made relating to her opening up to others was quickly shot down. She couldn't even hear me. I suggested she join a knitting circle since she said all she did was sit at home at night and knit. She said she didn't like driving at night. I suggested she take a desktop-publishing course since she said she liked working with computers. She rejected this, too, saying she saw no practical reason to do so. I suggested she attend some of the potluck dinners in her condo building. She said she was vegetarian and didn't like or couldn't eat the food others brought.

No wonder she wasn't in flight—she wouldn't even get on-board and let her Higher Self take off. She was stuck in her own self-reliant resistance. In truth, Bernadette was so afraid of being vulnerable that she refused to open the portal to her heart and allow others in. Without opening up, she would most likely remain in her misery on the sidelines of life, disconnected from the flow.

I understood. As a prideful "warrior" soul myself, I know how uncomfortable it can be, at least at first, to accept our vulnerabilities and allow others to see them. But if we ignore, deny, or suppress our vulnerabilities and stay in heart lockdown, we greatly inhibit our capacity to travel at the speed of love.

Travel with Friends

When we are unable to open up, be vulnerable, and accept love and support from others and the Universe, we not only fail to soar, but we end up broken, exhausted, and limping along in life instead.

My client Donald, an elderly man, was so determined to be absolutely self-reliant that he cancelled his flight altogether. Donald suffered a great loss when his life partner of 30 years passed away after a six-month battle with stomach cancer. Donald was the more dependent of the two in the partnership, so not only did he lose the love of his life, but he was also thrown into taking full responsibility for the maintenance of his life, including the finances and the house he and his partner shared—an assignment he was unprepared to handle. Emotionally distraught and financially unskilled, he was nevertheless prideful and refused all outreach from friends and family.

Instead, he walled himself off and began gambling on the Internet. Initially he had some minor success, which only fed his isolation and addiction. But soon enough the tide turned, and within a short time he had lost everything both he and his partner had created over the years. His house went into foreclosure, and he was forced into bankruptcy.

Still, he refused help.

The saving grace in all of this is that with his back to the wall, Donald finally gave up prideful control and let help in. He moved in with his niece and nephew in another state and became involved, once again, in life and love and the world around him. It cost him greatly to open his heart and spread his wings to love, but at the last moment, he did. He learned finally, as we all must, that love lifts us out of everything, every time. Without it, we have nothing.

Several years back, I was in Kauai with my spiritual family of ten blessed, healing teachers. In the past 12 years, we have organized an annual six-day healing event called Translucent You for an intimate group of people. The six-day experience involves intensive class work, but also beach time, bodywork, artwork, meditation; and a lot of dancing, movement, song, and play. Our goal is to wash away the psychic wounds of the past and fully liberate each spirit into Divine flight.

This particular year we had a participant who had an advanced case of multiple sclerosis. She could only walk with the use of crutches, and at times she couldn't even do that. She also experienced episodes of extreme pain.

We watched as she struggled through each day, and we admired her heroic strength in doing everything for herself throughout. She walked and hiked on her own, although she did move slowly, painfully, and stoically. She enjoyed the ocean and was very creative in the art room. Her greatest breakthrough, and the great breakthrough for the class as a whole, however, came on the fifth night, when she finally gave up control and asked the group to help her dance. We rejoiced and rushed in, lifting her up in the air and dancing her all around the room. Surrendering her need to do everything by herself, she cried with surprise and relief as she felt the support of her beloved mates. But we cried, too, so grateful for the chance to be of help to someone for whom we all felt great love and admiration. One person's acceptance of her vulnerabilities is every person's permission to do the same. We all healed a little more that evening.

Vulnerability is what opens our hearts. It is our liftoff point. Until we can view our vulnerabilities with love, we are in pride; and as we know, pride simply doesn't fly. It thumps to the ground like a cold boulder and blocks the way for everyone. That is why it's considered one of the seven deadly sins. It costs us our flight.

Know What You Need

For years I had experienced a lot of office drama. Every assistant I hired ended up causing me so many problems that I thought it was my personal curse to have to endure this daily mess, until one day I realized I only hired people who were unstable, needy, and, quite honestly, not capable of helping me in the way I needed. I was so busy being helpful to them that I didn't allow myself to notice how they were actually incapable of helping *me*. Then, one day, I'd had it. My assistant got into my computer and stole a manuscript I was working on and submitted it to a magazine under her own name. By the grace of God I discovered this.

Feeling furious and horribly betrayed, I let her go. But in doing so, I also looked at how I had created this situation and contributed to the problem. I could see, in retrospect, that I had lured her in, knowing full well she didn't really want to do the job. She wanted to do *my* job. I ignored this, and more important, I once again ignored my own needs.

After this fiasco, I finally made peace with my vulnerability and hired someone who could truly support me in the way I needed. He started work as my assistant eight years ago but is now my trusted and beloved business partner. The more I accepted his support, the more we both grew and the more we both became empowered. Traveling at the speed of love works that way. It's beautiful. And the assistant I fired is now writing and submitting articles of her own, which is what she really wanted to do all along. That, too, makes me very happy, as I know she is in flight, traveling at the speed of what she loves now as well. Her misguided act did us both a favor in the long run.

The key to accepting our vulnerabilities and being open to help is to ask for and seek competent and appropriate help. In other words, although a loving best friend means well and acts as your sounding board, you may actually need the support of a professional therapist. (Or if your home needs to be repainted, you may consider a professional painter over your brother-in-law, especially if the job is complicated or you need expert skill.)

Open up to what you really need to stay aloft and flying in the Divine flow of life. This is where the saying "Don't be penny-wise, but pound-foolish" comes into play. In other words, don't sabotage your intent to travel at the speed of love by being cheap with yourself and your needs. Be honest and humble by seeking the best, most reliable, most competent help available. Make your needs and vulnerabilities important. You don't have to build a shrine around them (and please don't), but do recognize that part of your ability to travel at the speed of love is to approach your needs in a grounded, practical, and loving way.

This includes engaging proper support for your body, mind, emotions, and spirit. If opening up to help is foreign, start opening up to support in small ways. For example, every time someone asks if they can help you, say, "Yes," and then accept their love. Rather than give a knee-jerk "I'm fine" retort that comes all too quickly, stop and acknowledge the open hand that is being stretched out toward you. By reaching your hand out and making a heartfelt connection, you'll tap into the universal flow.

The Spirit of Help

Sometimes we just fall into so much muck in our lives that accepting help is the only way out of the quicksand. With help comes hidden and blessed gifts as well.

Once while I was exploring the dark, exotic, winding alleys of the Khan el-Khalili, the famous bazaar in the heart of Cairo, I stepped forward and the ground underneath my feet completely collapsed. The next thing I knew, to my absolutely speechless horror, I was up to my knees in sewage water. And I was wearing sandals! Shocked, disgusted, and frantic all at the same time, the only thing I could do was start screaming and crying. Suddenly, seemingly out of nowhere, four women from inside a nearby shop rushed to my aid and gently pulled me out of the hole. They quietly began patting me, reassuring me, and calming me as I continued to cry in revulsion and confusion. They didn't say one word as they gently walked me into their shop.

Next, they led me to a back room where they motioned for me to remove my sandals and jeans, offering me a beautiful wool shawl to cover myself. I gratefully complied. They then silently scrubbed my shoes, my jeans, and my feet up to my knees with rose-scented soap, working all the while in smiling, reassuring silence. They then patted me down with gorgeous Egyptian aromatic oils, including my shoes and jeans. One offered me delicious mint tea and fresh water while they worked. Another stood guard at the door to the back room to ensure my privacy. Patrick waited nervously outside, not daring to enter this den of female angels.

In 30 minutes, I was better than new. My jeans were returned, wet but sweet and fresh, as were my sandals. My psyche was restored, by virtue of the love and the refreshing mint tea. My disgust turned into fascinated admiration for the attentive and loving helpers who rushed to my aid without a word. It was an extraordinary experience. I left feeling more loved and nurtured than I could have ever imagined.

Upon returning from this trip, I couldn't wait to share with others that the highlight of my vacation was falling into a sewer and then being rescued. I'd do it all over again.

In-Flight Check-In

Reflect on your vulnerabilities, those aspects of your flight where you need support, assistance, guidance, nurturing, and the help and wisdom of others. You can usually find these areas where you feel your life is stuck; where you are defended, guarded, brittle, rigid, or where you feel like a victim. Now with your notebook in hand, take a few deep breaths, and answer the following:

- What are my vulnerabilities?

- In what areas could I use more support?

- Am I open to receiving it?

- Can I trust others enough to gracefully accept their help in order to further elevate my journey?

- Where am I prideful?

- In what ways do I block others from helping me?

- In what ways am I still a victim and unwilling to receive help?

- In what ways have I been helped by others?

- Have I noticed the more subtle, silent, and private help I've received along the way?

- Where have I set myself back by asking for help from those who were not in a genuine position to do so?

Basic Flying Lessons

"Yes, Thank You"

Every single time a person asks if they can be of help, instead of saying, "Thanks, but no thanks," take a deep breath and say, "Yes, thank you. I'd love some help." If you have a clear idea of how you could use some help, ask specifically for what you need.

If you aren't sure of what kind of assistance you need, ask the helper what he or she can offer. For example, my daughter encountered a cosmetics salesman just the other day who asked her if he could be of any service. Normally she would have said no, feeling pressured to buy something if she got help, but this time she answered, "Possibly. I'm looking for a new mascara." He then asked, "What do you want your mascara to do for you?" Unsure of what he meant, she laughed and said, "Bring my boyfriend back and pay off my credit card. If it can't do that, what else can mascara do?"

They both had a good laugh at his question and her answer and instantly bonded. He then introduced her to several mascaras with all kinds of features she had no idea existed, then loaded her up with cosmetics samples of all sorts for her to take home without spending a dime. Normally she wouldn't have asked for help, but I had been encouraging it, so she accepted his outreach. She left with fun new makeup and a new friend at the cosmetics counter, something she had never experienced before.

Be gracious in accepting help or assistance, but don't be overly so. A warm and heartfelt "Thank you" works well for just about everyone. That's all that is required of you.

"Please Help"

Every day for at least a week, ask at least one person for some help. It can be anything from asking a person to hold open a door, to pick you up a cup of coffee at Starbucks, to take you to the airport, to lend an ear, or anything in between. When seeking help, don't be overly apologetic or feel as though you must justify asking for help by turning your need into a big drama. A simple "Excuse me, can you help me please?" will do. Notice how difficult this may be for you.

People don't mind helping, but they do mind long-winded, sad-sack stories that go along with the request. For example, you can ask someone to help you carry your groceries to the car, but spare them the details about your bad back and the surgery that went wrong. You can ask someone for a ride, but forego the need to share the details about your bunions and how difficult it is to walk.

Be perceptive, and ask for assistance from those who can help, over those who are clearly struggling themselves. For example, I would ask my neighbor to watch my dog, but I would not ask her for a loan. One she can do, the other she cannot. Also, be prepared to have someone decline your request for help and say no without taking it personally. Sometimes it isn't possible for someone to do what is asked for reasons you may not know of, so be a good sport if you get a negative response, and don't sulk. The point of this practice is to become more comfortable asking for help rather than going it stoically alone. Remember, most people like to be helpful and are happy for the chance. Give it to them. It is helpful to both of you.

Advanced Flying Lessons

The Good Samaritan

This week, assume the role of a Good Samaritan. Open your eyes and ears and notice situations where you can be of help to fellow travelers. It can be as easy as opening a door for an elderly person, offering to help carry your neighbors' groceries from the car to her apartment, assisting a young mother with her stroller, or helping a blind man cross the street. You don't need to do great, heroic feats, just little acts of genuine loving service: a simple smile extended toward a street person, being friendly and patient with the person ahead of you in the grocery line, or offering assistance to the foreign student interning at your office. Remember, we are in this journey together, and any small service toward another makes the trip lighter and more pleasant for all.

The Secret Fairy

Take the role of a Good Samaritan a little further and perform an anonymous act of service or good deed for at least one person a day for a week. The "feel good" part of this suggestion, the part that lifts you up in flight, is the "service" part. The fun part is the anonymous part. For example, pay the toll for the person behind you along with your own the next time you enter a tollbooth. Leave a gift basket of goodies on an elderly person's doorstep. Send anonymous flowers to someone who could use some cheering up. Pick up the tab for the person behind you in the lunch line. Pick up garbage, leave extra room for the car next to you in the parking lot, or return the carts to the cart-return area at the grocery store. Anonymously donate food to a food pantry, clothing to the local back-to-work program or any other cause that needs them, or an old computer to a school. Be creative, and have fun being the anonymous good fairy. Don't tell anyone what you've done. Just hold it close to your heart and enjoy the vibration as it lifts you into the flow.

Belated Thank-You Notes

Go to the stationery store and select a dozen thank-you cards, or just pick out some nice stationery. Next, visit a warm and inviting coffee shop and settle in. Order your favorite hot drink and handwrite thank-you notes to 12 people who have made a difference in your life. These thank-you's need not go to only recent kind helpers. Send a thank-you to someone you have failed to appreciate, even if this person's service to you was offered sometime ago. Describe how they helped you and the results of their help. Tell them how much you appreciate their influence in your life and what a positive difference it has made.

Thank friends, neighbors, children, good buddies, old or new teachers, even people with whom you've had a difficult rapport if the connection with them ultimately helped you. Especially call

to mind those who helped you when you were feeling exception-
ally insecure or lost, and be sure to include them on this thank-
you list. Avoid the temptation to skip the letter and just send a
text message or e-mail instead. There is something very respectful
and meaningful in a written letter that instant communication
just doesn't quite capture. Send these thank-you's out in the next
seven days.

Chapter 12

New Horizons

For reasons I cannot fully explain, I've always been terrified of water, especially the ocean. As much as I enjoy the sun and sand at the beach, when it comes to entering the water, I have absolutely no desire to have that experience, ever. I do notice, however, that many friends come back from romps in the waves feeling exhilarated, cleansed, joyful, excited, and filled with fascinating tales of all that the sea offers. I am especially drawn to stories of their discoveries under the sea, a place that terrifies me. They speak of exotic sea creatures, precious coral, and unusual plants—a world that commands their awe and electrifies their imaginations.

And for most of my life I have wallowed in the discomfort, fear, and resistance and have denied myself the experience of the ocean. That is, until recently. While attending a conference on the big island of Hawaii, I had a sudden change of heart.

Appreciating the gift of this warm and magnificent island, I decided that it was time to recognize what my phobia had been denying me and break free. I was suddenly ready to get into the ocean and experience it firsthand by snorkeling. My decision felt exhilarating. Refusing to give in to my anxiety anymore, I most emphatically put one foot in front of the other, one step at a time, and headed toward the water, fear and all.

Once at the water's edge, aware of my now seriously pounding heart and mounting sense of panic, I remembered a former teacher telling me that when you breathe into fear, it turns into adventure. So I did. I took many deep breaths as I faced the bouncy waves and, to my surprise, the adventure won out. I quickly secured snorkeling gear from a kiosk and asked for a guide. A beautiful young man appeared, smiling from ear to ear, and gently showed me how to put on my mask, flippers, and snorkel. It was easy enough, and soon we flippered into the freezing cold (to me) water. I was in up to my waist when my resistance kicked in and stopped me cold.

"Wait." I gasped. "I need a moment to get comfortable." I glanced around quickly, planning my escape.

But to my surprise, my guide grabbed my hand, and lovingly but firmly said, "No. Let's go." He then gave me enough of a tug that I instantly surrendered, discomfort and all, and found myself swimming face-first out to sea. With that tug began one of the most invigorating experiences of my life. Wow! An entire world that I never even knew existed—one that my fear and resistance had completely denied me all these years—was suddenly revealed to me, right before my eyes. All the reasons I'd ever had for denying myself this joy and wonder completely evaporated. I couldn't even remember what had kept me from this magical experience. The only thing I knew was that I was so fully present during this undersea discovery that I could not think of a thing. I could only breathe and be.

My snorkeling adventure completely changed my life. It showed me just how much my controlling mind had cost me. And it suggested that if I would only give up my fear and control, I could open myself up to entire new worlds that have been there all along but that my mind would not let me see.

Back on dry land and familiar territory, I couldn't help but wonder what other uplifting experiences my fearful mind was depriving me of. If there was that depth of beauty only 100 feet away in an ocean that I'd looked at countless times before, there must be a million other mesmerizing, mystifying aha's and wondrous discoveries right before my eyes in other areas as well, which might be revealed to me if I only surrendered in the same way. Looking at the ocean with fear blocked my ability to experience, let alone embrace, its beauty, gifts, blessings, mystery, and healing power.

The same is true for how we perceive other people. Our blinders of fear and suspicion prevent us from enjoying their beauty, blessings, magic, mystery, and healing potential. If you take away the blinders, you experience life and people in a whole new way. Cultivating this unedited, unmodified, uncensored view of the world around us means being open to adventure and discovery beyond fear. It means being open to learning about the deeper beautiful truth in everything, even ourselves.

When I was in the ocean, time stopped. Thought stopped. Mind chatter stopped. For that short time, I was just present to the beautiful moments unfolding before me. I entered a childlike state of wonder. What if I remained in that childlike state of wonder? Can you imagine?

Be Enthusiastic

Many years ago, I traveled to the southwest region of France with my husband, Patrick, and my then eight-year-old daughter Sabrina and nine-year-old daughter Sonia. When we arrived, the weather was atrocious. Although it was mid-June, the skies were a dark, angry gray. Cold sheets of rain poured out of them at 90-degree angles for hours without letting up for a moment during our entire journey from Paris to Dordogne. Patrick and I were quite frustrated and annoyed by this unlucky deluge. We drove for seven hours, then stopped for the night at a lovely country inn to get a break from the tempest. Once we checked in, the girls noticed that the inn had a swimming pool and were thrilled to no end. Within minutes, their clothes were in piles on the floor, their bathing suits and swim goggles were on, and they were running for the door.

"Wait!" Patrick screamed, intercepting them. "It's freezing cold and wet outside."

"So?" they answered back incredulously. "There's a swimming pool outside . . . and we want to get in. Get ready and come in."

Their enthusiasm overrode his resistance. Soon he too was in his bathing trunks and goggles, reluctantly swept up in their delight. The three of them disappeared into the now dark, drizzly cold to go for a swim. I expected them back in minutes. Instead, they were gone for almost two hours. And when they returned, shivering and blue with cold, they were squealing with delight.

I then realized that all three had lost their minds . . . at least the mind of control, resistance, fear of discomfort, and caution. Because of that, they'd had a glamorous, glorious, brilliant evening romp. They took warm showers and were in dry clothes in no time, the damp and cold forgotten. But the fun, the exhilaration, and the derring-do were amplified all the more.

Traveling at the speed of love is about pursuing what you love no matter what intellectual hesitations may arise and try to stop you.

The Adventure Is Now

Recently, my now 21-year-old daughter, Sonia, called me. Over the phone, I heard the same enthusiastic joy I had witnessed in her that gray evening after the swim in the pool in France 12 years ago.

"Mom, I have the best news!" she cried. "I joined a rock-climbing club two weeks ago. It starts with easy climbs, and you can advance to more challenging levels, clear up to ten, starting with beginner. I've been going three times a week, and now I'm no longer a 'B' for beginner. I'm already at level 1."

Her delight was so powerful that I burst out laughing. The accomplishment of advancing from Beginner to Level 1 may seem modest to the unexcited, unimpressed mind, but to the open heart this was a victory to celebrate. I felt her joy 3,000 miles away; goodness only knows how many people around her felt it as well.

Every person who chooses to travel at the speed of love helps those who are afraid to. They inspire those who want to open their hearts, try something new, or take a risk by doing what the fearful only dream of. The fearful see the daring following their dreams, and it gives them courage to try for themselves.

So every step you take toward love—even if it's a tiny one— every inch you move in the direction of your heart over fear, ripples out and adds lightness, brightness, and courage to the whole. That positive, loving vibration floating in the ether will find others unaware and give them the power to go past their fears, to choose love, and to reach for all the gifts life offers.

In-Flight Check-In

Take a few moments to quiet your mind. Breathe in deeply and relax. Get out your notebook now, and write down your answers to the following questions:

- What have you been fearful of trying, yet found the courage to do anyway?
- Where in your life has someone blazed a trail for you and given you confidence as a result?
- Where have you blazed a trail, if ever, for another?
- Where have you already traveled at the speed of love? On the job? In your relationships? Using your creativity?
- What have you attempted but quit too soon? Skydiving? Deep-sea diving? Belly dancing? Long-distance biking? Skinny-dipping? Trapeze? Karaoke singing? Public speaking? Driving? Playing an instrument? Taking a photography course? Pole dancing? Horseback riding? Getting close to someone? Speaking your truth?

Basic Flying Lessons

Get Ready, Get Set, Go!

Choose one adventure, wish, daydream, or longing you've held that has been unfulfilled. Feel the internal resistance that has blocked that chance and denied you the experience.

Create that undertaking for yourself, knowing full well that your fearful mind might screech with panicked resistance. Be intelligent. Even if physical risk is involved in your desire, ask for a capable guide, and then go for it.

50 Wonder-Full Ideas

Over the next week, in your notebook or journal, write down 50 things you wonder about. For example:

- "I wonder how many stars there are in the solar system."
- "I wonder how far it is to Istanbul from my house."
- "I wonder how long it would take me to stand on my head if I started practicing today."

Planet Earth

Purchase, rent, or borrow from the local library the DVD series *Planet Earth*. It will restore your sense of wonder and awe.

Advanced Flying Lessons

Take a Trapeze Course

Look in your local directory or search the Internet for the closest trapeze class in your area and sign up today. Don't dwell on the reasons not to do so, such as you're too old, it's too late, or it's too expensive. Just sign up and go without thinking. Trapeze will help you to face your fears and move through them in the shortest amount of time possible. Besides, it's also great fun.

Experience Watsu

Watsu is a form of massage therapy that takes place in water. In a Watsu session, the practitioner moves you gently through the water while you close your eyes and give over your trust completely. The session lasts about 50 to 60 minutes; and in this time, you learn to totally surrender control. Many spas now offer Watsu massage.

Horseback Riding

Horses are great teachers when it comes to surrendering your fear. They sense fear and will not allow it to move them, so if you are fearful when you ride them, they ignore you and do what they want. The only way to be in control when riding a horse is to let go of fear and trust the animal and yourself completely. It may take a few tries, but eventually you will no longer fear the horse, and it will begin to cooperate with you.

50 Solutions

Over the next week, in your journal or notebook, write down 50 solutions to either a personal, local, familial, social, or world problem. All ideas are acceptable, and the crazier the better. For example:

- *Problem:* Work boredom. *Solution:* 15 minutes of outdoor recess twice a day.

- *Problem:* Nuclear threat. *Solution:* All world leaders must fight naked in a bowl of Jell-O until there's only one man standing.

Work your creative muscles and let your imagination have fun.

Chapter 13

Turbulence

I was on my way to Boston, flying through clear skies, feeling perfectly relaxed and at ease, when suddenly the plane jolted and shook with the force of the gods, then dropped for what felt like thousands of feet. And so did my heart. Fear gripped my body as the plane continued to shake, rattle, and roll; and then, just as suddenly, it stopped and resumed smooth sailing once again. That was not the case with my heart. It pounded in anxiety, waiting for the next lurch to come our way. It didn't. All remained calm, and eventually my calm was restored as well.

Unexpected turbulence always catches me off guard, no matter how seasoned a traveler I consider myself. It comes out of nowhere and, quite frankly, scares me even when my logical brain assures me, *It's only turbulence, bumpy air, nothing more.*

Psychic turbulence has the same effect on me. The thing about unexpected psychic turbulence that throws us so far out of the flow is that it is surprising and, like bumpy air, can jostle our inner peace very quickly. Psychic turbulence is the sudden appearance of old wounds, unexpressed or buried emotions, and negative thought patterns that shake loose and rattle through our psyches, disturbing our inner tranquility.

As with turbulence on aircraft, when this happens, all we can do is navigate the bumps as best as we can, stay the course of our highest intentions, and breathe, knowing that these bumpy thoughts are not real and cannot actually harm us. We just need to tighten our mental seat belts and ride them out until they pass.

Not too long ago, I experienced some very intense and extremely unexpected turbulence. I was enjoying a casual afternoon with a new acquaintance in Seattle, when quite spontaneously, he took out his camera and started sharing with me a series of photos of him and his friends dancing and playing around a bonfire on the beach. The photos reflected the light in a surreal way and showed them enjoying themselves like crazy. I, too, was enjoying myself thoroughly when, all of a sudden, my mood changed, and I began to feel irritated, even a little angry, as I observed photo after photo.

Confused and embarrassed by my reaction, I forced a smile, acted overly interested, and pretended to be having a great time, although truthfully I wanted to reach out, grab the camera, and throw it across the room. My reaction caught me totally by surprise and threw me for a loop.

What on earth is wrong with me, for Pete's sake? I wondered. This reaction was so illogical and so unlike me, yet I was seized by it. Breathing in and trying to relax, I had no choice but to tighten the seat belt of my behavior and ride out the picture show as best I could. But my mind and emotions flashed in subtle irritation and distress beyond my control. No doubt about it, I had hit severe psychic turbulence.

We finished chatting, my new friend put his camera away, and our time together came to a somewhat poorly disguised awkward ending. Walking away, I was completely flabbergasted by my own reactions and emotions and honestly had no idea what had hit me. More interesting was the fact that, as intense as my emotions were in that moment and for a few minutes afterward, with breath, time, and distraction, my inner calm returned once again. Not one to allow a good upset to go unexamined, I began to review the entire episode in my mind, trying to discern why I was suddenly thrown into such agitation and upset when looking at those pictures. My feelings didn't make me proud; they were borne of jealousy, insecurity, and sadness, of all things. Why on earth did looking at a new friend's photos of a fun event evoke such a reaction from me?

After much reflection, prayer, and good old-fashioned mental detective work I realized those photos agitated some very ancient inner-child wounds buried deep within me. Looking at him and his friends playing with such abandon brought up old, buried feelings of having to postpone play so many times as a child in Catholic school. My inner child was still angry and sad about that. In order to continue the journey of light and flow, these old wounds needed to be unearthed and shaken free from my being.

The free-spirited picture show did that, and so my friend had just unwittingly assisted me on my journey. Once those old buried wounds were brought to my awareness, I was once again able to feel and then release them from my being, and in doing so, lighten my journey. I was also made aware that I clearly needed to allow myself to be more spontaneous and lighthearted and let my inner child come out and play a whole lot more. With that decision, all trace of irritation and jealousy transformed into excitement and joyful anticipation for me.

When traveling at the speed of love, whenever we encounter disowned fragments, injuries, psychic wounds, and incidents of separation from life and source, we need to reclaim or release them, as appropriate, for our wholeness. We meet unexpected turbulence on our life's journey in the form of spontaneous eruptions arising from our emotional body or emerging in negative thought patterns and dark moods that seem to come out of nowhere and seize us in their grip.

Dreary Day

Just last Christmas I was on vacation in Colorado, arguably one of the most beautiful places on earth, having lunch with my elder daughter, Sonia, who had just returned from a semester of studying abroad. We were laughing and joking in a sweet lighthearted state, when all of a sudden a cloud passed over my daughter's heart, and she suddenly became pensive and moody. Uh-oh! Unexpected turbulence!

"What's the matter, honey?" I asked, after her aura noticeably darkened and her joy leaked out.

"Nothing," she answered. "I'm just tired." We both knew she wasn't tired at all, but rather had just been tossed about by a little unexpected internal psychic turbulence.

Knowing the symptoms, I smiled and suggested, "Let's just breathe together for a moment or two and ride it out."

"Yeah," she answered halfheartedly. "Good idea." As we left the restaurant and got distracted by the beauty of our walk through the snow-covered town back to our rented home, Sonia lightened up a little and was quiet. As we turned the corner toward the house, the turbulence in her heart and mind eased a bit, and she suddenly had a spontaneous clearing of her feelings.

"I missed you when I was in France, Mom. And in just two days I'll be leaving for school in Portland, and it's all so fast. I just want to hang out and have fun with you a little longer and not be rushed," she blurted out. She was surprised by her own words and the revelation they carried with them.

"I know, honey," I answered. "It does seem too fast."

One of the underlying feelings that is always present when unexpected turbulence kicks in is fear, even if you don't immediately recognize it. One thing I've noticed is that when traveling at the speed of fear, time plays games with you. It is too slow, dragging endlessly and painfully along; or it is too fast, flying by and taunting you as you try in vain to catch up with it. Only when you acknowledge and release fear does time relax, stretch, and bend for you, and even suspend altogether. Once my daughter moved through the turbulence and expressed her fear, time stopped contracting and taunting her. She relaxed, we relaxed, the mood of the day relaxed, and we were back to enjoying ourselves once again.

The only way to get to the speed of love is through the turbulence of fear. The only way to work through turbulence is to breathe through it and reenter the moment. When psychic turbulence overtakes you, it is important to recognize that the disturbance is not rooted in the present, so it is of no use to look for a reason in present time to justify it. Inner turbulence is almost always the resurfacing of an ancient wound asking to be healed. It is a good thing to experience turbulence, as it gives you the opportunity to heal old wounds. It's what you do with that opportunity that matters.

When turbulence does arise in you, do some detective work to discover its true origin. Begin with breathing. This relaxes your body and calms your emotions. Next, ask yourself what you are feeling. Sad? Angry? Jealous? Abandoned? Hurt? Betrayed? Scared? Afraid? List every emotion you can think of until you hit upon the one buried underneath the turbulence of the moment. Then ask your inner self what it wants in order to calm the turbulence. Voice the answer to this out loud if possible, as the inner self will often surprise you with the answer it gives. If it's not possible to answer out loud comfortably, take some time alone and pose your question to yourself in your journal. I have found that often it only takes a little detective work to gain huge insights that calm the bumpy ride of psychic turbulence fairly quickly. Once the source of turbulence is discovered and expressed, the inner self becomes calm, satisfied that it has been heard.

Fearful Imaginings

At times of radical shifts and changes, our fearful imaginings cause the greatest turbulence of all. As I'm writing this, a powerful series of violent storms are passing over my neighborhood, bringing with them 50-miles-per-hour winds, knocking down trees, downing power lines, and flooding the streets and basements all around. They've been coming and going all day. One minute we're huddled in the corner scared to death; ten minutes later the storm is gone, the air is clear, and we are safe and sound.

Needless to say, our imaginings have been all over the place today. At times, our fear was so powerful that we nearly scared ourselves to death with worry about what could happen. The basement could flood. The trees could crash down on the car. The electrical wires could kill someone. The winds could blow out our windows.

Yet in these short few minutes, the storms have once again passed and it's calm outside. This reminds me of something Mark Twain is reported to have once said: "A lot of horrible things have happened to me . . . some of which actually occurred." This makes me laugh as I think of all the tragedies I have suffered in my own imagination, including today, and how few of them ever manifested, such as believing I might not get into college; fearing I would get rejected by the airline when I applied; being convinced I might not ever get a book published, fall in love, get married, have children, or see them grow up; or worrying I'd see my house fall down in the storm today. I've seriously suffered a million other fleeting fears in my imaginings that felt real at the time and made me sick with anxiety, yet were only a bad dream.

Even today, as we all know, life around the world is bobbing up and down, with economic markets undergoing radical and wildly vacillating shifts, foreign countries testing nuclear weapons, unemployment at an all-time high in some areas, record numbers of homes going into foreclosure, and people everywhere being bombarded with daily deluges of negative news. It seems as though no matter how much we breathe, how intent we are on being in flow, how valiantly we choose love over fear, we cannot gain enough altitude to rise above the worldwide waves of negativity and fear crashing over this planet. That, at least, is what our fearful imaginings would have us believe, so we can remain vulnerable to being discouraged, weakened, and easily manipulated into powerlessness.

Each one of us has the capacity to draw everyone we affect into the powerful force of the flow just by being who we are. The more of us who refuse to be manipulated and frightened by appearances and stay focused on the flow and connected to the heart, the more quickly we not only liberate ourselves from the fog of negativity hanging over this planet, but the more we help liberate those around us as well. The key is to live our lives with the clear wisdom of our heart and the empowered eyes of our Divine creative intelligence rather than through the emotionally reactive, defensive, scared, and ultimately powerless negative imaginings that fog our brains from time to time. We must remember that everything (yes, everything) in our lives originates in our own creative thoughts and choices. That means if we have created tremendous problems, we can also create massive solutions. And we *will* if we lift the fog by remembering we are creative Divine beings, and we use the power of our imaginations properly to guide us toward solutions and away from fearful projections.

Get Past Illusions

Not everyone on this planet is miserable. There are those who are finding ways, no matter what their external conditions are, to travel in dignity, peace, and love. They succeed because no matter what is surrounding them, they face it with calm confidence. They can do this because they see the goodness of life. They know that with love, they can always create something new, better, stronger, purer, sweeter, more confident, and more empowered than ever before, and they do.

We all come to this awareness sooner or later. Using the power of the imagination, we can either scare ourselves or heal ourselves, depending on what we choose. We can choose to create healing and positivity if we stop imagining the worst; take a breath; realize we have a choice; and then, with our breath, make a healthy, loving, self-empowering, joyously imagined choice. Or we can create a nightmare.

When I was around ten years old, a 3-D horror movie came out, and everybody in town lined up to see it as fast as they could. I begged my mom to let me go as well, because I didn't want to miss out, but the answer was a flat-out "No" because the price of a movie simply wasn't in the family budget. I was one of seven kids, and if one went, we all went. Frustrated that I was missing out, you can imagine my delight when my best friend invited me to go with her and said her parents would pay. With that unexpected invitation, I was off and running to the movie theater that very weekend.

173

When we got there, my friend's dad treated us both to a large bucket of popcorn and a half-gallon Coke. Loaded down with goodies, I approached the movie entrance door, put on my 3-D glasses, and waited for her dad to open the door. As I turned to face the theater, Coke and popcorn in hand, glasses in place, he swung the door open. To my utter shock and horror, a ghoul with bloody teeth, long fingernails, and black bloody eyes was lunging right into my face. This ghoul was coming at me so fast, and I was so surprised, that I screamed and threw both my popcorn and my Coke right at it with all my might.

"Ew! What the—?" I heard from the theater. I had just drenched the unsuspecting audience with my Coke and popcorn. Confused, embarrassed, overwhelmed, and scared beyond belief, I immediately turned, glasses still on, fearing the ghoul was at my back and still lunging toward me, and ran straight out of the theater. Once outside, I realized my mistake. But I couldn't reenter—and frankly, I didn't dare.

I laugh at that ridiculous memory today, knowing now that it was just an illusion scaring me at the time. But it felt so real to me then that I reacted as though it were. If I had only known then what I know now, that I just needed to remember that I was looking at an illusion and that I was safe all along, even if my perception was seeing something else, I would have probably enjoyed the fright and, if not that, at least my popcorn and Coke.

Fear Pulls Us Like Taffy

In a way, the scary world lunging at us right now is no different from my experience as a kid at the movie house. We are getting scared in the theater of life because we forget we are Divine creative beings who always have a choice and a chance to make life anything we want it to be. We become mesmerized by the ugliness of life and fall asleep to our creativity.

Life is just like the theater with the illusion that we are victims waiting to be pounced upon. But more than that, fear is a force that pushes and pulls us in all directions, sometimes pulling us right into it, and sometimes pushing us away from it.

In the theater that day, I was pushed away from the fun and excitement I could have had. In fact, fear pushed me right out the door! More recently, my fear pulled me toward it. I got out of my car and went to feed the parking meter here in Chicago, where I live, when I realized I had no quarters. So, afraid I'd get a ticket, I quickly set about finding change for a dollar at one of the nearby shops. I went into a dress store and stood waiting while two women spoke. Not wanting to interrupt because a sale was in progress, I stood patiently and waited for them to finish.

As I waited, my fear grew. The newspapers have been writing about the new parking meters in Chicago for weeks, and the entire city was in an uproar about how closely they were being monitored and the record numbers of tickets being issued. I caught the bug on this one and was fearing a ticket myself as I stood in line. By the time the woman got to me and I was able to ask for change, I had waited for nearly ten minutes. And sure enough, by the time I got back to the meter to put in the quarters, I had a ticket on my windshield, just as I had feared. I couldn't believe it as I watched the meter man casually waltz over to the car next to mine to give it a ticket as well, smiling at me as our eyes met.

Yet . . . I *could* believe it. While I was in the store, I was busy attracting this ticket with my fears. Christ warned us about this in the Bible when he said, "And their fears shall come upon them." He was right. They do. And fast.

The secret to traveling at the speed of love in the face of fearful turbulence is to imagine daily that you are rising above your fears with ease and joy. The more we imagine that we are rising above the clouds on the horizon, that instead we are really loving life and life is loving us back, fear gives way to fun. As I've said before, "When you breathe into fear, it becomes adventure." It does. Hard for you to imagine it works that way? Try it and see for yourself.

In-Flight Check-In

Once again, it's time to take out your notebook and spend a few minutes thinking about each of the following questions. Breathe deeply and get centered and grounded before you begin. This time focus on your past experiences and how they might still be affecting you today. Rather than simple *yes/no* answers, delve into your emotional body and include examples of when your past experiences might be affecting certain reactions or behaviors today. The more attentive you are to these questions and exercises, the more benefit you'll get from them.

Think about the last time unexpected turbulence took you off course.

- Can you recall a time you felt a sudden shift into anger, moodiness, or despair? Or you became agitated, impatient, restless, or just plain fearful out of the blue?

- Can you connect any of those mood shifts to a deeper awareness of your neglected needs?

- What need might be trying to come to your attention now?

- What scary things do you imagine?

- What wonderful things can you imagine?

- How do you use your imagination? To scare you? Or to inspire you?

- Have you attracted something in life that you've feared lately (such as the ticket I received)?

- Have you changed a fear into an adventure lately by facing it instead of running from it?

- Are you ready to try?

- What have you feared in the past that you now laugh at?

- What is causing genuine turbulence that you must ride out?

- When feeling threatened, does your inner child act out? How?

Basic Flying Lessons

Lions and Tigers and Bears . . . *Oh My!*

In your notebook, write down all the past fearful imaginings you've entertained that have not occurred. Number them, and then next to each one write down how long that particular fear consumed your life. For example:

1. I feared I would not get accepted into college—2 years

2. I feared I would not find a partner in life—8 years

3. I feared I would not have enough money to pay my bills—10 years

4. I feared I would not get the job I wanted—6 days

Once you go through this list, add up the time these imagined fears have wasted in your life and the cost to you. Be aware of the price of fear when you are tempted to scare yourself again. This tends to reduce fear quickly.

Surprise!

Again, in your journal, write down all the wonderful things that life has surprised you with, especially around the things you feared. For example:

- I was surprised to meet a wonderful partner.

- I was surprised to find a job that I love.

- I was surprised to have three beautiful children, two of whom are stepchildren.

- I was surprised to be included on a trip to Europe by my company.

- I was surprised to learn to play the piano at age 40.

- I was surprised to live in a beautiful home.

- I was surprised that people at work like my creative ideas.

Write down at least three surprises a day.

Reassure Your Inner Child

When you experience the turbulence of a dark mood coming upon you, do some detective work. Review when exactly it came up. What were you doing? How did it manifest? Were you suddenly irritable? Angry? Tearful? Anxious? Needy? Next, ask your inner child what it was feeling. What does your inner child fear? And what does your inner child want from you now? You cannot undo the past, but you can address unwanted needs in the present. If your inner child wants reassurance, be the parent and reassure it that you are here and will take care of it. If your inner child wants more fun, agree to a playdate in the form of a fun experience such as going to see a play or to a comedy club, or just take a day or even an afternoon off. If your inner child is insecure about the future, reassure it through journal writing. Just acknowledging your inner child and assuring it that you are aware of and interested in filling its needs will lift your mood and invite calm to return.

Box It Out

Inner turbulence builds up adrenaline, and this causes a great deal of stress and tension in the body. If this stress and tension is not released, it leaks out in argumentative and irritable outbursts at others, who are often innocent bystanders. To release the tension, yell in the shower, hit pillows with your fists, go to the beach and scream at the ocean, or do all three until you feel the tension lifting. The key is *not* to scream, yell at, or hit other people.

Walk Through It

Nothing lifts the tension and sullenness of inner turbulence from the body and spirit better or faster than moving. It releases fear from bones and muscles right out of the body. When you feel overcome with fear, put on your walking shoes and walk it off. Walk until you feel the tension lifting. Walk as fast as you can, and if you have a walking partner, talk about your fear as you walk. It will drain away as you go and be replaced with a positive inspiration or solution to bring you back to the present.

Advanced Flying Lessons

Get in Water

One of the best ways to clear your mind of negative moods, old patterns, self-doubt, accumulated negativity, and other emotional stress and mental turbulence is to get into water. Ideally, the water you get into is the ocean, but a lake, a pool, or even a bathtub will do. In a tub, add a quart of Epsom salts to the water and soak for a full 20 minutes, if not more. Turn off the phone, dim the lights, and play soft music, or sit in silence while you soak. Water clears your body, mind, and Spirit of negative charges, refreshes you, and brings you back to the moment.

Ride (Write) It Out

Sudden inner turbulence arises to signal to your conscious mind that old energy, unfinished business, and childhood wounds are in need of being noticed and released. One of the best ways to ride out turbulence is to do what is called the Ocean Breath. This breath cools the mind and heats the body. A cool mind allows you to become detached and releases you from the energetic effect of the turbulence. This breath also heats the body, which then can actually burn the pattern out of the body.

To do the Ocean Breath, inhale through the nostrils, expanding the lungs to capacity, and on the first exhale, open the mouth and make a "ha" sound, as if blowing steam on a mirror.

Inhale once more to capacity, and then exhale through the nostrils while constricting the back of the throat and making the same "ha" sound, this time with the mouth closed.

It sounds a little like sounds like you are about to say "hot" without the *t* when you breathe like this.

After a few of these breaths, quiet your mind and focus on what is causing emotional or mental turbulence. Take your journal and write down all patterns and feelings that come to mind.

Next, breathe the Ocean Breath a few more times, imagining with each exhale that you are releasing these patterns from your life. They belong in the past and have no purpose in the present. Use your intention to let them go. If they resist, ask what purpose they serve and what they want from you. A change of behavior? A different decision? Setting better boundaries? Speaking your truth? Forgiving someone? Breathe and listen. Be aware. And acknowledge what is being asked of you from these patterns by writing it down in your journal. The frustrating energy will transition, if not immediately, then soon. Trust and go back to the present. Relax.

Speak Up

Nothing is more influential on your subconscious mind (where negative patterns and unexpressed feelings reside) than the sound of your own voice. Using a small voice recorder (often now available on many cell phones) express your pent-up, fear-based, unhappy, unappreciated, angry, wounded feelings. Do not hold back. List everything you're unhappy about. After recording this list of woes and fears, rewind the recorder and listen to yourself. If these complaints are legitimate and warrant a change from you or others, you will hear it in your voice. If you're simply acting like a victim and airing an old story without taking any responsibility for your present needs, you will hear this in your voice as well.

Next, again on the recorder, speak the truth of what you want to experience. Ask your Higher Self to speak to you and through you and guide you past the turbulence you're presently encountering to a higher, more peaceful state of being. Listen to this recording often and let it guide you through the bumpy ride.

CHAPTER 14

Mechanicals and Maintenance

This past summer at 6 A.M., I had just checked in for my flight to Albany, gotten my boarding pass, and was heading to the gate when I heard over the public-address system that the flight had just been unexpectedly canceled due to an airplane "mechanical." I was not happy to hear this because I was on my way to teach at a workshop at the Omega Institute in upstate New York and was expected to start my class that evening. I needed to get there and didn't have much time to spare.

Racing up to the desk (as was everyone else) to ask for more information, including the availability of alternative flights, I quickly overheard that there were no other available flights to Albany on any airline that day, and that all we could do was wait for the plane to get fixed. So wait we did, for five hours to be exact. We finally took off just before noon and, luckily for me, arrived in time for my workshop after all.

While en route after the long delay, I couldn't help but reflect on how infrequently, if ever, we anticipate disruptions as we go along in life. We act so surprised, yet unexpected disruptions— the "mechanicals" of life—do occur all the time. Not only do we experience mechanicals on airplanes, when it comes to the journey of life, we experience our own disruptive physical mechanicals in the form of illnesses, injuries, accidents, and other body breakdowns of all sorts. And as we all know, when the body breaks down, our journey is definitely interrupted.

Three years ago, I had a huge and unexpected physical breakdown. My "aircraft" blew apart. This happened right before a long-planned two-week adventure with my family, my sister, and her daughter to go to India. We were to leave the day after Christmas and were extremely excited to go. That is, I was until three days before Christmas, when out of the blue I pulled something in my back while at my morning yoga class. By that evening I was in so much pain that I couldn't even move. A trip to the emergency room and an MRI later revealed that I had somehow herniated a disc. No wonder I was in such excruciating pain.

Blowing out my back was definitely not in my holiday plans, and besides being in terrible pain, I was now afraid that I had blown my trip to India as well. No amount of chanting or meditating or praying brought me an ounce of relief. The only thing that worked was an epidural followed by copious amounts of pain relievers.

Not one to give up easily, I did manage to go on the trip after all, but not without being extremely challenged and at times unable to move. Three years and hours of rehabilitation later, I am still mildly incapacitated on certain days and walk very carefully so as to not aggravate my disc all over again.

This unexpected injury reoriented my priorities with lightning speed. What I took for granted, such as being able to stand up, turn over in my sleep, or walk across a room, was now the main purpose of my life. Success in any of these efforts brought near tears of relief to my eyes on a daily basis and suddenly seemed to be the only thing that really mattered.

This painful episode taught me a long-overdue lesson: that unless I took loving care of my body and gave it the proper attention and maintenance it required and deserved, I couldn't expect my journey to flow without interruption.

My personal "mechanical" caused me to stop and reevaluate how well I took care of my body as a general rule, and I honestly had to confess it was not as well as I should have been, by any means.

Although I was taking yoga, I had been pushing myself way beyond my natural limits for weeks because I wanted to be able to show off my yoga skills in India (as though anyone there would care). In trying to stand on my head before my time, I was now unable to stand at all. Humbled, I placed my full attention squarely on my body's needs with newfound respect.

My body told the truth. What I was doing was not good for it, and it let me know. I was not totally taken by surprise. I'd had many warnings before the fall. Ignoring signs of mechanical wear and tear for months, I kept up my unreasonably intense pace, including my yoga practice, my mind pushing me way beyond my body's limits for way too long, which is how I go about a lot of things in my life. I just ignored the increasingly loud warning signals until my body walloped me to get my attention, and boy did it ever!

Once through the crisis, I considered myself lucky to have only suffered a herniated disc. When adding up all the ignorant neglect and abuse I had put my body through over the years—the endless diet of lousy junk food, the cigarettes I smoked as a teen, the lack of sleep, the stress of overdoing—it's a wonder my body could get up and go at all, let alone as well as it did. This experience was the first time I had connected my behavior to my body's reaction, because up until this time it had run like a champ. This injury and the lengthy time it took for my recovery earned my greatest respect for my body, and how it works alongside mind and Spirit to move me through life with ease. Up until that time, I'd believed life to be more mind and Spirit, and that the body was the least important of the three. This crash changed all of that. After all, if my body didn't work, the plane couldn't fly.

This is in no way meant to imply that all body "mechanicals" are the result of carelessness and poor judgment, only that mine was. In fact, most of our physical illnesses or mechanicals, so to speak, are really no one's fault. They are simply the result of the hazards of traveling this Earth plane.

There are viral mechanicals, bacterial mechanicals, genetic mechanicals, and structural mechanicals; mechanicals that result from accidents, wear and tear, and old age; mechanicals due to consuming lousy fuel; and even mysterious mechanicals that no one understands or can fix.

This makes it all the more essential that we give our bodies the best proactive regular maintenance and care as a means to help avoid and reduce the number of mechanicals we face in life. Good maintenance will also help us get through incidents we do face as fast and as well possible so that we can continue our journey through life with minimal interruptions, staying in flow. Just as aircraft need regular attention and high-quality maintenance to go the distance they are asked to travel, so too do we need to keep up the best maintenance if we hope to travel long distances without unexpected interruptions of service.

Fuel for the Road

The best quality maintenance begins with consuming high-octane fuel, the kind that can fuel your body at the cellular level. As spiritual beings, our consciousness permeates our entire being from the nuclei of our cells to the edges of our auras. Our physical bodies carry the imprints of every single experience we've ever had on Earth from our first breath to the present moment.

As we begin to awaken; expand; and elevate our consciousness from a fear-based, mortal frequency to a higher, love-centered, spiritual frequency, every brain, muscle, tissue, and bone that does not resonate with love must be detoxified, cleansed, and purified of limiting and wounded frequencies in order to achieve, sustain, and vibrate to the frequency of love.

I know that sounds daunting. It certainly felt that way to me as I worked to elevate my own vibration to that of love. Although transforming your physical energetic field requires attention and effort, it can be done. And once you begin to clear yourself of past negative imprints, you'll feel so good that you won't consider living any other way.

Transforming negative energy in your body into a more powerful loving frequency begins with your breath, diet, movement, and rest. I've already talked a lot about breath (see Chapter 3), so let's move on and talk a little bit about diet and movement.

Alkaline vs. Acidic Foods

All foods that go into the body are like fuels that go into an engine. Just as there is a difference between grades of fuel for aircraft, there are also varying grades of fuel for the body.

Foods that produce an acidic effect on the body create more of a lower, sometimes fear-based vibration than foods with an alkaline pH, which have an overall higher, more life-affirming, positive effect on the body. Ideally, the body functions best at a pH level of around 7, which means an alkaline state. (You can get urine strips at the local pharmacy to test your pH level.) So it only makes sense to concentrate on fueling your body with more alkaline foods than acidic foods to stay at that optimal pH balance. It's that simple. The question is, which are alkaline foods and which are acidic foods?

Alkaline and acidic foods are found in all food groups, so it's best to check a food chart, found on the Internet or at any health-food store, to get a thorough idea of which foods are which. You don't have to follow the chart to the letter. Just glance at it to get an idea of what are mainly alkaline and what are mainly acidic foods in each group, and try to lean toward alkaline foods over acidic ones. The alkaline foods tend to be greens, nuts, whole grains, seeds, and certain fruits, while acidic foods tend to be red meat, processed foods, packaged foods, and sugars. Again, this is a very broad categorization and only intended to get you thinking. In the back of the book in Appendix II, you'll find a chart of alkaline and acidic foods to get you going in the right direction for optimal energy travel.

Fast Foods Drag You Down

Especially toxic to the body are chemical-filled, processed, and "fast" foods that are marketed to us everywhere. These "faux" or false foods fail to sustain the life and light force in our cells and seriously lower our positive loving frequency. In fact, a regular diet of fatty, processed, unnatural food is so toxic to the energetic field that you will hardly be able to travel at all, let alone at the speed and frequency of love.

I know that this conversation is challenging to a lot of people because they simply don't want to change the way they eat, especially when it comes to giving up their beloved greasy, salty, fatty, processed foods. I know because I don't want to hear that I should give up my French fries. Yet the reason we love these foods is the same reason they're so hard to give up: they're laden with addictive chemicals that make your body crave them.

If you're a junk-food junkie, you are in fact being manipulated by an addiction to toxic, light-destroying, vibration-lowering fare. All you have to do to determine whether you're addicted to toxic, life-draining foods is to pay attention to how you feel both toward yourself and others, physically and psychically, after you eat. If you feel peaceful, energized, lighthearted, satisfied, calm, and quiet, both inside and out, and your digestion flows smoothly and often, then most likely you are in an alkaline state and vibrating at the frequency of love.

If, however, you feel fatigued, bloated, gassy, irritable, anxious, tired, heavy, and depressed, or have indigestion, constipation, diarrhea, or low blood sugar, then you have most likely drifted to a more acidic state, which creates a lower, fear-based energetic frequency and drains both you and those around you.

Once you start eating a more consistently alkaline diet, you will experience several other very exciting benefits as well. For one, your heart chakra will open as your body, feeling so well supported, begins to move out of "survival mode" and relax. You will become far more receptive to the positive energies that are in the ethers. It's a simple "like attracts like" dynamic: as you feel better, the world you live in feels better. As you elevate your vibration, you begin to intercept others who have elevated theirs as well.

Another benefit to eating a more alkaline diet is that alkaline food activates the upper chakras and, in particular, the pineal gland, which is the master gland and the key to entering the highest frequencies of spiritual love. When fueled with loving sustenance, you vibrate to loving expression.

Moving into an alkaline frequency doesn't mean you have to give up the foods you love. It just means you must eat more alkaline foods than acidic ones. As a red wine–, cheese-, and baguette-loving Francophile, this is good news for me. I love these acidic foods in moderation, and enjoying them brings forward a tremendously loving vibration in my heart. I just don't eat like this every day.

The same goes for eating meat. I've gone back and forth on meat over the years, sometimes eating it, sometimes not. I always enjoy it, but the more I focus on traveling at the speed of love, the less I want it. It does seem to lower my vibration, so I choose to eat red meat far less often. I do have spiritually bright friends who carry a beautiful vibration yet continue to eat some meat. Not a lot, though; and if they do, it is usually organic meat. Ultimately, the decision is yours. Pay attention to your vibration, and make decisions based on how you feel.

Eat Mindfully

Pay attention to subtle energy shifts to know how best to fuel your body's needs. One of the greatest challenges to our bodies is eating too much food. Breathe between bites and give your body a chance to respond to the food as you ingest it. Do not allow your mind to race you through your meals, as though a contender in the Indy 500. The speed of love is a gentle, easy pace, not a frantic, urgent, intense one. The addicted brain, on the other hand, is frantic, urgent, intense, and oxygen deprived.

Slow down, breathe between bites, and notice how each food affects you. Traveling light means inside as well as outside, so go easier on the amount of food you take in at once. The engine in life's flight is your digestive system; and it runs best when fueled in small, slow, steady doses of high-octane fuel.

One way to retrain the brain and recalibrate the body to a higher fuel efficiency is to eat only half of what is on your plate at any time and leave the rest. Do this for every meal. Smaller meals keep more oxygen going to the brain than to the stomach, which will elevate your awareness and sensitivity, ease your digestion, and keep things moving along.

Most spiritual traditions encourage people to eat mindfully, and that's also the message conveyed on the popular reality-TV show *The Biggest Loser.* While on the surface it appears to be merely a weight-loss contest, the show is really rooted in people making conscious, self-supporting choices designed not only to help them lose unwanted weight, but more important, to get rid of unwanted negative patterns, imprints, and habits that keep them living in fear and self-loathing. As the contest unfolds and the weeks go by, each contestant shifts from a predominantly acidic to an alkaline diet, and right before our eyes, they heal and love permeates their being, for self and others. And in that transformation, they heal the people watching, as well.

All in Moderation

If you want to elevate your personal vibration, give up foods that clearly don't offer any evidence of love. Food that is canned, packaged, frozen, sterile, and stale is loveless and will make you unhappy. If you are uncertain about a food, feel it in your heart. Ask yourself if that food offers a positive, life-affirming, loving vibration, or not. If you feel *yes,* then enjoy it. If you feel *no,* then avoid it. If you are unsure, eat only a little and move on to more certain things. Believe it or not, when you decide to travel at the speed of love in life, many of these choices become second nature.

The point is to give ourselves the proper fuel to be able to travel at the speed of love. Although we are spiritual beings, we are traveling in physical vehicles, and they need the high-octane fuel to travel to the heights to which we aspire.

Blessing

A wonderful way to upgrade all fuel at no extra cost to you is to offer some form of blessing to our great Creator before eating. Doing this energetically elevates our food and drink to a vibrational level of gratitude for the support we are given, which is one of the highest, most healing vibrations the body can experience.

Take a moment before eating, or even drinking, to thank God for the gift of your sustenance. We are so blessed every day with the most basic of things, and taking a moment to be grateful for and appreciative of the things that keep us alive and well is fuel for the spirit. Add blessings and prayers of gratitude to the daily ritual of eating and drinking, and your journey will improve greatly.

Say a blessing over all that goes into your body, and you can elevate the vibration to one of great love and light. This alone will make the daily ride a great deal more pleasurable. Pray in joy and gratitude for your life and the things that keep you alive. This is just as essential to your journey as food and water.

One of my favorite blessings is: "We thank you, our Beloved Creator, for the wonderful bounty of this meal, and for the goodness of you, God, to provide it. May it nourish us body, mind, and spirit and give us the energy to serve the world with love and kindness throughout this day. Amen."

Water

In addition to an alkaline diet, we also need to fuel ourselves with lots and lots of water to enter into a heightened state of vibration. Being dehydrated keeps us vibrationally grounded in lower frequencies and, consequently, in a lower-grade, fear-based flow. Dehydration also lessens our intuition and cuts us off from our control tower. All engines need some water to run, and we are no exception. If we are dehydrated, we cannot stay strongly connected to Source and quickly fall out of flow.

Only drinking water keeps us properly hydrated. Coffee, sodas, energy drinks, lattes, caffeinated teas, and alcoholic beverages don't create the vibration of love in the same way.

Masaru Emoto, who wrote *The Healing Power of Water,* testifies to the potency of water and how it absorbs and reflects energetic intention; we can actually infuse it with the power, through intention and prayer, to transform negative energy in the body and flush negative frequencies from the body and surrounding energy fields. Simply hold any water you drink in your hands before you drink it and suggest to it that it clear, purge, flush, purify, and detox your body and energy field of all negativity. Fill your water with love and appreciation for its goodness and ask the water to refresh, refuel, and regenerate every cell in you so that you can journey through your day in the blessed flow of love. Then drink up and enjoy as the water goes to work for you. As for how much water you should drink, my dear friend Dr. Michelle Robin, a gifted healer and the director of Your Wellness Connection in Kansas City, a center for positive wellness, says it is best to drink at least half your body weight in ounces every day, preferably before 8 P.M. This means if you weigh 150 pounds, you should drink 75 ounces of water a day. If you weigh 100 pounds, you should drink 50 ounces of water a day. Do this for a week, and you will feel such an improvement in your energy, you won't believe it.

Super Greens

If you want to give your diet and water an added boost, you can add the alkaline punch of spirulina, green barley, or any super blue-green algae to your water, and you will really feel energized.

Algae come from the sea, and the sea vibration is pure love and light. Adding this frequency to your water introduces this loving vibration to your body. It is extremely fortifying and energizing and significantly raises your vibration.

You can find super greens at your local food store in the "super greens" section. They usually come in powder form. You don't have to add a lot of these algae to get the desired boost. Just a teaspoon in water once a day does the trick. They don't taste bad, usually like a very weak pea soup. You can add these greens to a morning shake as well if the taste in water doesn't appeal to you.

Exercise

In addition to an alkaline diet, proper hydration, and super greens, we also need to exercise in order to keep the energy of the body at its highest level of vibration. Moderate movement every day assists the digestive process, which is key to reaching higher and higher positive levels of vibration and living in the flow of love.

The body is the vehicle through which we journey in this lifetime, and it is intended to move. It simply doesn't work as well when it doesn't move enough. Just last week, I asked my husband to take my car in for a checkup, as it was acting funny. The mechanic who worked on it gave it a complete overhaul, then surprisingly said the problem with the car was that I didn't drive it enough (which is true, because I travel a lot), and sitting on the street had caused it to rust underneath. "Cars are made to be driven," he said. "Get behind the wheel and go." I believe the same goes for the body.

I've traveled through many foreign countries where the modern world has not snatched away the need to move around on foot, and the people look incredibly fit and strong. I've seen old women in India walking with the equivalent of a small houseful of goods being transported on their heads. They cruise down the roads in bare feet while joyfully laughing and singing, not showing a single sign of distress. I've seen old men riding rickety old bikes up steep hillsides in Italy and France with large parcels in the baskets without even breaking a sweat, their faces to the sun and their expressions relaxed and at ease.

In the modern world, I see people huffing and puffing up a few steps, preferring an escalator or an elevator to move them rather than using their own steam. These conveniences lower our vibration and deprive us of the need for the body to be in motion. We are happier when we move, plain and simple, and happier means we are in the flow.

I have a beautiful client named Mary who was born without fully formed hands, legs, and feet. She must navigate the world in a specially designed wheelchair, and wherever she goes, people jump to assist her by pushing her wheelchair for her. Yet again and again, I've seen her decline their offers and joyfully exercise her own upper body as she moves through the world. We can all find a way to move if we want to, and we will be far happier if we are blessed with vehicles that can and do move easily and often.

Don't let your physical vehicle become rusty due to lack of movement. Just as cars were made to drive, your physical vehicle is made to move as well. No matter how much you move, make up your mind to move a little more than the day before, unless of course you just finished a marathon. The point is that to travel at the speed of love is, at the foundation, to travel; and to travel is to move.

Walk around the block. Take the stairs. Park your car away from the entrance to the mall or grocery store and walk the extra distance. Turn on some music and dance your way through doing the dishes. Get on a bicycle or Rollerblades. Take up a sport such as tennis, basketball, or swimming. Make up your mind to move for at least 15 minutes a day, 30 is better.

If you already are in the habit of exercising, shake it up a bit and try something new, such as yoga, Pilates, or belly dancing. Embrace the idea that moving the body is exhilarating and joyful, and no matter how you feel before you move, you always feel better after you do.

Rest

Another thing essential for proper maintenance of our bodies is at least eight hours of rest every night. Yet it's not enough just to get eight hours. Because our bodies are tuned into the natural rhythms of life, they have inner clocks that rest and rejuvenate the organs in sync with the natural world, which means between the hours of 10 P.M. and 6 A.M. So in order to fully rejuvenate while we sleep, we must get those eight hours of rest between those hours. Therefore, if a person goes to sleep at 2 A.M., his body will only rejuvenate until 6 A.M., even if he sleeps until 10 A.M. This is okay once in a while, but if we make a regular habit of it, our bodies become depleted and run into the ground. If we want to travel at the speed of love, we have to be able to lift off . . . starting with lifting our faces from the pillow every morning, and this means going to bed by 10 P.M. as often as we can.

Essential Maintenance

I've mentioned proper eating, the need for water, even the importance of an alkaline-based diet in past books, but only in passing. I believe now, in retrospect, that although I was aware of the importance of these things to living in the higher flow of love, I never realized just how important these choices really are to our ability to live in a sustained vibration of love.

What I do know now is that these basics are essential to traveling at the speed of love. You simply cannot achieve this higher vibration if you poison your body. It goes without saying that this includes drinking alcohol excessively; disturbing your natural pH with recreational or unnecessary drugs; or overburdening your body with too much food and drink, and too little or too much sleep at the wrong time.

All these things sabotage your ability to travel at the speed of love. They bog you down because unconscious choices such as these are born in fear, and therefore fear will resonate throughout your vibration. It's really about common sense. It's just that we've gotten away from common sense in our overthought, modern world.

If the thought of changing your diet, eliminating toxic substances, eating smaller meals, drinking more water, adding super greens, exercising more, and going to bed earlier seems overwhelming to you or you simply don't want to bother, try any one of these suggestions in small doses and see how you feel before you deny yourself the benefits altogether.

For example, make an alkaline smoothie in your blender for breakfast once or twice a week and see how you feel. Give up one of your two or three cups of coffee, juice, or soda in exchange for a large glass of fresh water; and better yet, drink water fortified with greens such as dried barley powder in its place and see how you feel. Eat a smaller lunch than usual and then go for a five- or ten-minute walk afterward. Fuel the journey as best you can one day at a time, as that is the only way you can journey anyway. Go to bed earlier one day a week. Let your elevated life experience be your confirmation. The better you feel, the easier the journey.

Sudden Breakdown

When a mechanical breakdown does occur in the body and you find yourself facing illness, injury, or any other sort of weakness and cannot get up and go, then stop, rest, and recuperate without guilt. Just as airplanes need consistent maintenance and, at times, complete overhauls, so too do our bodies need consistent attention and extra support from time to time. No matter what causes the "mechanical," the first step is to move through it and recover when you get sick or hurt in some way. The second step is to look for the cause and take steps to remove it in the future. The third step is to set up a solid prevention and maintenance plan to keep your vehicle flying high through the friendly skies with love. These three steps will help support a peaceful journey.

In-Flight Check-In

Take a deep breath and get centered. Next, take out your notebook and set it by your side. Stand up and stretch and get ready to focus again on some important questions that will assist your flight progress. Before you begin, get a tall glass of fresh water to sip as you work through the following questions. In between questions, stand up and walk around the room, or even around your home, for two to three minutes before proceeding. As always, take your time and do not feel pressured to answer all these questions at one time. You can revisit them throughout the day or over a period of several days if you prefer. The important thing is that you give each question your full consideration as you answer.

- How alkaline is your diet?
- Do you generally eat fresh foods and enough greens?
- How much water are you drinking every day?
- Are you drinking enough fresh water over other beverages?
- Are you overeating?
- Is your body stressed by consuming a poor diet?
- Do you exercise? How often?
- Do you enjoy moving?
- Does your life encourage enough walking in a day?
- Have you ever noticed how food affects you?
- Are you a fast eater?
- Do you pay attention to what you are eating, or do you eat mindlessly?
- Do you get enough rest?
- What time do you go to bed?
- Would you benefit from going to bed a little earlier?
- Do you give thanks before you eat? Privately or openly?
- If your body were a car, would you say it runs well, or does it need a tune-up?
- Does it need a minor tune-up or a major overhaul?

- Are you suffering from any mechanicals now?
- If so, what are they?
- How are you trying to heal?

Basic Flying Lessons

A Week of Health

Eat three servings of fresh fruits and vegetables for every serving of starches and protein. Drink a minimum of half your body weight in ounces of water a day. That means if you weigh 200 pounds, drink 100 ounces of water a day. If you weigh 160 pounds, drink 80 ounces of water a day. Go to bed in time to get eight hours of sleep, preferably before 10 P.M. Walk for ten minutes every day at a brisk pace.

Shake Your Booty

The happiest way to move is to your favorite music. Get your favorite CD or Internet music or just sing . . . and dance for 15 full minutes every morning before getting dressed for work.

Since time may be limited, you can do the singing and dancing in the shower (be careful not to slip), in the kitchen while making coffee or breakfast, or while getting dressed. Be creative and turn anything you must do into a dance routine. The key is to let go, belt it out, bust a move, and shake your groove thing with gusto, *as if no one were watching,* as the famous country song says. Most of all, have fun. Even tying your shoes can become a dance routine with a little imagination. If you have kids, ask them to join you. If you have teenagers, give them something to roll their eyes over. If you have a partner or housemate, reach out and ask him or her to dance with you. A little samba while waiting for the toast to brown can be a deliciously fun way to start the day. A quick watusi or a Michael Jackson moonwalk over to the coffee pot will kick the day off to a brilliant start. And once the engine kicks in at the speed of love, it keeps going all day long.

Be Aware Before You Act

Awareness is key to traveling at the speed of love. Before you eat, breathe and be aware of what you are about to eat. Will it support you or drag you down? Before you drink, breathe and be aware of what you are about to drink. Will it refresh you or dehydrate you? Before you turn on the TV in the bedroom, breathe and be aware of what time it is. Is there time to watch TV and still get a rejuvenating night's sleep? When you go shopping for groceries, as you place things in the cart, breathe and be aware of what you are selecting. Are you selecting life-supporting foods that will keep you in an optimal alkaline state? Before you sit down, breathe and be aware. Is sitting the best thing for you, or would it better serve you to move a little bit?

Stretch

One of the best things you can do to keep your earthly vehicle in good repair is to stretch every part of your being. Start by stretching your lungs. Breathe in as deeply as you can, and then take a few more little sips of air, stretching your lungs a little more. Next, yawn and stretch your mouth wide open and let out the biggest yawn sound you can. Reach your arms above your head and stretch your arms up to the ceiling as far as they will go. Next, gently bend over from the hips, bending your knees if necessary so that there is no strain on your back, and reach to touch your toes, stretching as far as your fingertips will go, and then slowly come back up, vertebra by vertebra. Take your time so that you don't get dizzy. Then stand tall and drop your arms to each side of your body; and then lean to one side, stretching your arm alongside your body and sliding it as far down the side as possible without strain. Do this on the other side as well. Place your fingers in front of you and stretch your fingers as wide open and as far as they will go. Then try stretching your toes. Finally, stretch your imagination and think of doing one new thing today that you haven't done before, such as trying a new food, taking a new way to work, listening to someone you normally dismiss, or entertaining an opinion you generally discount. Stretch. Stretch. Stretch. Enjoy the expanded you.

Advanced Flying Lessons

For the Rest of Your Life

Do everything I suggested above . . . forever.

Yoga

Do yoga three times a week for 30 minutes. If possible, go to a class so that a competent instructor can guide you through the proper way to do the asanas, or postures. If not, work with a yoga video. These can be found at local fitness stores or at the local library. Also, check your local television listings. There are many yoga programs on TV throughout the day.

Clear the Mind

Give up all alcohol and recreational mood-altering substances for one month.

Going Green

Go on a 24-hour fast to give your digestive system a rest. (Check with your doctor first on this one.) Eat only fresh greens, grains, and fruits for the next three days, along with lots of fresh water.

Quiet Time

Quiet is the best possible foundation for recovery of injury, sickness, and pain. If you are experiencing a mechanical, be kind to yourself and take the time to allow yourself peace and the quiet you need to recover, free of guilt. Don't fight your condition. It won't help. Accept your situation with patience and love, and take the time you need to heal.

Seek the Best Mechanics

Seek the best possible mechanics you can find in the way of healers, doctors, and caretakers for the body when you are injured, sick, or feeling weak. Your body is your vehicle for traveling at the speed of love. It is a precious gift from God and works miracles for you every day. It deserves to be maintained and cared for with the highest degree of respect and love possible. This doesn't guarantee you won't experience a mechanical along the way, but it will greatly reduce the number and intensity of mechanicals you do experience, as well as move you through them quickly and help you get back in the flow.

Extremely Advanced Flying Lesson

Stop complaining about exercise, diet, your weight, your physical appearance, or your physical condition and love yourself completely *as is*. When asked, "How are you?" respond, "Feeling good and in the flow." (Yes, I know this sounds silly, but try it anyway . . . it's fun!)

Chapter 15

Drifting Off Course

Several weeks ago, my friend Debra, a gifted healer and teacher, felt the sudden intuitive impulse to offer a two-day workshop on energetic healing to several clients who had shown an interest in the topic. It felt right; and she was flooded with enthusiasm, creative inspiration, and confidence—three clear indications that she was in the flow in her intention to share her gifts.

Never having put on a workshop before, Debra wasn't exactly sure how to proceed, a concern she voiced to one of the interested participants. Wanting to help, her student immediately offered to assist and began to share all kinds of ideas. She suggested that Debra hold the workshop in a Chicago-area hotel so that it would be convenient for people to come from out of town. Debra agreed. She recommended that Debra invite 30 to 40 people, that they create special ceremonies for healing at night, and to have a healing circle with drums. All of these ideas sounded great, so Debra went along with it. Yet the more complicated and ambitious the workshop became, the less inspired and enthusiastic Debra felt.

She tried to write a curriculum for her class, but as the plans developed, her commitment shrank. Confused about her reticence, especially since her student was being so supportive and was doing so much to help her, Debra felt guilty and kept going along with "the plan." Finally, after two weeks of preparation, Debra was asked to sign a contract with the hotel to seal the deal. Everything was set in place, looked good on paper, and sounded great to Debra's ears. Yet she suddenly realized that what started out traveling at the speed of love was now dead in the water for her. Debra didn't want to continue. It just didn't flow for her any-more, and she wasn't sure why. She loved her work and especially enjoyed sharing it with others, she loved her client and was genu-inely grateful for all she had done to set up the workshop week-end, and she loved teaching and wasn't afraid. Clearly, she knew something was "off," but what?

Allowing herself time to review, reflect, and meditate on her resistance, she suddenly realized what was wrong. Her spirit was ready to host a small, organic class in a simple setting for a few of her dearest clients. The vision her student was creating was not one that Debra was inspired to fulfill . . . at least not as the first class she was to offer. It was too ambitious and was overreaching her true desire. She canceled the reservation with the hotel, asked another good friend if she could host the class in her office space, invited a handful of students, and all of this was done with a few phone calls after dinner.

The pressure to create a large workshop dissipated, and every-thing was in place in a matter of minutes. Debra was once again excited, yet at the same time relaxed, confident, peaceful, and, well, back in the flow—all except for one minor glitch. What was Debra going to say to her helpful student? How was she going to reject everything the student had done?

Taking a deep breath, she called and explained her change of direction. Rather than feeling offended, it turned out that her student was relieved as well.

"All I wanted to do was be of help to you, Debra," she said. "But personally, I'm thankful it's going to be more intimate and casual. That's so much more like what I had hoped it could be." Her student's reaction further convinced Debra that she had made the proper course correction, and she was now on track with what would work best for everyone involved.

Her resistance gave way to creative inspiration, and after two weeks of agitation, she suddenly envisioned how she was going to lay out the entire course in one complete swoop, another clear sign to Debra that she had caught the Divine jet stream and was on her way to a fantastic creation.

Where Are You Going?

It's important, when on your own journey, to be alert for signs that you may be drifting off course as well; and if you do drift, that you catch yourself before it's too late, before you lose your way and fall away from the flow. There are several ways to do this. The first is obvious to any good pilot about to embark on a flight, which is to have a clear idea of where you want to go and what kind of experience you desire.

This may seem like a paradox, because going with the flow seems to be the exact opposite of clearly choosing a destination or intention. Yet they do not contradict one another at all. My mother clarified this best for me once when I asked the very same question: "If I'm clear on my intentions and destination, then how can I go with the flow?"

She answered, "Easy. Tell the Universe what you want, but don't tell it how to deliver it. Let the Universe show you the way, and follow the signs." That made sense, so I gave it a try. It worked.

For example, years ago I told the Universe I wanted to travel easily all over the world. It told me, through my intuition, to join the airlines, which I did. And then, to my great surprise, just before I was about to quit, I was offered a buyout contract that afforded my family and me free travel in exchange for quitting. Wow—talk about Divine flow!

Read the Map

The Universe is set up to guide us to flow toward the highest good on a soul level for all concerned. The deal is that we must know what kind of experiences we want to have on our journey, and the Universe, like our very own fantastic Universal travel agent, will set up the connections to get us there. We set the intention. The Universe sets up the way. It's important to know that intuition only supports our most authentic, spiritually aligned intentions, however; only the spirit can travel at the speed of love. The ego is not welcome on this journey.

The Universe sends us directions through our intuition; and we receive them through an inner voice, a tug in the heart, a sense, a vibe, a deep inner thought, a feeling, a certain subtle knowing, or an energy that directs us along the way. We each feel this intuition in a different way, and because it is subtle, it can be elusive. Nevertheless, if we pay attention, we can all feel it in the center of our hearts, flowing through our veins, and in our bones, like a deep inborn guidance system wired to God.

It may be tricky to describe intuition, but it's not hard to feel it. Just focus on the middle of your heart. Like a subtle blinking light, when you take notice and follow its signals, you feel satisfied, quiet, calm, certain, relieved, confident, and, most of all, in alignment with your authentic self. Ignore this heart-based beeper and you'll feel restless, anxious, uneasy, disturbed, and not quite yourself. To feel your heart vibration, breathe deeply, quiet your thoughts for a moment, put your hand on your heart, and listen for its pulse. It's so subtle that you may doubt that what you're feeling is real. Don't. It is.

Allow yourself one full day to be guided by your intuition. During the day, whenever you're faced with a question, decision, or choice, put your hand on your heart and say out loud, "My intuition says . . . ," and then answer out loud.

Next, follow the response your intuition gave you. For example, you may wonder how to get to work the fastest way. Place your hand on your heart, and ask your intuition to guide you. It may say, *Take the train today,* even though you usually drive. For that day, go ahead and take public transportation. You may discover by doing this that you miss a major traffic jam and sail straight through to work. Whether you have that assurance or not (you probably won't), follow your vibes anyway. Be a good sport in following your intuition fully all day. Be open to what surprising new things may occur.

If we are travelers, and our body is our vehicle, our intuition is the radio signal along the way or the radar on the instrument panel that keeps us on track. We cannot travel at the speed of love without it, because we'll get lost. If we are on track, it hums along smoothly and we feel at ease, in the flow, right with ourselves and the Universe, and at peace as we go.

If we drift off course and out of alignment with our authentic selves, however, the radar starts to beep, causing tension in our heart, our chest, the back of our neck, our stomach, and throughout our nervous system, leaving us feeling unsettled—as though we have "ants in the pants," so to speak. This feeling is our indication that we have drifted from our true intention and must reexamine the direction in which we're flowing to get back on track.

When we first deviate from our course, the vibration that alerts us is subtle. The further we drift, the more intense the energetic alert becomes. It is up to us to pay attention to our inner world and notice if we are at peace and at ease with our choices, or if not, to reevaluate and be willing to make the changes necessary to get back in the groove of our authentic self.

The signals are not that difficult to read. "Good vibes" mean we are in the flow. "Bad vibes" mean we are drifting. All we must do is pay attention to our vibes, trust them, and follow them.

Watch Your Inner Radar

A long-term client, Kim, a 37-year-old pharmaceutical saleswoman, envisioned meeting and sharing her life with a soul mate. She longed to be completely herself with that person and be accepted and celebrated for it. She also envisioned having great fun with her intended beloved, and great sex as well.

She met Marcus, a young medical intern, at a co-worker's birthday party, and the chemistry was instant. They got along well, laughed a lot, and had great sex from the first night they met. Encouraged after two months of fun, Kim felt she was flying high, surely at the speed of love. She then took steps toward an even deeper, more authentic intimacy with Marcus and began to share her more private hopes and dreams and her spiritual and religious views. Suddenly, the flow between them stopped. Marcus withdrew—a little at first, and then altogether.

Kim was confused, alarmed, and panicked. Refusing to believe their "love" had dissipated so quickly, she began all sorts of manipulations to get Marcus back into the flow with her again. She called him constantly and left text messages on his cell phone. She wrote him letters and pretended she didn't notice he was AWOL. When she called me, she insisted they were soul mates and it was only a matter of time before he'd come to his senses and realize it.

When she asked me if this was accurate, I paused, then asked, "How does it feel between you two? Is this a glitch or a bust? You'll know if you check in with your heart."

That's when Kim burst into disappointed tears. "I feel so awful," she cried. "I hate to admit it, but our connection feels so over! He loved the romance but clearly did not want a commitment, and I ignored the signs all the way because *I* did."

I was quiet. When traveling at the speed of love, your compass—or radar, gauge, or instrument panel—is your intuition. It senses whether you're on course or if you've drifted off. Simply be still and feel the vibration within. Suddenly, Kim sighed. "Weird," she said. "As devastated as I am about my dreams with Marcus not materializing, I somehow feel lighter and relieved. At least now I'm not kidding myself and forcing *my* way over the natural way."

Trust Your Intuition

All I know for sure, as Oprah would say, is that the only way to travel at the speed of love is to listen, trust, believe, and follow your feelings and the truth of what they convey, even if that truth is disappointing or not what you want to accept. In other words, if something feels off, it is. If something doesn't feel right, it isn't. If something, however subtle, feels dissonant, pay attention. Examine it closely and study what it's trying to tell you. Honor what you're feeling because your feelings are a conduit from the spiritual realm.

The vibration of love is ease and flow. When you are in the flow, even through turbulence, challenge, upset, and dark clouds, you still feel resonant progress toward peace. The vibration of the ego, of control, of fear, is just the opposite. It feels like struggle, conflict, and, most of all, resistance. Whenever you feel any of these vibrations, take them as a huge clue that you're drifting off course.

Debra felt resistance to her student's plan for her class. Kim felt Marcus's resistance toward her life plans with him. Following your feelings and surrendering to your need to understand them is fundamental to traveling at the speed of love. Although your logical mind may not understand what's going on, the vibration you feel always conveys something, and that something is important or you wouldn't have picked up on it.

When you feel the vibration of resistance, for example, this is a signal that it's time to take a step back, take a time out, and reverse or suspend your course, depending on how you feel. If you feel warm and positive in your heart, this is as good as a green light, urging you to carry on, go for the experience, and take the opportunity into your heart with confidence.

Resonant or Dissonant?

If you aren't fully clear about your intention, zero in on what kinds of feelings you're experiencing. If your intention and your feeling resonate, leaving you peaceful, relaxed, and at ease in your body, you are in Divine flow, traveling at the speed of love.

If not, note the difference and use calm breathing to get reoriented toward the experience you seek. If you feel a vibrational pull that makes no logical sense but resonates in your body, heart, and mind, surrender all need to control and follow your feeling. If it diverts you away from your conscious intention, trust the feeling anyway. It is your Divine Spirit overriding your plan with a better one.

A single client of mine, Nancy, booked a cruise to Mexico and was looking forward to going, when all of a sudden she got the strong sense that she shouldn't go—although she had no logical reason to feel this way. She fought the feeling for three days and then decided to trust it and stay home, even though she would lose the money she'd paid for the vacation because it was too late to get a refund.

Nancy went out to dinner with her best friend the day after the ship left. They ate at a local restaurant, and sitting next to them were three handsome men from Norway, all engineers in town on business. They struck up a conversation, and to make a long story short, Nancy hit it off with one of the guys. They were in town for three more days before they went back to Stavanger, where they lived, so Nancy offered to take the man she'd befriended around town the next evening.

This was this beginning of a great romance between them, and by the time he left, he had invited Nancy to Norway to visit him in the fall. She accepted and went, the romance blossomed into love, and they married the following spring. Had she been on that cruise, Nancy would not have met the man she calls the love of her life. She didn't know why she wasn't supposed to go at the time, but evidently her Higher Self did, and it gave her the direction not to miss the real "ship" she was hoping for in life: a committed, loving relationship.

The key to trusting this process is to be honest with yourself and set true intentions. Change course only if you truly feel the vibration pulling you in a new direction, not if you're trying to force something unnatural or out of the flow to go your way.

If you do drift off course, don't panic. Just make a correction by coming back to your breath, to your heart, and to your authentic intentions. This may require being calm and quiet so that you can get back in touch with Divine flow.

Wishful Thinking vs. Intuition

Many of my clients have asked me how to tell the difference between a true intuitive vibration and wishful or fearful thinking. There are several ways: wishful or fearful thinking jumps and changes from moment to moment, like a kangaroo in a cage, while a true intuitive vibration stays the same morning, noon, and night and doesn't waver, no matter what. Another clue is that a true intuitive vibration leaves you feeling calm and satisfied in your heart and chest area and causes you to breathe easier when you listen to and honor it. Something inside settles down and relaxes, as though its mission is accomplished. Wishful or fearful thinking never quite settles the body, no matter what. A third way to tell an intuitive vibe from wishful or fearful thinking is that a true vibration arises from the heart in the middle of your chest, while a fearful or wishful thought feels as though it's arising from the middle of your head, even your sinuses at times, as though stuck in the middle of your head. It doesn't feel solid, while an intuitive vibration does.

To tune in to intuition, slow down, breathe, take five, pay attention, and listen to your heart. Focus on your heart and ask your intuition to guide you. Pay attention to how you feel, especially to the energy coursing through your body. If your intuition is supporting a direction or course of action, it gently pushes you toward it by conveying a warm, calm, magnetic feeling. If your intuition is trying to divert you away from something, it will convey this, too, by causing a subtle agitation throughout your body. Intuition feels like a low hum, almost like an electrical buzz or current running through your tissues, sometimes in the heart or chest area, sometimes in the stomach or in the throat.

If in doubt about your intuitive guidance, another way to check is to speak your feelings out loud and then observe how the words affect you. If they are true guidance, your body will feel the buzz of confirmation, especially in your heart area. If what you voice is not true intuition, but rather wishful thinking or fears, you will feel a slight restless agitation pulsing through your body. This is all very subtle, as I said, but like sand in your eye or a pebble in your shoe, you know if something feels off.

In-Flight Check-In

Once again, it's time to take out your notebook and spend a few minutes thinking about each of the following questions. Breathe deeply and get centered and grounded before you begin. This time, focus on your past experiences and how they might still be affecting you today. Rather than simple *yes/no* answers, delve into your emotional body and include examples of when your past experiences might be affecting certain reactions or behaviors today. The more attentive you are to these questions and exercises, the more benefit you'll get from them.

- What, if anything, might you be feeling resistance toward in your life right now?

- What are you forcing that isn't working?

- What is your intuition trying to tell you that you're ignoring or denying?

- What are you refusing to acknowledge that's costing you peace of mind?

- Stop right now and check in with your feelings. Are any of them dissonant?

- Do you express your intuitive feelings?

- Where in your body does your intuition get your attention? In your gut? In your heart? In your chest?

Basic Flying Lessons

Pay Attention

If you're disconnected from or unfamiliar with your intuition, you may need to practice paying attention to your feelings to sharpen your awareness.

A good way to hone your feeling apparatus is to stop what you're doing for a few minutes every hour or so and tune your attention fully to your body, and in particular, your heart.

Then ask yourself out loud, "Am I doing what I want to be doing, or am I being swept away by someone else's intent? Or by my own ego?"

As a guideline, you can ask:

- Do I feel peaceful?
- Am I being creative?
- Am I speaking my mind?
- Do I enjoy what I'm doing?
- Why am I doing what I'm doing?
- Could I stop if I wanted to?
- If not, why not?
- Am I doing what I'm doing because I want to or because I have to?
- If I'm doing something because I have to, what is the benefit?
- Am I anywhere near where I want to be?
- Am I happy?
- Are my choices in harmony with my intentions and desires?

Flight Plan

You can avoid drifting off course by setting clear intentions, knowing where you want to go next, and staying present. Just as a pilot knows where he's going and follows a flight plan to get there, so too must you know where you want to go so that your intuition can assist in creating the route to get you there.

Create your flight plan today. In your journal, answer the following:

- What do I want to experience next . . .
  . . . in my business or job?
  . . . in my relationship?
  . . . with respect to my health?
  . . . with my friends and family?
  . . . while adventuring in life?
  . . . in my personal growth?
- What new vistas would I like to explore?
- Where am I going now?

Next, set your intentions based on what you discovered with these questions. For example, if you wrote: "I want to experience a stronger, happier marriage," then you might intend to spend more quality time alone with your partner. If you want a better-paying job, you might intend to start exploring new opportunities and going on interviews. Just know that intuition works best with clear intentions. The better the intentions that you set are, the more intuition can guide you to manifest them.

Advanced Flying Lessons

Pocket Journal

For two weeks, carry a small pocket notebook with you at all times, and in it write down every single gut feeling, hunch, bright idea, hit, or intuitive flash you have as it comes up or soon there-after. Simply record your feelings and don't worry about interpret-ing them—they will reveal themselves over time. Be patient and trust that all your intuitive flashes will come to make sense even-tually. For the moment, just observe, and write everything down. The more you notice and document your intuitive feelings, the more often and more clearly they will guide you. At the end of the two weeks, look over your journal entries and notice if any of them make more sense now that time has passed. Check them off as they come to make sense. This practice teaches you to listen to intuition all the time rather than dismiss it, even if it doesn't make logical sense in the moment.

Check Your Intuition

Throughout the day, ask your intuition what it feels about the situations you face, especially when you have to make decisions. Be direct. Simply tune inward and say, *Hmm. What does my intuition say about this?* Take a few quiet breaths and then answer out loud. If what you say truly is your intuition speaking, your body will feel relaxed and calm. If it isn't, but rather wishful thinking or your fretful mind, you will feel that in your body as well, this time as subtle agitation and restlessness. This practice teaches you the difference between intuitive guidance and mental energy.

Sleep on It

Fear and confusion tend to lift after a good night's rest. If you find yourself confused, led by others' feelings over your own and unable to tune in to your intuition, give the whole situation a rest and sleep on it. It may not seem advanced to sleep on a problem, but it *is* in that it's often difficult for the mind to let something go enough to actually sleep. So when I suggest that you sleep on it, I mean really sleep. Let your confusion and worry slip from your mind, knowing that while in a deep state of rest your Higher Self can make contact with you and download guidance in the form of a dream or a refreshed and clear perspective in the morning. Trust that sleep will clear away the confusion and restore you to your authentic self. It is from this place that you can connect with your Higher Self and feel its guidance keeping you on course.

Chapter 16

Hijackings

Yesterday I was enjoying a particularly lovely day, traveling at the speed of love, experiencing delightful synchronicities, witnessing the beautiful people around me, even hearing the birds' first songs of spring in the air as the long, harsh winter was slowly making way for spring. My heart was fully open as I walked home from work at 3 P.M. My day couldn't have been more gorgeous until, halfway through the crosswalk on the busiest street I cross to get home, a red van ran the stop sign and raced straight toward me. The driver laid on his horn, thrust his head out the window, and screamed at me to get the !*&^ out of the way. Then he flipped me off and squealed past me going 90 miles per hour. This psychic assault almost gave me a heart attack. I physically escaped harm (save for the near-deadly amount of adrenaline shooting through my veins), but I could not say the same was true energetically. My nerves were shot, my heart was pounding in my chest, and my emotions raced from outrage and indignation.

All I could think was, *Where did that come from?* One minute I was happily flowing with life; the next, a crazy person had burst into my lovely experience and hijacked me. No longer in the flow of my lovely day, I was overwhelmed, whisked away into the crazy driver's terror and drama before I knew what hit me. I never saw the psychic hijacker coming. He descended upon me so fast that I didn't even have a chance to protect myself from his assault.

It took me several more blocks of walking to recover my stolen breath, pick up the pieces of my shattered composure, and redirect my nose to the jet stream of love once again; and while I wanted to jump right back into the flow, it was more like I limped back into it, worse for the wear and tear. Psychic hijackings occur every day, and like all travelers, we're vulnerable to them and their sneaky, energetic ambushes and must be on guard.

Psychic hijackers carelessly throw their bad behavior, aggression, rage, self-pity, self-absorption, indignation, entitlement, addiction, blame, anger, self-centeredness, and impatience around freely, without awareness of or regard for how they affect others. They are so into their own crazy drama that they believe it's the only thing that matters to everyone.

Psychic hijackers are the road ragers, rude store clerks, arrogant neighbors, snotty adolescents, impatient co-workers, cranky old folks, overworked middle-agers, manipulative family members, and self-absorbed drama kings and queens. They are the aggressive or unconscious general population at large who are so filled with drama, negativity, and fear that they intrude upon others at full speed and dump their mess all over, like a toxic oil spill, taking everything and everyone in their path down with them.

Psychic hijackers are everywhere, yet are rarely as obvious as the speeding maniac who nearly ran me over. Often, in fact, they look quite benign, even pleasant. Yet when they begin to dump their negativity and fear on you in copious amounts, they catch you off guard, sweeping you up in their vortex before you even know what hit you. You get dragged off your path and hijacked, like a hostage.

Held Hostage

Traveling from Chicago to Kona, in Hawaii, to accept an invitation to become a member of the Transformational Leadership Circle (a group of progressive spiritual teachers from all over the world), I was seated in front of a woman who spoke nonstop at the top of her lungs to the bleary-eyed, boundary-challenged seatmate next to her. At first I tuned her out with my iPod and noise-canceling headphones, but soon my batteries gave out, and once again, I was subjected to her endless stream of negative ranting.

I heard about her mother's bathroom habits; the sales at Wal-mart versus K-mart; the obnoxious ways of her last three husbands; and the troubles she had with her dentures, hemorrhoids, cataracts, bunions, and wrinkle-cream allergies. She didn't come up for a breath. Her voice was grating on my nerves like fingernails on a chalkboard. Desperate for relief, my eyes darted around the plane for an empty seat to escape to. No luck. Every seat was taken. Trying to divert my attention, I picked up my book, hoping that it would distract me from the endless drone buzzing in the back of my head. I couldn't even concentrate on one sentence. As if held prisoner, all my mind could do was wince at her every word, secretly plotting a million ways to turn around and scream, "Lady, will you *please shut up!*" The irony of going to be elected as a spiritual leader while secretly plotting to strangle the lady behind me was not lost on me.

The choice was simple. I could travel in psychic misery and suffer the indignity of being subjected to her banal blabber and victimized by her merciless drone, boiling in frustration and irritation until I could hardly restrain myself; or I could travel at the speed of love—peaceful, calm, and at ease. Honestly, the choice wasn't easy. I was "in it," meaning my ego had been sufficiently agitated and the beast had been let out of her cage. I was upset and wanted to let her know it.

It's interesting to note just how intense being seized by the ego's irritations can be. I had to make a choice. I turned around, looked the woman straight in the eye, and placed one finger in front of my lips, as if to suggest "Shh . . . be quiet!" She looked at me as though I had slapped her, and she stopped talking. I relaxed, *Whew!* Yes. Quiet. I turned around. Two short seconds later, she tapped me sharply on the shoulder.

"Excuse me. Are you implying that I'm talking too loud?"

Surprised, and just a little scared, I nodded my head, smiled, and whispered, "Just a little."

"Well," she snapped back. "I never!" Then she began to stage-whisper a loud, harsh "Screw you, lady" diatribe against me, which lasted a full five minutes, before she jumped back to her previous discourse and continued her nonstop babble at full volume.

What to do? How do you travel at the speed of love when you have someone behind you irritating the hell out of you, and they either don't know or don't care?

This is exactly the time to reach for the escape hatch from the ego and lift up. In other words, bring your attention to the energetic portal located in the very center of your heart, and begin to vibrate on a higher level. The way to enter the portal isn't difficult. Just breathe and, with focus and concentration, open your heart. Breathe and connect with your Spirit. Breathe and accept, rather than fight what's going on. Study the difficult situation you find yourself in with compassion, and find love for it all.

I turned around and sneaked a peek. The woman was anxious and lonely. She filled her emptiness and fear with words. She didn't want to feel her anxiety, so she talked over it. Words were her drug. She was so frightened of her loneliness, she was unaware of anything else. I was grateful that I wasn't in her position.

Compassion replaced irritation. I understood her compulsion to talk and freed myself from being angered by it. She was simply self-soothing. I needed to do the same. The enraged beast of my ego gave one final inner growl, but then returned to its corner and quieted down. As soon as I realized her behavior wasn't meant to be so obnoxious, I calmed down. I returned to myself. I found the portal to my heart and up I went. My heart expanded. My imagination shifted to peaceful images. I focused on the approaching island: the beauty, the ocean, the flowers, the dolphins, the sweetness of the earth. I drifted into my own daydreams. I breathed into my peace. I became lost in the beauty of my imagination for a long time. My eyes closed; eventually my mind relaxed. I felt quiet, an aura of calm surrounding me. It was peaceful. Moments later, I realized that light was flowing throughout my entire body.

The chattering woman was sleeping, and glancing backward, I could see she had a peaceful look on her face as well. With my newfound peace came some newfound insight. The first was that we cannot change another person, ever. Moreover, when aggravated by another, we cannot fight the situation either. All we can do is remember that there's an escape hatch from all that bothers us in life, a secret portal through which we can slip into tranquility; and once we do, everything that's bothering us will cease to irritate. That portal is one of love, and it's located in the center of the heart. Once we focus on the heart, we begin to spiral up into a vortex of positive energy, leaving the aggravation far below.

Relative Misery

My girlfriend Evelyn is visiting her 83-year-old mother this weekend, something she's been doing once a month ever since her father died last summer. Evelyn truly wants to be there for her mother during this transition time, as she's having a great deal of difficulty coping with life alone. Evelyn goes to see her with a lot of love in her heart.

But showing up with love in her heart and loving the experience of actually being with her mother are two very separate things. Evelyn loves her mother. She loves being of service to her mother. She loves reorganizing her life to be with her mother, but no sooner does she walk through the front door than the extremely challenging experience of actually being with her mother kicks in. This is because Evelyn's mother is a fearful, cantankerous, whiny, irrational, and extremely controlling woman. For example, her mother lives in an area where temperatures rise, at times, to over 100 degrees. Yet she insists that all the windows and doors remain sealed shut and refuses to turn on the air-conditioning or open windows during the hotter months because she doesn't like drafts. So Evelyn, who's going through menopause, is forced to sweat through her hot flashes and heat waves every day she's there. She says it makes Bikram yoga feel like a cool mountain stroll.

Evelyn's mother has also lost her appetite since her husband's death and eats very little. Her cupboards and refrigerator are bare, yet she doesn't want to eat at restaurants because she doesn't like to go out. She also refuses to buy groceries because she says they'll go to waste. Nor does she want Evelyn to go to

221

a restaurant or the grocery store without her, insisting that her daughter content herself to exist on the same stale crackers and slices of dried-out salami that she eats. If Evelyn wants to eat anything other than that, her mother gets angry, passive-aggressive, or sulky and doesn't speak to her.

Next is the issue of the guest bedroom where Evelyn usually sleeps when she's there. The last time Evelyn arrived at her mother's home, she found that her mother had emptied every single closet and drawer in the house and spread the contents all over the guest-bedroom bed and floor, leaving no place for Evelyn to sleep. When Evelyn asked to move the stuff, her mother told her to sleep on the couch or on the floor instead because she didn't want Evelyn to disturb her "project."

On top of all this, her mother constantly criticizes Evelyn, calling her fat, suggesting her hairstyle isn't attractive, lamenting the fact that she's not married, and saying she should try harder to find a man. I'm sure you're beginning to see just how obnoxious and unbearable Evelyn's mother can be and why she doesn't love visiting her. In fact, being with her mother pushes nearly all of Evelyn's "buttons" to the absolute limits of her patience. Evelyn bites her tongue, takes regular deep breaths, and tries not to take the insufferable behavior personally.

Yes, it is difficult for Evelyn to visit her mom, but that's beside the point. Love is sometimes difficult, especially when dealing with crazy, wounded, grieving human beings; and Evelyn knows that. The point is that she loves her mother and realizes that so many of her challenging behaviors are the result of profound grief, disorientation, and fear. Although some are just plain obnoxious, and ones that her mother has always possessed, Evelyn looks past these irritations as best she can. That's what traveling at the speed of love is all about.

It is in facing difficult people with patience, and having the ability to roll with the challenges they bring with them, yet still remaining in loving service in spite of it all, that we express love best. Love is about rolling with the ups and downs of life with an open, tolerant, patient heart. When in the flow, we don't allow the challenges or difficulties to derail our good and loving intentions. Traveling at the speed of love means having the ability to face life's difficulties and difficult people and still remain in a calm, loving, high vibrational frequency. After all, it's easy to love when the circumstances and people are easy. But that's traveling at the speed of comfort, not love. It's when we are able to give love to unlovable circumstances, unlovable behaviors, unlovable conditions, and unpleasant people—and still keep our heart open—that we are truly elevating our vibration and traveling at the speed of love.

Hostage to Your Own Perceptions

To travel at the speed of love, you must be willing to give life your all. This includes having a positive, grateful attitude and a willingness to be a good sport. It means taking the high road and forgiving, overlooking, ignoring, laughing at, and fully embracing all that comes your way—especially the crazy people—as part of the journey of being alive. All of this requires energy, so you have to make sure you have an adequate amount of fuel in your tank.

I spoke to a woman named Ariel several months ago. A 33-year-old unmarried nurse, she was frustrated in her job and said she felt as though she were being smothered to death. She was deeply involved with her sister who had a disabled child whom she helped several times a week, but secretly felt trapped and unable to follow her own heart's desire because of it, although her sister encouraged her at every turn to take care of herself.

Ariel also lived near her father and regularly engaged with him, even though they fought all the time. She hadn't ever been in a serious relationship and was worried that her biological clock was running out. She gave a lot to her patients and family, but from a place of depletion, exhaustion, and resentment; and it didn't feel good to her or them.

She was lonely, yet every man she went out with failed to ask her out for a second date. She was trying to travel at the speed

223

of love, but her self-neglect prevented her from lifting off into a higher orbit. Ariel couldn't understand why, with such good intentions, she felt so unappreciated, unfulfilled, and stuck.

It was clear the problem was that she was giving way more than she was honestly able to give. She was running on an empty gas tank and had been for a long time, so everyone she helped was in fact becoming sickened by the negative vibes of resentment and overextension that she put out. She would have done herself, her patients, and her family a huge favor to quit helping them so much and focus on pursuing a job and a life that felt fun and fulfilling to her instead.

I suggested about ten ways Ariel could make her life more relaxing, more fun, more fulfilling, and still be able to help her sister, work part-time, and pay her bills, but they fell on deaf ears. She ignored every suggestion I offered before she fully heard me out, convinced it wouldn't work, which only verified that she wasn't receptive to taking care of herself or making the necessary changes. She would continue to suffer on the path of helping others, and make them suffer for her doing so. The only journey she was taking was around and around in a vicious cycle.

I knew Ariel was paralyzed with frustration and so did she, but not enough to reach deeper into her heart and honestly change her strategies for life. She knew suffering. She knew sacrifice. She did not know fun or joy or satisfaction. Rather than take a risk and follow her heart, her logic (really, her fear) ruled and she remained stuck. She refused to acknowledge that she had a choice about how her life was unfolding. She would not allow a shift toward self-love, personal care, and the promise of a new direction.

Drama Hijacks Peace

Another signal that you're getting hijacked (or you're hijacking others) is experiencing or causing drama. Drama is the ego's attempt to take over the flow and force it in another direction. It never works, and it always leaves the traveler mired in negative energy.

Whenever you encounter drama, be on guard and refuse to engage. I realize that this is the equivalent of asking you to back away from a million-watt vacuum sucking you in, but be determined and stay strong. Drama never, ever, ever delivers loving, positive results. All it does is blow your circuits and propel you into reverse.

Drama is an attempt to block the flow with an unproductive stance. It's a vain attempt by the drama maker to play God. It doesn't work. It does great damage, and after the dust settles, it's embarrassing. I know because I've been the victim of my own and other people's dramas so many times that I'm not confused about where this road leads anymore. I've screamed and been screamed at. I've cried and been cried to. I've argued and been argued with. I've felt victimized and been accused of victimizing others. I've resented and been resented. All of this is drama, plain and simple. It's acting like a victim instead of moving toward a creative solution. It's sitting in the soup of suffering instead of making the situation into a feast of opportunities to grow. It's a drag on you and everyone else.

It's a hijacker of all that is positive, creative, and loving. And it's a waste of time.

The key to dismantling drama is to be logical, grounded, and clear about what you want, and honest enough to admit it. When, if ever, can you say drama felt good? Yes, I know it feels good for a second or a minute—okay, even an hour. But once it's passed, the only vibration that remains is either embarrassment or resentment or both. There's a wonderfully descriptive word for drama. The word is *yuck!*

If you feel yourself being hijacked by the "yuck" of drama, yours or another's, take many deep, long, slow breaths. This is because drama can't survive with breath. Drama is only possible without breath. It feeds on breathlessness like a demon. Breath fights drama.

It's awfully difficult to be hysterical and breathe deeply at the same time. It's also difficult to be angry, irritated, injured, or insulted and breathe deeply. Try it. You simply can't do it.

Drama especially likes to sneak in when a person is fatigued, hungry, rushed, or being pushed too hard or too fast. The solution, therefore, to being drama free is to pace your life intelligently, sustaining yourself as you go. Most of all, the key to avoiding drama is to not allow your ego to trick you into believing it has power. Drama is not powerful. It has volume. It has intensity. It has passion. But it has no true power.

Blow Off Steam

When you get hijacked on your journey, the psychic hijacker succeeds because he wrests the control away from you. The only way to get back into the jet stream is to take back control.

First, look at the drama or conflict, not the person causing the drama, as the hijacker. Using your full power of intention, focus your breath into your belly until you feel full of breath. Do this several times more. In fact, do this 10 or 20 times, all the while noticing, even studying, the details of the drama as though you're watching a horror movie of a tornado-like vortex trying to suck everything around it into its devilish whirl.

As you breathe in, look the negativity straight in the eye and, using the power of your mind, say to yourself and the drama, *I'm not afraid of you.* Then breathe out.

Do this several times, and take your time. Fear is always in a hurry, riding your rear end like a cattle prod, trying to push you along faster and faster until you feel totally manipulated, overwhelmed, and out of control.

Next, breathe in and say to the negative situation, *I see you . . . but I won't engage with you.* And then don't. Refuse. Cover your solar plexus, your belly, as you do this, because in the center of your stomach, in the gut, is where fear seeps in and pulls you down.

When traveling at the speed of love, you can always protect yourself from negativity by covering your solar plexus, looking the problem or person in the eye, and refusing to engage in the drama. This takes practice because negativity and drama tend to taunt us like little demons until they get a reaction. A person pro-voking drama wants a reaction because when you blow your lid, his or her negative tension gets dispelled. It's literally toxic relief.

If you get sucked into the negative vortex, the negative energy flows into your body through your solar plexus, seeps into your nervous system like a toxic electrical current, and slams your heart shut. This instantly takes you into rapid descent and out of the jet stream of loving flow.

A psychic hijacker works best by effectively creating conflict, but if that doesn't work and you don't engage, be warned that he or she will amp up the negativity and try even more aggressive and passive-aggressive tactics to get a reaction.

So when your husband or wife has an outburst of rage and drama, or a co-worker or boss unloads on you, rather than taking the bait, say to yourself, *I see/feel this drama.*

Breathe and cover your solar plexus (your belly). Say, *I refuse to engage.*

Breathe and don't engage.

The "don't engage" part is the key, and it's where you want to focus. It may take practice and there will be setbacks. Don't mind them. We are here to learn, and if we keep up our practice, we will experience setbacks less and less often.

Positive Protection

A good defense measure against hijackers is to actively culti-vate the habit of positive thought and expression. By this I don't mean that you want to become artificially saccharine sweet. What I mean is to train your attention to notice what is genuinely good about any given moment or experience, no matter what, and say so out loud.

For example, right now, Patrick and I are both undergoing many challenges with our vulnerable, aging parents. My in-laws were recently involved in a car accident and both were seriously injured. They are choosing to be positive, strong, and intentional, and to fight to extend and enjoy even more the life they so love. As their children, Patrick and I are learning just how precious our parents are to us, as well as coming to see and accept the inevitable vulnerabilities of aging, which have softened our hearts and sharpened our focus on appreciating our own lives.

Look at the challenges facing you and reframe them in a positive perspective. Life only brings gifts, albeit in strange wrapping at times. Look for gifts; acknowledge gifts. And finally, practice looking at your own patterns of fear, control, negativity, low self-esteem, and victimhood without reacting. See how these energies pop up like ducks in an arcade game. But don't get seduced into knocking them down. Even if you do knock some down, other negative patterns pop up and replace them.

That is the nature of the lower mind. It just keeps on parading negativity across the mental landscape. Rather than attack these patterns, do your best to ignore them. Unless you go after them, unless you give them power by paying attention to them, they will pop up and then move on.

In-Flight Check-In

It's time to take out your notebook and spend a few minutes thinking about each of the following questions. Breathe deeply and get centered and grounded before you begin. This time, focus on your present experiences and your reactions to day-to-day life. Rather than simple *yes/no* answers, delve deeply into your emotional body and include examples of how drama might be affecting certain reactions or behaviors today. The more attentive you are to these questions and exercises, the more benefit you'll get from them.

- Where in your life do you cause drama?
- Where in your life would it serve you to be more patient?
- Whom in your life do you consider difficult to deal with?

- Who in your life is high maintenance?

- Where in your life are you being asked for a lot more than you can honestly give?

- Are you able to go the extra mile for those who need you right now, or are you honestly unable to extend any farther?

- What in your life is filled with drama?

- How do you take care of yourself so that you have patience for those whose demands are high?

- Are you extending yourself too far and suffering for it?

Basic Flying Lessons

Walk It Off

Whenever you reach a limit and find yourself feeling irritable, impatient, angry, temperamental, annoyed, unreasonable, and ready to lash out or withdraw in a sulk, go for a ten-minute walk instead. If you are at work and must explain your absence, say you don't feel well, if necessary (because it's true), and take this break for yourself.

Count to Ten

When your patience is challenged, take a deep breath and remember: the situation is what it is. Having an outburst over it will most likely not change it for the better. If anything, it will probably make it worse . . . for you, especially. Instead, count to ten with a breath in between each number. By the time you get to ten, the crisis of emotion will have passed.

Advanced Flying Lessons

The Key to Safety

Fearful or intense emotions flood the body with adrenaline, triggering what is called "fight-or-flight syndrome," where you either want to attack or run away. Once you start to head in this direction, you temporarily lose touch with your Higher Self, and consequently can quickly spiral out of loving flow. If you don't act fast to intercept this adrenaline surge, it's very difficult to reverse.

When you find your adrenaline pumping too fast, remember to breathe slowly and focus your eyes on the physical world around you. When you get highly emotional, you'll tend to turn your gaze inward, which then causes your sense of emergency or threat to amplify. If a person is causing you to feel angry or upset, look at things other than that person in your immediate surroundings to get grounded. If possible, and if they're handy, place your hand on your keys and take a few steps back and forth, keys in hand.

For reasons I cannot fully explain, having your keys in hand when feeling overwhelmed or threatened gives a sense of power and calms you down quickly. If you stand frozen when upset, you'll start to feel trapped, and this only makes your adrenal glands flare even more. So with eyes focused on the physical world, pace slowly back and forth, farther than a few steps if you can, and keep breathing. If you can do this for at least three to five minutes, you can keep the adrenals calm and reestablish contact or remain in touch with your Higher Self.

Take Comfort

When I have been fortunate enough to travel in business class over the years, I've always been given a complimentary toiletry kit filled with a few handy niceties designed to make my flight more comfortable: a small toothbrush, a comb, lotion, toothpaste, and a small sample of cologne. It is nothing much, really, but it makes me feel pampered. And whether or not I use it, I love that I have it.

When traveling through your days, it helps to create a comfort kit of your own. You may not need it, but just knowing it is there in case you do provides great comfort. And if you find yourself stressed or overextended, reach for your comfort kit and indulge in one or all of the soothing remedies inside to help you navigate the challenges at hand in a gracefully grounded manner.

My personal kit has a small bottle of lavender aromatherapy, which helps ease stress; a bottle of the flower essence Rescue Remedy, which calms my tattered nerves and overtaxed emotions (both are available at any local health-food store); a small piece of dark chocolate, which elevates good, positive endorphins in the brain; and a few chamomile tea bags, because chamomile assists in good sleep. I also like to keep my meditative music and noise-canceling headphones handy on flights.

Think about what you might like in your kit. In my friend Lynn's kit, she has her favorite pillow, a nonfiction book that inspires her, jellybeans, fashion magazines, cashews, and warm fluffy socks. Perhaps you might like a crossword puzzle, sudoku, or other games to relax your mind, or a good novel to get lost in. My friend Mark likes to read technical magazines, while another friend Julia likes to soothe herself by writing in her journal. The point is to create an emergency kit of some sort that you can reach for anytime you need to regroup, disconnect from the stress of the outer world, and relax. Reach for it whenever you feel overwhelmed, irritable, anxious, moody, impatient, and overtaxed. It will keep you traveling at the speed of love when you are at the greatest risk of crashing into negativity.

CHAPTER 17

Round-trips

Not long ago, I was in South Africa on a book tour and fund-raising event for an organization supported by my publisher, Hay House, called NOAH: Nurturing Orphans of AIDS for Humanity. There are millions of orphans and AIDS victims there, and NOAH creates day cares for them and provides at least one meal a day—the only meal most will eat that day.

While in Johannesburg, my Hay House host took me to visit one of the crèches, or day-care centers, for about 150 children from the ages of one to about five, just outside the city. When I arrived, the director, Sino, and her assistant Rebecca met us and began to show us around. The place itself consisted of six basic four-walled structures without proper doors, windows, or any sort of color or beauty, and certainly no toys or games. It was lunchtime when we arrived, so we were escorted to a small room filled with about 35 children (babies, really), each sitting with a very small bowl on his or her lap filled with soupy white potatoes, a small amount of yellow corn, and a few peas. That was it. They ate quietly and greedily, shoveling the warm mush into their mouths as fast as they could; blinking and looking up at us silently, not smiling and not interested in us at all, intent only on their need to get their nourishment as quickly as possible.

I couldn't help but think of all the times my mom said to me as a child to finish my plate of food and be grateful because there were kids starving in Africa. Looking at these sweet, silent faces, I realized she was not exaggerating; there really are millions of kids starving in Africa.

My heart breaking, we moved on to the sleeping room, where about 75 toddlers who had just finished lunch were lying down on a hard concrete floor—no cots, no pillows, no blankets—huddled facedown, pretending to sleep, while in fact stealing glances at us sideways as we peeked in.

I wanted to scoop these children up by the handful and bring them home with me as I looked upon them. I was then escorted to the playroom, where I was met by yet another shy, quiet group of toddlers who lined the walls of the room, staring suspiciously at us as we walked in.

The director spoke to the kids in a language I couldn't understand for about two minutes; and then suddenly, as if a lightbulb had turned on inside the kids, they smiled from ear to ear, jumped excitedly to their feet, and got into a dance formation of three lines. The next thing I knew, the director turned on an ancient CD player, and a song started playing through the speakers. These shy, quiet babies sprang into a lively chorus line worthy of Broadway. They sang at full, openhearted volume and danced with so much exuberance it made my heart dizzy; all the while they were looking me directly in the eye and giving me absolutely everything they had to give and more.

Their transformation from somber, abandoned wallflowers to a brilliant performing dance team took my breath away. They danced in perfect sync, sang in perfect pitch, and shared their spirits with expansive generosity for the next 15 minutes.

I was mesmerized and humbled as I took in their loving performance. When they finished, I laughed, clapped, and asked for an encore. I felt as though I had just been showered with pure, unconditional love. My heart opened and tears filled my eyes. These small, innocent children, some of whom had experienced unthinkable horrors in their barely beginning lives, filled me with more sweetness and love than I had experienced in a long, long time. I was under the illusion that I was there to offer something to support these abandoned children when, in fact, it was quite the opposite. These innocent children had never seen me before and would never see me again. Yet they gave me the most generous and precious gift—the greatest outpouring of love and service that I had ever witnessed or received before.

They were so spirited, so abundant in sharing and giving, that I was humbled to silence. My coming to South Africa was not in service to them. It was in service to me. As I stood before them, filled with loving sweetness and grace from their blessed beings, I could only thank God for my good fortune.

I left thinking about how things really turn out so differently from what we expect sometimes. I had arrived full of my personal intention to help support these children when, in truth, it was they who gave me the conscious depths of my humanity back. The sweet dance of these children reawakened in me a humility and gratitude for the vast abundance of my own life, something I had lost along the way. To be in the presence of that much need and that much dignity awakened me to the fact that to need is not to be weak. It is a gift to those who forget to give. God had orchestrated this event to remind me what is truly important in life. I was not the giver this day. I was the gifted.

Leaving the crèche, I was perfectly clear that the only thing that matters in life—the *only* thing—is that we love and serve all of humanity as best we can, every day, as those children did. I was reminded that service does not require grand or heroic efforts. Those children were masters of love and service. Without parents; safe homes; fresh clothes; or basics like food, running water, or toilets, they were rich in their capacity to share what they could, their song and dance, without holding back one single drop of themselves. They gave their complicated, compromised, deeply frightening lives their all—their full, loving hearts. That is all any of us have to do to catch up and join them in traveling at the speed of love. Just give our full hearts to the lives God gave us and share our love as they did.

Give Your All

I walked away thinking of all the times and places where I could have given more. It was not in my work—I always give my all there. But I could see that with my friends, I could take more interest and keep in touch better. It would be such a gift to me if I made the effort. I could also make myself more available to my siblings. I know, and they know, that I love them; but in my busyness, I sometimes forget or neglect to give my all to my relationships with them. Not because I "should," not because "it's the right thing to do," but rather because, as I was so succinctly reminded by those magnificent babies, to give from the heart is to enrich beyond measure.

Sitting quietly in my hotel room, reflecting on my experience at the crèche, I got it. Being of service to others, in every way we can possibly be, is the only way to travel at the full speed of love. Our giving to others is the greatest illusion of all because every smile, every outreach, every effort is a gift that keeps on giving back. It is the fuel that fills our tanks. It doesn't even matter if the gift of our service is received, recognized, or appreciated at all. The true recipient of all the giving we do is, in fact, ourselves. Giving is the first-class ride, the instant upgrade from struggle to flow. What we give doesn't matter either. It can be time, effort, donations, money, or simply living our agreements and commitments with great love. I left the crèche rich in blessings and inspiration. These children were my role models, my guides. They were masters in sharing everything they had with exuberance, confidence, and joy. If only I could do that every day with everyone, I'd be flying high.

Angels in Disguise

Years ago, fresh out of college with a psychology degree, my husband, Patrick, got his first professional job at the Dubuque County Mental-Health Center where he lived in Dubuque, Iowa. His job was to check in on the psychiatric patients in the center, see how they were doing, chart their progress, make sure they were

236

taking their medications, and give them counseling each day. It was a sad job in a sad place for a young man, and he wasn't sure it suited him. Yet he was told by several influential people in his life that he was lucky to have a job in his field at all, and this was as good as it got. So he went to work every day, pushing aside all the other hopes, dreams, and ambitions he might have had, trying to feel the gratitude he was told he *should* have.

One day he went to check in on an old woman who was particularly difficult and had a history of angry outbursts and severe tantrums. When he first popped his head into her room, he found her lying in the fetal position, perfectly still, not moving a muscle.

"Hello," he said, in a low voice, not wanting to startle her, "I'm Patrick Tully from the Dubuque County Mental-Health Center. I'm here to check in on you and see how you are today." She didn't move, and from the look on her face, Patrick wondered if she had died.

He came closer, still speaking barely above a whisper. "Hello, ma'am. I'm Patrick Tully from the Dubuque County Mental-Health Center to check in on you."

Still she did not move. She lay there like a small, shriveled-up bird. He became even more worried that she, in fact, might have expired. It wasn't unlikely since she was rather old and had been there for quite a while. He moved in even closer.

"Hello ma'am. I'm Patrick Tully," he said, now hovering right above her bed. Still nothing. He leaned very close, wanting to check to see if she was breathing. "Hello, ma'am," he continued. "I'm . . . " Just then she reached out like lightning and grabbed him by the tie and yanked him close, choking him as she spoke.

"I don't care who you are!" she snarled. "You see me here shriveled up like a prisoner? You'll soon be lying here just like me, dying without ever living your hopes and dreams." Then she released his tie and closed her eyes once again.

Shocked, Patrick stood up and took a deep breath. She was right. That could be him one day. In fact, it was his biggest fear. He leaned over and whispered, "Thank you," and quietly left the room. As he did, he looked down at the chart he carried, where he made notes on his patients. He wrote: "Patient is doing just fine." He turned in the doorway and looked back at her. As though feeling his gaze, she opened her eyes, stared at him for a second, and closed them once again. Patrick turned around, reflecting on what she had just said. Next, he went straight to his supervisor, turned in his clipboard, and said, "I quit."

He walked out, took off his tie, and went straight to the Dubuque Travel Center and, with his savings, bought a ticket around the world. He'd secretly dreamed of this for a long time but was worried it was way too big a dream for him to ever imagine actually creating. Two weeks later, he left on the greatest adventure of his life. He traveled for an entire year. He reflected on the elderly woman often as he circled the globe. He believed when he began that job that he was there to help the patients. Instead, it was she—an angry, insolent, troublesome old woman—who not only helped him, but freed him to live the life of his dreams.

That's how it goes when traveling at the speed of love. Every moment, in every situation, we are all in the position to receive incredible gifts. But often they come in curiously disguised packages, and we can only receive them if we are open. In everything we do, every service we share, every task we execute for another, we stand to receive everything a ten thousandfold, lifting us up and spreading our own wings in flight.

Angels Are Everywhere

My daughter Sonia goes to college in Portland, Oregon. One day she had an assignment to take pictures of interesting people for her photography class. Wanting very much to do a good job and stretch beyond her comfort zone of friends, children, and people she knew, she headed to a park known as a place where the homeless and the drug addicts of the city congregated. As she approached the park, she noticed a disheveled man in his 60s sitting on a bench and caught his eye. Looking straight back at her, he said, "Hello." Overcoming her shyness, she approached and explained her assignment.

"I'm supposed to take photos of interesting people. You look interesting. May I take a photo of you?"

Expecting a grudging "No" or an indifferent nod, she was surprised when he jumped up and starting mugging for the camera, striking various poses and trying his darnedest to look interesting. Laughing and caught a bit off guard by his sudden animation, she began to click away. After a few minutes, he wanted to see the shots, so she stopped and showed him what she had gotten on camera. These photos were quite silly, a homeless man posing like a runway model. They both laughed, and he started talking with her and sharing his life story.

Being Sonia, she felt it would be kind to sit and listen, so she relaxed and put her camera aside. First he talked about growing up in the country and joining the Army, where he was sent to Vietnam. He fought in some of the most intense battles, he said, saw many close friends die, and came home all *&^$ed up and with what his shrink later called post-traumatic stress disorder.

He then told her he had to take drugs to fight the trauma, but they messed him up. He also said he got married and had a daughter; but his wife was killed in a car accident, and because of her death, he had become very depressed. His daughter was 17 at the time and moved away.

He was rambling a bit, and then suddenly he stood up and said, "Come on. I want to show you something." Sonia blindly followed him, not sure where they were going or why. A couple of blocks later, he dashed into an empty bar. Once inside, he headed for the corner and then down the stairs. Sonia followed him, not completely afraid because there were a couple of people present and he seemed, behind his drunken condition, like a very sweet man.

Once downstairs, he headed straight to the back of the bar where there was an old dusty piano. He sat down and immediately started playing beautifully. He performed three songs for her, all of which he said he had written for his daughter, whom he hadn't seen in 20 years. Each one was more exquisite than the one before.

He finished playing and said, "You can't take a picture of music, but that's the real me, not the bum you see in the park."

He then stopped playing, and they both walked upstairs. He turned and saw some flowers in a window box in the bar window and spontaneously ripped them out, handing them to Sonia, saying, "Thank you for treating me like a human."

Sonia was so moved she was speechless. She thought she was doing him a favor by listening to him, when, in fact, it turned out that he was the one who gave her the gift that day. He reminded her of one of the greatest lessons: never judge a person by appearances.

Her decision to dignify him by listening was far surpassed by the gift of him sharing his life's journey with all its courageous turns and devastating losses, and the beauty of his talent, which shone through all the debris he was buried under. She got up and applauded him, thanked him profusely, and walked out, her life's perspective changed forever. She even wondered if he was real. Maybe he was really an angel showing her something important in life.

He had awakened something in her heart that hadn't been quite as alert before. She walked for a while before she could fully discern what it was. Finally, she understood. It was a deep and profound sense of compassion for him and all people who were suffering. It was a gift that opened her heart in a way she'd never known was possible.

Traveling at the speed of love is always a round-trip journey. When on this trip, we learn that there is no such thing as giving to another that isn't really the "other" giving to ourselves. To give is one of our greatest expressions of love, and it doesn't require material abundance. Whether we give our time, our energy, our assets, our interest, our support, our talents, or our skills, underneath it all we are sharing our hearts. Those in need are our angels. They invite us to rise to greater heights, to soar up into a higher altitude. Everyone with a pressing need who appears on our path is really an angel in service to our hearts. The journey to giving is perhaps the easiest one to take.

In-Flight Check-In

Once again, take a few deep, cleansing breaths and stretch for a few minutes. Next, take out your notebook and get comfortable. Look over and ponder each question before you write down your responses. Recall moments all the way back to your childhood to find the answers. Reflect on how each answer energetically affects you to this day, and make a note of that as well.

- Recall the times in your journey of life when you offered your service to someone or something.

- What gifts or benefit did you receive from your efforts?

- Which were the obvious gifts?

- Which were the more subtle or surprising gifts?

- What difficulties arose as a result of your choice?

- Where in your life did you think you were the giver, but actually found yourself instead on the receiving end of love and support?

- How did it surprise you?

- Where in your journey today might you elevate your energetic altitude by giving more than you presently are?

- What treasures of spirit can you share even more?

- What efforts in service can you step up to?

Remember, every journey into generosity and service is a first-class, round-trip ticket to love. The more you give, the more you get. Service is the gift that keeps on giving.

Basic Flying Lessons

Get Involved

Volunteer to help your community this week. Remember, your community encompasses all of humanity, and all sentient beings. It's not just your neighborhood. And it's not just people, but animals as well. We are all connected to all living things.

You can call Meals On Wheels in your city and deliver meals to shut-ins. You can join or organize a neighborhood cleanup of garbage or help remove graffiti from the garages and streets in your area. You can call your local church and help serve lunch or organize and hand out food to the poor in the neighborhood. Walk for breast cancer. Join a fund-raiser and contribute. Teach Sunday school. Volunteer to help foreigners who do not speak or read English well. Coach the local kids' volleyball games. Adopt a pet from the humane society. Donate to protect an endangered species. If there is a will, you can find plenty of needs and ways. Do it once and see how you feel. How high are you flying when you finish? Try it to find out the answer to this question.

Share

Go through your home and collect any useful things that can help another family through a crisis and donate them to the cause. This includes clothes, dishes, furniture, shoes, toys, and even books. Share what you have with those who don't have as much.

Advanced Flying Lessons

Mentor

If you have any special skills, offer your services to mentor those who don't have the support they need to succeed. Reach out to someone at work who is behind you in status and skill and offer your assistance, guidance, and help. Join a mentoring group and share your talents with those who are in desperate need of your assistance.

Tithe

Tithing is the practice of giving back 10 percent of your income to those who have helped you succeed in life, whether it's a person, a church, a school, or a cause. You can also tithe your energies, your talents, and your gifts to anything or anyone that has added to your happiness and success in life in some way or needs your assistance. Notice what's around you. To tithe money, simply write a check to your cause for 10 percent of your income, be it by day, by week, or by year, and donate it. You can do it anonymously, but it's not necessary. Just do it without any strings attached.

Try tithing three times before you decide if it's worthwhile. You may discover that the more you give, the more you receive in return. It almost seems odd that giving away your money actually amplifies your abundance, yet it does. To tithe your effort, just put energy into assisting others without strings attached.

Live Your Dreams

Whatever you dream of doing, do it now. There is no greater gift you can give to this world than your happiness. If you're flying at the speed of love toward what you love, others will catch your enthusiasm and courage and begin to take off in their hearts' direction as well. Don't waste time playing it safe, because you don't know how much time you have. If you want to travel, pick up the phone and book your reservation today. If you want to paint, sing, dance, write, act, hang out and watch sunsets, or backpack across the Amazon, do it, please. This world is populated with enough miserable souls who have lost altitude and crashed into the ditches of their own misery due to lack of imagination, courage, permission, or inspiration.

In response to this, my teacher Dr. Tully once said to me, "If you want to be of service to this miserable world, don't be one of them." Be courageous and authentic enough to break free of old ideas, expectations, and fears; and go for the glory of the life you want to live now, even if you're afraid. Don't waste any more time thinking about it, waiting for the perfect moment. As my basketball coach would say to the team in high school, "Just take the ball and run like mad, and don't look back."

If you do, you will soon discover you are no longer running away from fear, but rather you are flying high toward your joy.

Epilogue

Our Final Destination

In the fall of 2008, my life changed forever in a way I never expected. In the span of six weeks, my seemingly healthy older brother, Bruce, and my perfectly healthy father both died suddenly and without warning. Bruce died in his sleep, and my father from a blood clot in his lung. My life as I knew it, my family matrix, my worldview, even how I saw myself, died along with them.

I was caught completely off guard by their deaths, and my unconscious complacency about life was shattered. Suddenly all that I took for granted, including my very next breath, became a precious, unpredictable gift and was no longer a given. Intellectually, I have always known that we are here for a very short time, but that knowledge somehow got shoved way back into the corners of my mind. Until these two deaths, I had forgotten that life is a gift that can be taken back by God at any minute. I had forgotten the fact that we are travelers visiting the Earth plane and that this is not our home. I had forgotten that we are visitors to life; on a journey; and here to explore, expand, and discover, but nevertheless here as spiritual travelers destined to move on.

It was humbling to remember. Peering at my father's plasticized body in the casket at the funeral viewing room brought this message home to me. There was his body, yet the spirit of my father was no longer in it. His journey had called him onward, perhaps home. Who knows? Not me. All I knew was that he was no longer with us, his family.

I was reminded again of the fleeting nature of our journey as I stood with my remaining family at the cemetery mausoleum, placing my father's ashes next to my brother's, and was told the remaining little boxes would be reserved for my mother and, if I desired, for me as well. I was acutely aware of the fleeting and precious gift of life when asked to stand next to the urns of my brother's and father's ashes and say a few words, when in my exuberance, I threw my arms out while speaking and knocked the lid off my brother's urn, freeing his ashes to be scattered in the wind. Thank goodness for the quick steps of my younger sister, who saved him from such a maladroit ending.

Over the past few months, I have since managed to assimilate and deal with the fact of their near-simultaneous deaths and have even been able to find a few gifts in my devastation. I received the gift of being reminded of what a great family I have and how I can count on them in times of extreme pain and loss. I received the gift of reevaluating how I use my time and reconsidering my priorities to allow for more free time, family time, and fun time. I received the gift of appreciating life more than I ever have before, conscious now of how precious it is and how we gamble in believing that it's there forever.

And I am deeply reminded that our life's journey is a gift, not a given, and that we can never truly know how long the journey will last. All we can do is decide how it unfolds. My brother's journey unfolded as a wild ride, an adventure dedicated to testing the edges; challenging the limits; and exploring sensuality, music, art, and love. As a drummer, he rock-and-rolled. As an artist, he created lasting works of art. As a sensualist, he cooked gourmet food, created the most beautiful environments, and painted the most elegant paintings. All that mattered, of course, but what mattered most is how he loved. He was intense, passionate, reckless, crazy, foolish, and exuberant in his love for family, friends, and lovers. Even for his kitty, Winter Girl. That is what he was remembered for. That is what mattered.

The same is true for my father. He was the quintessential good man. He was a steadfast worker, father, and friend. He fixed things; kept our home sound and beautiful; and was the rock for his children, grandchildren, and countless neighbors, customers, and even strangers. All that mattered. But what mattered most was that he loved his wife, my mother, with his whole heart, soul, and being and it showed in all he did. What he left us with, and what carried him on to the next experience, whatever that may be, was his love. It lives on in his children. Because of him, we all became lovers of life and lovers of being in love just like he was. His physical accomplishments were modest but significant, yet they pale in the light of what he achieved by simply loving with complete commitment and abandon as his life's way.

Looking back over my dad's life, my brother's life, my family's life, and my life from this new vantage point of lucid awareness that life is a journey—and by all accounts a brief one—I can honestly say the only thing we take with us and the only thing we leave behind is the love we received, lived, expressed, and shared.

Our physical life is temporary. The love we accept, choose, and share while traveling is not. In fact, the whole point of embarking on this journey is to love and to keep expanding our capacity to embody and embrace love.

We are the only species on the planet that seems to have a choice in how we direct our lives. We can live in fear, control, anger, doubt, or hesitation, waiting for the perfect conditions before we take flight. But if we do, we risk never taking off at all. Traveling through life is something we are all here to do. How we travel is something we choose. As I said in the beginning of this book, the journey through life leads us all back to the same destination, Spirit, in the end. We can either travel this journey in fear and miss the adventure, or travel at the speed of love and have the times of our lives. You choose.

Happy Travels. All my love,
Sonia

Dear Fellow Travelers,

To keep you traveling at the speed of love on this great adventure called life, I have created a CD of first-class spirited music called, not surprisingly, "Traveling at the Speed of Love." Following are the words to the title song. You can download this song for free as an mp3 file by visiting my Website at: **www.trustyourvibes.com**. You can also order the entire CD on my site. I hope you enjoy this small gift of lyrics, music, and loving spirit from me to you.

All my love,
Sonia

*As you know life's illusion
And we choose how we fly
Fear no more dark confusion
Lift your eyes to the sky
And we're not simply victims
Who get lost in the fray
We are travelers of light now
At the speed of love today . . .*

*We're on a great adventure
Come join the ride
We're on a great adventure
We're Flying high . . .*

*Maybe you worry it's too late
But fear no one
Just let your heart open wide
The time has come . . . the time
has come . . .*

*We're on a great adventure
Come join the ride
We're on a great adventure
We're Flying high . . .*

*Maybe you worry it's too late
But fear no one
Just let your heart open wide
The time has come . . . the time
has come . . .*

*We're on a great adventure.
We're on a great adventure . . . yeah!
We're on a great adventure . . . yeah!*

*So don't waste another thought
Just step up and get on board*

*No matter what you know
Love's the only way to go*

*Turn on your brilliant light
Give up the endless fight
Don't hold back and get left behind
Free your heart and free your mind*

*So don't waste another thought
Just step up and get on board
Flying high . . . flying high*

*No matter what you know
Love's the only way to go
Flying high . . . flying high . . .*

*Turn on your brilliant light
Give up the endless fight
Flying high . . . flying high . . .*

*Don't hold back and get left behind
Free your heart and free your mind
Just fly high. Flying high . . .*

*We're on a great adventure
Live life from above*

*We're on a great adventure
Flying at the speed of love . . .
The speed of love . . . the speed
of love . . .*

We're on a great adventure . . .

Appendix I

Flight Attendants

Healing Helpers and Workshops to Keep
You Flowing at the Speed of Love

Below are some of the best resources and people I know for keeping you happily in flight. Among them are superb healers, helpers, guides, wellness experts, and soul teachers who are there to keep you on course. They have all helped me and can help you as well. In addition, I am available by phone for **Personal Intuitive Consultations** to get you back on track and in the flow of your authentic self and soul purpose. I also offer many vibrant healing classes and workshops. Please visit my Website at **www .trustyourvibes.com** to see my class schedule or book a personal intuitive consultation appointment with me online.

Debra Grace Graves: Shamanic journeying and healing, psychic-pathway mentoring, soul retrieval, and intuitive readings; **debra.grace@gmail.com**; 636-233-2526

Cuky Choquette Harvey: Profound energetic bodywork, professional-level training, ancient lomi lomi energetic healing, and soul unwinding; **www.translucentyou.com**; 913-681-5602

Sabrina Choquette Tully: Life-path intuitive guidance readings; **www.sabrinatully.com**

Shamrock Holtz: Shamanic energetic clearing, profound healing bodywork, and breakthrough intuitive healing; **www.back2the body.org**; **shamrockholtz@me.com**; 808-635-8669

Sonia Choquette Tully: Intuitive coaching, readings; www.soniatully.com

Erica Trojan: Evolutionary astrology; **eetrojan@yahoo.com**; 847-275-2785

Lu Ann Glatzmaier Ph. D.: Spiritual and soul guidance counseling; **spiritualvoice@earthlink.net**; 303-394-3056

Dr. Michelle Robin: Holistic chiropractic and wellness; **www.YourWellnessCenter.com**

Mark Welch: Sound and vibrational healing; **www.musicbymarkwelch.com**; 805-927-2416

Crystal Jenkins: Spiritual and action-oriented counseling, life coaching, Hoffman instructor; **www.YourWellnessCenter .com**; 913-269-5175

*Inner Wisdom In-Depth Trainings
and Workshops with Sonia Choquette*

Levels 1–4 Certification Training: Four-day professional in-depth intensives for developing a deep connection with intuitive source, for personal guidance and professional guidance; **www.trustyourvibes.com**; 773-989-1151

Ask Your Guides In-Depth Workshop: In-depth intensive for establishing a deep connection with the spirit world and your personal guides; **www.trustyourvibes.com**; 773-989-1151

Translucent You: Six-day intimate healing experience on the island of Kauai led by Sonia Choquette, Cuky Choquette Harvey, and the Translucent You healing team; **www.translucentyou .com**; 913-681-5602

True Balance: An in-depth workshop for creating activation and alignment of the chakra energetic system; **www.trustyour vibes.com**; 773-989-1151

Online Courses with Sonia Choquette

For the following courses, please visit: **www.trustyourvibes .com** and **www.soniachoquette.com.**

Psychic Sit-ups: One-year online intuitive development and personal mentoring with Sonia Choquette; available in English, Spanish, French, Portuguese, and more

Heart's Desire: Nine-week online in-depth personal mentoring course with Sonia Choquette for creating the life you really want; available in English, Spanish, French, and more

The Answer Is Simple: Nine-week online course for elevating vibration and living free of obstacles

Balancing the Chakras: In-depth online chakra-balancing course

For the following courses, please visit Psychic University: **www.ConsciousOne.com.**

The Psychic Pathway: Introductory online course on developing your intuitive gifts

True Balance: Introductory online course for understanding and balancing the chakras

Heart's Desire: Introductory online course for creating the life you really want

For Your Love of Life and Nurturing Food

The Chakra Chefs: A seven-chakra course on how to create loving and lovely meals that correspond to the chakra system in order to balance and nurture your, body, mind, and spirit; presented by my husband, Patrick Tully, and his best friend and fellow chef, Craig Kinzer; **www.chakrachefs.com**

Appendix II

Acidifying and Alkalizing Foods

ACIDIFYING	ALKALIZING
Acidifying Vegetables	
Corn	***Alkalizing Vegetables***
Lentils	Alfalfa
Olives	Barley grass
Winter squash	Beets
	Broccoli
Acidifying Fruits	Cabbage
Blueberries	Carrots
Cranberries	Cauliflower
Currants	Celery
Fruits, canned or glazed	Chlorella
Plums	Cucumbers
Prunes	Dandelions
	Dulse
Acidifying Grains,	Edible flowers
Grain Products	Eggplant
Amaranth	Fermented veggies
Barley	Garlic
Bran, oat	Green beans
Bran, wheat	Greens, beet
Bread	Greens, chard
Corn	Greens, collard
Cornstarch	Greens, wild
Crackers, soda	Kale
Flour, hemp seed	Kohlrabi
Flour, wheat	Lettuce
Flour, white	Mushrooms
Kamut	Mustard greens
Macaroni	Nightshade veggies
Milk, rice	Onions

ACIDIFYING

Noodles
Oatmeal
Oats, rolled
Quinoa
Rice, all
Rice cakes
Rye
Spaghetti
Spelt
Wheat
Wheat germ

Acidifying Beans & Legumes
Beans, black
Beans, kidney
Beans, pinto
Beans, red
Beans, white
Chickpeas
Lentils
Milk, soy
Peas
Soybeans

Acidifying Dairy
Butter
Cheese
Cheese, processed
Ice cream
Ice milk

Acidifying Nuts & Butters
Cashews
Milk, almond
Peanut butter
Peanuts
Pecans
Tahini
Walnuts

ALKALIZING

Parsnips
Peas
Peppers
Pumpkins
Radishes
Rutabagas
Sea veggies
Spinach
Spirulina
Sprouts
Sweet potatoes
Tomatoes
Watercress
Wheatgrass

Alkalizing Oriental Vegetables
Daikon
Dandelion root
Kombu
Maitake
Nori
Reishi
Shiitake
Umeboshi
Wakame

Alkalizing Fruits
Apples
Apricots
Avocados
Bananas
Berries
Blackberries
Cantaloupe
Cherries, sour
Coconut, fresh
Currants
Dates, dried
Figs, dried
Grapefruit*

ACIDIFYING

Acidifying Animal Protein
Bacon
Beef
Carp
Clams
Cod
Corned beef
Fish
Haddock
Lamb
Lobster
Mussels
Organ meats
Oyster
Pike
Pork
Rabbit
Salmon
Sardines
Sausage
Scallops
Shellfish
Shrimp
Tuna
Turkey
Veal
Venison

Acidifying Fats & Oils
Avocado oil
Butter
Canola oil
Corn oil
Hemp seed oil
Flax oil
Lard
Olive oil
Safflower oil
Sesame oil
Sunflower oil

ALKALIZING

Alkalizing Fruits
Grapes
Honeydew melon
Lemon*
Lime*
Muskmelon
Nectarines
Oranges*
Peaches
Pears
Pineapple
Raisins
Raspberries
Rhubarb
Strawberries
Tangerines*
Tomatoes
Tropical fruits
Umeboshi plums
Watermelon

Alkalizing Protein
Almonds
Chestnuts
Hemp protein
Millet
Tempeh (fermented)
Tofu (fermented)

Alkalizing Sweeteners
Stevia

Alkalizing Spices & Seasonings
Chili pepper
Cinnamon
Curry
Ginger
Herbs, all
Miso
Mustard
Sea salt

ACIDIFYING	ALKALIZING
	Tamari
Acidifying Sweeteners	
Carob	***Alkalizing (Other)***
Corn syrup	Apple-cider vinegar
Sugar	Bee pollen
	Juice, fresh fruit
Acidifying Alcohol	Juice, green
Beer	Juice, veggie
Hard liquor	Lecithin granules
Wine	Molasses, blackstrap
	Probiotic cultures
Acidifying Foods (misc.)	Soured dairy products
Catsup	Water, alkaline antioxidant
Cocoa	Water, mineral
Coffee	
Mustard	***Alkalizing Minerals,***
Pepper	***Examples***
Soft drinks	Calcium: pH 12
Vinegar	Cesium: pH 14
	Magnesium: pH 9
Acidifying Drugs & Chemicals	Potassium: pH 14
Aspirin	Sodium: pH 14
Chemicals	

Acidifying Drugs & Chemicals
Aspirin
Chemicals
Drugs, medicinal
Drugs, psychedelic
Herbicides
Pesticides
Tobacco

***Acidifying Junk Food
Examples***
Beer: pH 2.5
Coca-Cola: pH 2
Coffee: pH 4

*Although it might seem that citrus fruits would have an acidifying effect on the body, the citric acid they contain actually has an alkalinizing effect on the system.

— ♥ ♥ ♥ —

About the Author

Sonia Choquette is a world-renowned author, storyteller, vibrational healer, and six-sensory spiritual teacher in international demand for her guidance, wisdom, and capacity to heal the soul. She's the author of several best-selling books, including the *New York Times* bestseller *The Answer Is Simple, Ask Your Guides, Trust Your Vibes,* and *Soul Lessons and Soul Purpose;* and numerous audio programs and card decks. Sonia was educated at the University of Denver and the Sorbonne in Paris, and holds a Ph.D. in metaphysics from the American Institute of Holistic Theology. She resides with her family in Chicago.

Website: **www.soniachoquette.com**

NOTES

NOTES

NOTES

NOTES

NOTES

NOTES

NOTES

NOTES

Notes

NOTES

Hay House Titles of Related Interest

YOU CAN HEAL YOUR LIFE, *the movie,*
starring Louise L. Hay & Friends
(available as a 1-DVD program and an expanded 2-DVD set)
Watch the trailer at: **www.LouiseHayMovie.com**

THE SHIFT, *the movie,*
starring Dr. Wayne W. Dyer
(available as a 1-DVD program and an expanded 2-DVD set)
Watch the trailer at: **www.DyerMovie.com**

The Art of Extreme Self-Care: *Transform Your Life One Month at a Time,*
by Cheryl Richardson

From Stress to Success . . . in Just 31 Days! by Dr. John F. Demartini

The Healing Power of Water, by Masaru Emoto

The Intuitive Advisor: *A Psychic Doctor Teaches You How to Solve Your Most Pressing Health Problems,* by Mona Lisa Schulz, M.D., Ph.D.

Led by Faith: *Rising from the Ashes of the Rwandan Genocide,*
by Immaculée Ilibagiza, with Steve Erwin

Recipes for Health Bliss: *Using NatureFoods & Lifestyle Choices to Rejuvenate Your Body and Life,* by Susan Smith Jones, Ph.D.

28 Days to a More Magnetic Life, by Sandra Anne Taylor

Your Soul's Compass: *What Is Spiritual Guidance?*
by Joan Borysenko, Ph.D., and Gordon Dveirin, Ed.D.

All of the above are available at your local bookstore,
or may be ordered by contacting Hay House (see next page).

We hope you enjoyed this Hay House book. If you'd like to receive our online catalog featuring additional information on Hay House books and products, or if you'd like to find out more about the Hay Foundation, please contact:

Hay House, Inc., P.O. Box 5100, Carlsbad, CA 92018-5100

(760) 431-7695 or (800) 654-5126
(760) 431-6948 (fax) or (800) 650-5115 (fax)
www.hayhouse.com® • www.hayfoundation.org

Published and distributed in Australia by: Hay House Australia Pty. Ltd., 18/36 Ralph St., Alexandria NSW 2015 • *Phone:* 612-9669-4299 • *Fax:* 612-9669-4144 www.hayhouse.com.au

Published and distributed in the United Kingdom by: Hay House UK, Ltd., 292B Kensal Rd., London W10 5BE • *Phone:* 44-20-8962-1230 • *Fax:* 44-20-8962-1239 www.hayhouse.co.uk

Published and distributed in the Republic of South Africa by: Hay House SA (Pty), Ltd., P.O. Box 990, Witkoppen 2068 • *Phone/Fax:* 27-11-467-8904 info@hayhouse.co.za • www.hayhouse.co.za

Published in India by: Hay House Publishers India, Muskaan Complex, Plot No. 3, B-2, Vasant Kunj, New Delhi 110 070 • *Phone:* 91-11-4176-1620 *Fax:* 91-11-4176-1630 • www.hayhouse.co.in

Distributed in Canada by: Raincoast, 9050 Shaughnessy St., Vancouver, B.C. V6P 6E5 *Phone:* (604) 323-7100 • *Fax:* (604) 323-2600 • www.raincoast.com

Take Your Soul on a Vacation

Visit **www.HealYourLife.com®** to regroup, recharge, and reconnect with your own magnificence. Featuring blogs, mind-body-spirit news, and life-changing wisdom from Louise Hay and friends.

Visit **www.HealYourLife.com** today!

HEAL YOUR LIFE ♥

Take Your Soul on a Vacation

Get your daily dose of inspiration today at **www.HealYourLife.com®**. Brimming with all of the necessary elements to ease your mind and educate your soul, this Website will become the foundation from which you'll start each day. This essential site delivers the latest in mind, body, and spirit news and real-time content from your favorite Hay House authors.

Make It Your Home Page Today!
www.HealYourLife.com®